Scotland in the Age of Improvement

Scotland in the Age of Improvement

Essays in Scottish History in the Eighteenth Century,
edited by N.T. Phillipson and Rosalind Mitchison
at the University Press, Edinburgh

© Copyright 1970
EDINBURGH UNIVERSITY PRESS
22 George Square, Edinburgh
North America
Aldine Publishing Company
529 South Wabash Avenue, Chicago
ISBN 0 85224 183 6
Library of Congress
Catalog Card Number 75 129106
Printed in Great Britain by
R. & R. Clark Ltd, Edinburgh

Contents

Abbreviations

SRO   Scottish Record Office

PRO   Public Record Office

NLS   National Library of Scotland

EUL   Edinburgh University Library

HMC   Historic Manuscripts Commission

SHS   Scottish History Society

DNB   Dictionary of National Biography

References are published in Edinburgh unless otherwise stated

Introduction

N.T. PHILLIPSON AND ROSALIND MITCHISON

The history of eighteenth-century Scotland offers its historians the most noble prospects. In that century Scotland was bound to England by the sort of incorporating union that has been so often projected in European history, and which has so often failed. By the middle of the century she had at last found the political stability which had for long eluded her and was entering a period of economic growth little short of miraculous for its speed and intensity. Indeed that economic recovery is as important and instructive for the understanding of a commercial world on the eve of industrialization as is Japan's post-war recovery for the understanding of mid-twentieth century capitalism. The second half of the century, too, was the time of the Scottish enlightenment, that remarkable outburst of intellectual life in which, almost overnight, Scotland was snatched from the relative cultural isolation in which she had passed the seventeenth century and placed in the centre of the thinking world.

But how few of these prospects have been explored! In the place of a historiography which explored Scotland's relations with a wider world, most of the interest of Scottish historians and their public of the nineteenth and twentieth centuries has been focused on a study of those forces which affected Scotland in isolation, and which attempted to perpetuate her solitariness. Attention was paid to Jacobitism and to the movements within the Kirk which attempted to keep in the forefront of men's minds the narrow sectarian and theocratic issues of the seventeenth century. All too often the act of union has been treated as the *terminus ad quem* of Scottish history. Without a parliament, historians appear to believe, there can be no nation, and without a nation no history, and all that is left for the historian is the study of nationalist movements aiming at a lost independence or those angry eruptions such as the Shawfield riots of 1725 or the Porteous riots of 1736 which demonstrated the dangerous weakness of the London government when faced with any large-scale public disorder. Some more daring historians have tried to overcome the difficulties posed by the union by ignoring it as far as possible. Scotland, after all, retained many of her traditional institutions after

B

the union, and these were harnessed to a way of life that is fondly believed to have been peculiarly Scottish and which doggedly withstood attempts to assimilate it to the wider world. Indeed, of so little importance is the union to most historians that in recent works on modern Scotland there is an almost complete indifference to the changing pattern of economic, political and administrative relations created by it, within which the history of modern Scotland has since developed.

Historiographical surveys are always personal, and therefore subject to disagreement. Not all, if any, of the other contributors to this volume would subscribe to the one we have offered. But all of us have accepted, often implicitly, that the union is a fact of life. It is not the union of so many of the text-books. For if Scotland lost her parliament she did not lose her independence. Not only did she retain her legal system, her kirk, her schools and her colleges, she retained her electoral system and her local government structure. Moreover, shortly after the union there was built up a set of administrative and political relations with England that was to leave her in a state of semi-independence which had marked resemblances with that of the American colonies or of Ireland. Within this complex political and administrative framework she achieved stability, prosperity and cultural excellence, and she did so, paradoxically, at the hands of a landed oligarchy whose past fractiousness had so often been one of the main reasons for Scotland's state of near anarchy.

The first three essays in this collection deal with various aspects of the growth of political stability in Scotland. Mr Cregeen deals with the pacification of the Highlands and with the process by which a tribal society was dragged into the modern world by the coercion and persuasion of the house of Argyll. It is interesting that this was the work of a great nobleman and not of the government. Indeed, as Mrs Mitchison shows, government in London was so remote from the Highlands both in terms of geography and understanding that it could offer little in the way of competent action when confronted with the rare major crises of the eighteenth century – the Jacobite rebellions. The best it could do was to muddle along, trust the dukes of Argyll, and hope. The handling of the Highland problem showed how improvised were the ordinary relations between centres of government in London and Edinburgh, and these relations are the subject of Mr Simpson's essay. In telling the story of how patronage was dispensed in those first, critical, fifty years of the union, he shows that while there was in some sense a 'Scottish system' which gave to particular individuals at particular times powers which were almost viceregal, the extent and limits of these powers were always dependent on the wider distribution of power in British politics as a whole.

But the success of the union was not simply the success of the great families in ruling an unruly country. It is impossible that the union could either have been achieved or become a success without the intervention of that interesting class, the gentry, and it is they who are the subject of the next three essays. Dr Smout continues his earlier work on their role in the story of economic and social improvement, Dr Janet Adam Smith studies aspects of the ideology with which they were associated and Dr Phillipson investigates the political implications of their growing public consciousness. For all three writers the gentry are rational improvers. For Dr Smout they show themselves as town planners and economic innovators whose stamp on the small towns and villages they created marks the face of modern Scotland. Improvement was closely linked to patriotic desires for the regeneration of their country, and as Dr Adam Smith shows, this could give rise to a patriotism that was confident, sometimes even aggressive, and yet periodically unnerved by the nagging suspicion that improvement was being achieved at the cost of national identity. Such an ideology and such tensions could have political implications, as Dr Phillipson shows in a study of a curious nationalist outburst, reminiscent of the recent revolt of the thirteen colonies, over a minor reorganization of a treasured national institution, the legal system, the structure of which has been carefully guaranteed by the Act of Union.

What exactly was the effect of the union on the country's national institutions, the legal system, the kirk and the educational structure? Professor Stein shows Scotland entering the union with a system of jurisprudence strongly influenced by the natural lawyers of Holland, gradually acquiring a maturity and independence under the influence of the sociological thinking of the Scottish enlightenment, before succumbing, in the early nineteenth century, to the English influence which has so strongly influenced it since. Mr Withrington deals with the development of education, showing an astonishing efflorescence of new types of advanced classical and practical education which could only have happened in a society with a profound feeling for education as necessary preparation for the ordinary business of life in a secular and progressive country. Dr Clark, too, writes about the pressures for modernization, this time operating on a kirk famed for fanaticism and bigotry. Manipulating the constitutional structure of the kirk, a small group of Moderate, secularly-minded clergy sought to harmonize the interests of church and state without falling prey to erastiansim. Both the organizers of education and the Moderate clergy here studied, accepted the implications of union, economic progress and political stability, as their personal aims, and confined their arguments as to the best way to bring these about. The book concludes with an essay by Professor Clive on the Scottish enlightenment, which shows how closely and integrally that movement was connected with the society of the country, and how closely the country's institutions and its aspirations had blended by the middle of the century. In particular this essay shows how the kirk was the first of Scotland's institutions to abandon the stifling priorities of the previous century.

Perhaps the most persistent and interesting theme to emerge from these essays is that of 'modernization' and 'improvement'. A whole ruling class, the great nobility, country gentlemen, lawyers, ministers, educationalists, philosophers and men of letters singly, but more often collectively, can be seen trying to adapt a given social, economic, political and ideological infrastructure to promote economic growth and social progress. They rested their faith not in the inexorable laws of a theological or secular determinism, but in the belief that progress lies in the exploitation of the advantages offered by a potentially rewarding environment. In a curious way they can be seen creating their own environment from the materials before them. In 1767 Adam Ferguson wrote this in his *History of Civil Society*:

'If we are asked therefore, Where the state of nature is to be found? we may answer, It is here; and it matters not whether we are understood to speak in the island of Great Britain, at the Cape of Good Hope, or the Straits of Magellan. While this active being is in the train of employing his talents, and of operating on the subjects around him, all situations are equally natural.'[1]

It is an observation that perfectly captures the spirit of the ideology of those who directed Scotland's fortunes in her age of improvement.

NOTE

1. A. Ferguson, *An Essay on the History of Civil Society, 1767*, ed. D. Forbes (1966), 8.

1. The Changing Role of the House of Argyll in the Scottish Highlands

ERIC CREGEEN

There is no more profound division within Scottish society than that between highland and lowland. In the sixteenth and seventeenth centuries the highlands formed an area which was culturally and politically more or less autonomous, the pattern of whose life was dictated by the system of clanship. By the end of the eighteenth century, the political and legal force of that system had been destroyed and the highlands had been drawn into the mainstream of contemporary life. It was to be the historical function of the house of Argyll, the senior branch of clan Campbell, whose chiefs were, almost without exception, men of great native ability and energy, to lead and control this revolutionary process.

The house of Argyll rose to pre-eminence by service to the Crown. In the late fifteenth and sixteenth centuries it had been charged with the 'daunting' of the highlands – that is, reducing them to obedience. In effect this meant the destruction of clan Donald, the chief rivals of the Campbells, whose vast territories formed what was virtually a semi-independent kingdom, more than one-third of the size of Scotland. By 1607 the operation had been completed and the Campbells were richly rewarded with the lion's share of the Mac-Donalds' mainland possessions. The process of expansion continued further when the first Marquis of Argyll took advantage of the financial difficulties of the MacLeans, to add their extensive lands to the Campbell empire.

By 1700 the house of Argyll was formidable indeed. Its rent-paying lands had quadrupled in size and covered at least five hundred square miles. Besides this, the Earl was overlord, or feudal superior, of most of the chiefs and landholders in Argyll and parts of western Inverness-shire, whose estates extended over an area of about 3,000 square miles. As hereditary sheriff of Argyll he represented the law of Scotland in the west highlands and was charged with the administration of justice, while as hereditary lord-lieutenant of Argyll he had control of its armed forces.

By 1700, however, the alliance, which had long existed between the house of Argyll and the Stuart kings, had broken down in the political and religious crisis of the seventeenth century. It was Argyll, more than any other man in Scotland, who in 1638 brought about the breach between the Covenanters and the Crown which led to the great civil war. When the revolution of 1688 finally expelled the Stuarts and established the Protestant succession, it was the tenth Earl of Argyll who administered the coronation oath to William and Mary at Westminster.

It was appropriate that he should have been rewarded with a dukedom in 1703. His house had assumed the role of creating and leading a new order in church and state. This had brought about the dissolution of its traditional and close alliance with the Scottish crown, but, by forging a new alliance with the Presbyterian cause and eventually with the Whig party, the house of Argyll had maintained itself, through many vicissitudes, as the controlling force in the west highlands and as the indispensable agents of the central government. After 1688 the interests of the government and the Argylls were interdependent. Without the loyal support of the Argylls, the new dynasty and the Whig interest would have been left practically without a friend in the highlands.

It is ironic, however, that if it had not been for the house of Argyll, there would probably not have been a Jacobite cause in the west highlands. The political and religious alignment of the highlands was decided in the seventeenth and eighteenth centuries by clan relationships. The anti-royalism of the Campbells swung their enemies over to the King's side, and since the expansion of the house of Argyll had deprived numerous branches of the western clans of their lands, a great legacy of hatred and distrust towards the Campbells was channelled into the Jacobite movement.

II

To appreciate the political situation in the highlands at the beginning of the eighteenth century and the social revolution which the house of Argyll effected, some notion must be given of the traditional clan structure and its relation to land-tenure. Until land became commercialized in the highlands its function was to support the clan. A chief reckoned his wealth not in sheep, cattle, or acres, but in the size of his following. This was made up of his clan and 'dependers'. The inner core of the clan consisted of the chief's immediate kinsmen, the gentry of the clan or '*daoine uaisle*'. They depended on the bounty of the chief to provide them with land and originally enjoyed their benefices, usually one or two extensive farms, without leases and over several generations.

The '*daoine uaisle*' were the chieftains of the clan, responsible for organizing it as a fighting force. They were essentially a military caste, for whom courage and prowess were the ultimate values and war and cattle-raids a way of life. In default of opportunities of serving their chief at home they sought employment in the Continental armies. Manual work they despised but cattle-dealing, being in a sense a natural extension of the cattle-raid, and often indistinguishable from it, was regarded as an acceptable pursuit. They had servants and sub-tenants to do the work of their farms.

The highland clan included commoners as well. They might hold land direct of the chief as joint-tenants of a farm, but usually they lived on a tacksman's land as sub-tenants or as servants, paid their rent and labour services to him and followed him in the clan war array. Among the commoners were men claiming descent from former chiefs and chieftains and proud of this kinship, attested by their lengthy patronymics and genealogical lore. But many had no such blood ties with the clan proper. They might be descended from earlier occupants of the land or from ancient allies of the chief, or from fugitives and 'broken men'. They could nevertheless claim protection and support.[1]

The chief was served by hereditary functionaries of high status, like the seannachie, the bard and the piper, who were usually not of the name but by preserving and propagating the traditions of the clan were essential to maintaining its morale and sense of identity.[2]

The chief, as representative of the clan founder, exercised an auto-cratic but not an arbitrary power. He was expected to fulfil the traditional obligations – to provide land, to give protection, to relieve want and to exercise liberal hospitality. Under a weak or illiberal chief, the unity of the clan might be threatened by rival contenders for power but not by social divisions. A widely diffused sense of kinship and a tradition of long-continued friendship and mutual support gave to the following of a highland chief, despite its diverse origins and caste-like structure, a remarkable degree of unity.

The Duke of Argyll was chief of clan Campbell and feudal superior of many vassals holding their estates of him in return for military service or on other terms. From among his clan and vassals he could muster well over five thousand men in the early eighteenth century. But, because of the success of his forbears in annexing vast areas from other clans, his estate harboured numerous tenants who, whilst they might grudgingly admit him as landlord, were followers of other chiefs.

To counteract the danger, the newly annexed lands had been partially settled by colonists either belonging to clan Campbell or allied to it. In Kintyre in the mid-seventeenth century the Marquis settled not only his own clan and dependants but Covenanting

lowland gentry and farmers. His successor, the ninth Earl, in annexing the MacLean lands, assigned them in extensive tracts to tacksmen
(i.e. leaseholders) who were of the gentry of his own clan and one or
two reliable MacLeans. The actual colonists were their sub-tacksmen
and sub-tenants, and were frequently their kinsmen. The sub-
tacksmen, with their own sub-tenants and servants, moved into the
annexed areas as outposts of the clan Campbell and part of the security
system whereby the house of Argyll maintained its hold over widespread and hostile territory.

A petition submitted to the third Duke in 1749 by John McLauchlan of Kilbride reveals something of the danger which the settlers ran.
It shows that they themselves undertook the task of seizing their
lands from the old possessors. McLauchlan's grandfather had been
assigned the Garvellach islands in the Firth of Lorne on a 'wadsett'
(a sort of mortgage) 'and although he met several obstructions yet at
length he forcibly obtained possession of these islands which for
several years made no return to the family of Argyll'. Thus until
McLauchlan seized them, the earl's annexation had been purely
titular, and he had not succeeded in collecting any rents. 'Although
the MacLeans did for some time smother their resentment on account
of my grandfather's having thus dispossessed them, yet at length a
band of them came fully armed under cloud of night and in a hostile
manner and most riotously plundered and carried off the whole effects
and bestial on these islands to the value of 3,000 merks, and after
destroying the houses and byres, stript the possessors of their vivers
and left their wives and children stript naked and exposed to the
inclemency of the weather....'

Over the annexed MacLean lands acts of overt hostility such as this,
as well as innumerable acts of secret revenge, ranging from cattle-
maiming to arson, were going on fifty years after the actual annexation.
The position of the tacksmen in Morvern became so untenable that
it was hopeless to let farms to any but the original occupants. As will
become clear, the existence of widespread 'disaffection to the Family'
within the estate was a factor of considerable political and also
economic importance throughout the eighteenth century.

III

It is commonly held that the old highlands died on the field of
Culloden in 1746, and that the subsequent statutes abolishing hereditary jurisdictions, military followings, highland dress, and the rest,
destroyed the clan system. This is a naïve and superficial view. What
destroyed the old highland social and political structure was its growing involvement in the general cultural influence of neighbours to the

south, England and Scottish lowlands. This influence, expressed in speech, manners, clothes, religion, political sympathy and activity, trade, seasonal migration, and so on, was at work in the highlands a long time before 1745, and reached its climax considerably after.

Already by the end of the seventeenth century much of Argyll had, through the work of the house of Argyll, adopted the Presbyterian order in the church and the Whig politics of its leader. A new economic outlook can be seen in the estate management of much of the Campbell lands, as in the MacKenzie lands further north, long before 1745. Floods of impoverished highlanders are found seeking work in the lowlands in periods of crop failure. Highland chiefs are found selling their poorer tenants as indentured labour in the American colonies.[3] If in the period following 1745 there seems to be a speeding up of change in the highlands, it is because the whole of Britain, indeed of Western Europe, was passing into a more active phase of development with everywhere a sharp upsurge in population growth, an expansion of trade and industry, the achievement of new technology. The economy of the highlands changed radically, so that its near-independence was transformed into almost total subordination to the demands of lowland industry. By the early nineteenth century the supply of cattle and sheep, wool, kelp, and labour to the southern towns had become the specialized function of the west highlands.

This abandonment of an economic condition approaching, though never attaining, self-sufficiency created rural problems of a kind familiar in the enclosure movements in France and England. The depopulation of large tracts of country and the disappearance of ancient farm-towns was accompanied by an unaccustomed mobility of labour, by the rise of new villages, by intensified development of coastal areas (associated with fishing and kelp-burning) and by the emergence of what was in effect a rural proletariat, engaged in wage-labour, kelp manufacture and fishing. Inevitably the disintegration of the traditional social structure was accompanied by the growth of a new pattern of relationships based on commercial values. The chief became a landlord, often a non-resident one, treating the land no longer as a means of supporting a warlike following but as a source of revenue and as a commodity to be bought and sold. His clansmen, released from their military services and labour dues, became simply rent-paying tenants, or, losing their stake in the land, turned to wage-earning employment or emigration. Sentimental ties between chief and clan became progressively weaker.

It can be argued that the legislation that followed Culloden hastened the processes of change by predisposing chiefs to accept the values of the militarily successful and politically dominant south. As Samuel

Johnson, whose account of his highland journey in 1773 contains probably the most profound analysis of the social changes taking place, remarked : 'The chiefs, divested of their prerogatives, necessarily turned their thoughts to the improvement of their revenues, and expect more rent as they have less homage'... 'When the power of birth and station ceases, no hope remains but from the prevalence of money.'[4] This seems profoundly true, but it is to be understood not simply in the context of the aftermath of 1745 but in the whole of the preceding century. MacLeod of Dunvegan's financial embarrassment and his demand for higher rents dated from his becoming a Member of Parliament in 1741, and many another chief was lured away, first from his estate, then from his clan, by becoming involved in English politics and society after the Union. It was this spectacle that made Dr Johnson declare : 'Sir, the Highland Chiefs should not be allowed to go further south than Aberdeen. A strong-minded man like Sir James MacDonald may be improved by an English education, but in general they may be tamed into insignificance.'[5]

True to its family traditions as pioneers and innovators, the house of Argyll assumed a new revolutionary role as leader of economic and social change in this setting and can be found introducing agricultural improvement in the early decades of the eighteenth century. The Dukes revolutionized the whole basis of land tenure on their estate before 1740. They built a castle at Inveraray in the new Gothic style, one of the earliest examples in Britain of this fashion, laid out parks, gardens and woodlands. They built new towns and villages, piers and canals, established new industries and encouraged schemes of re-settlement in the highlands to prevent emigration. One after another, with remarkable consistency, the eighteenth-century Dukes pursued this new economic policy, making Inveraray the main focus of change and 'improvement' in the west highlands.

The pioneer role came naturally to them. Their political activities made them normally resident in London, so that their visits to their highland estates were usually confined to a few summer months. Their social activities, tastes and expenditure were those of the great Whig magnates. The possession of five thousand fighting men as a personal following no doubt lent a certain romantic grandeur to the Duke of Argyll in the eyes of his peers, but the spending of five thousand pounds a year was more necessary if the Duke was not to appear down at heel among the Russells, the Stanhopes and the Pelhams. A perennial need for revenue characterized the estate management of the Dukes of Argyll in the eighteenth century.

Although the execution of their programme of agrarian re-organization was sometimes in conflict with immediate political objectives, both stemmed from the same underlying philosophy. When, in his instructions to the Chamberlain of Tiree in 1756, the third Duke, requiring that tenants should henceforth pay a part of their rents in spun yarn and that their womenfolk should spin diligently, wrote : 'I'm resolved to keep no tenants but such as will be peaceable and apply themselves to industry. You'll cause intimate this some sabbath after sermon[6]', he was speaking as a good Whig. In the schemes for 'civilizing the highlands' which occupied the Duke and his friends in government after 1745, projects for linen factories in remote areas, associated with the cultivation of flax and domestic spinning, bulked large. The economic virtues of hard work, thrift and sobriety were constantly urged upon the highlanders, and were regarded by the Duke and his friends as an excellent antidote to Jacobitism and disaffection, which thrived on idleness and intemperance.

The encouragement of such virtues, however, went beyond a purely political purpose. Industrious, sober and enterprising tenants were required if the estate was to yield a steadily increasing rent. This would be beneficial not to the Duke alone, but also to the tenant. Until the period of the second Duke (1703–43), the tenurial structure of the Argyll lands had been, in spite of rent rises, indistinguishable from that of any other large highland estate. The second Duke dramatically changed the whole basis of land-tenure. First in Kintyre, about 1710, then in his other lands in 1737, he offered tacks of farms in open auction to the highest bidders, whoever they might be. The Duke's agent, Duncan Forbes, Lord President of the Court of Session, declared war on the tacksmen, convened the sub-tacksmen and sub-tenants of the various districts, and 'acquainted them with your Grace's favourable intention of delivering them from the oppression of services and herezelds (heriots) and of encouraging them to improve their farms by giving them a sort of property in their grounds for nineteen years by leases, if they showed themselves worthy of the intended favour by offering frankly for their farms such rent as honestly and fairly they could bear'.

By skilfully driving a wedge between the tacksmen and their dependants, Forbes succeeded in raising the rents substantially and letting most of the farms either to the previous sub-tacksmen, who were gentlemen farmers, or to joint tenants. The increases in rent were obtained, according to Forbes, without adding to the tenants' burdens, since their labour services to the former tacksmen had been abolished. The commutation of rents in kind followed.

Almost at a single stroke of the pen, clanship and vassalage ceased officially to count in the tenurial system of the largest highland estate, and this a decade before the '45. In future, the deciding principle in the allocation of land was, in intention at any rate, to be a financial one. At first, the public auction, with open competitive bidding, was customary. By the mid-century, finding that it led to frequent quarrels and disorder, the third Duke introduced in its place a system of private offers, which permitted other factors besides the financial one to be given weight, in particular the willingness of candidates for farms to undertake certain improvements.

Competition had been established as the ruling principle in the allocation of land. The ancient tenants could no longer presume on long attachment or kinship to the family of Argyll but must make good their claim by offering high rents, substantial improvements and the certainty of prompt payment. Clansmen had to submit their offers on the same terms as the rest in the hope that, other things being equal, their attachment and that of their ancestors to the house of Argyll would sway the issue. John Campbell, 'tennent in Ballinoe in the island of Tirrie' in 1755 wrote his petition for a farm in these words:

'Humbly sheweth – That the said John Campbell, his father and grandfather have been tennents in the said island since your Grace's family obtained the property thereof, and were the first Campbells who settled in it. As I have four sons, three whereof are married but have no possessions, I humbly propose for myself and sons to take a tack of Kilchenichmore, one of your Grace's farms in the said island, and to pay yearly therefor...seven pounds, eleven shillings sevenpence farthing sterling...'[7]

In practice claims of kinship and loyalty contined to influence estate management, but their scope was much restricted. In the long run the new criteria being applied to tenancy on the estate winnowed away many ancient families. Some emigrated to the colonies and established their whole following of sub-tenants and dependants there. Others succeeded in retaining their lands, at any rate for a period, but their function, if not their outlook and values, had changed. They were no longer the military leaders of the clan, counsellors of the chief and masters of a numerous sub-tenantry, but gentlemen farmers, owing an insecure possession of their land to the efficiency with which they promoted the improvement of the estate. Dr Johnson found them a harassed and vanishing class, and lamented equally the disappearance of their feudal virtues and the social vacuum that their going left.[8]

Gradually, in the late eighteenth and early nineteenth centuries, large-scale tenant farmers began to replace the *'daoine uaisle'*. They grazed cattle and, later in the century, sheep for Lowland and English markets, applied themselves to the improvement of their extensive holdings, and rarely had sub-tenants. This new type of enterprising farmer and dealer is typified by the family of Gregorson or McGregor who, in the second half of the eighteenth century, acquired the lease of several large farms in Mull and Morvern and of the inn at the ferry between Mull and the mainland, together with the monopoly of transporting cattle from this important grazing area to the mainland. This concentration of economic opportunities enabled Angus Gregorson to pay the fifth Duke larger rents than any other tenants on the estate.

Depopulation frequently resulted from the grazing activities of the new tacksmen. Cattle and sheep needed less attention than crops. In Morvern generally, grazing farms maintained on the average no more than twenty-two people in 1779, in contrast with the traditional mixed arable and grazing farms, where the population averaged fifty-six. This contrast between densely populated and depopulated farms became sharper as sheep-farming spread in the later years of the century.

Between the new tacksmen and the small tenantry there was not the close attachment that had bound together the '*daoine uaisle*' and their dependants, even where the original families remained. For the first time military recruitment became difficult in the highlands. As a highland minister wrote in 1792 : 'A military spirit prevails much among the gentlemen of this country; they wish to keep the men, but their lands give so much more rent by stocking them with sheep that they cannot withstand the gain.'[9]

IV

The second Duke's new leases had established a larger body of direct tenants on the estate than had been there before. It was clearly intended that the former sub-tacksmen and small tenants should benefit from the removal of the tacksmen. Indeed the Duke saw himself as their protector.[10]

What were the actual results of the competitive system on this tenantry in the long run? The population of the highlands was increasing fast from about the middle of the eighteenth century. This fact, combined with the extension of cattle rearing and the arrival of sheep-masters, who bid strongly for farms, meant a steadily increasing demand for land and consequently rising rents. Rents were pushed up even higher than they need have been by fierce rivalry between different clans. The rent of the Garvellach islands rose, when the lease was open to competitive bidding, from about £14 in 1749 to £42 in 1757, owing to traditional antagonism between the two contending parties, McLauchlan of Kilbride and McDugald of Gallanich. Such situations, in which clan feuds expressed themselves in ferocious bids and counter-bids instead of in pitched battles and cattle-raids, were occurring over much of the Argyll estate until the end of the eighteenth century.

Tenants were often ruined by the high rents resulting from the competition for land. More than half of the small tenants who received new leases in 1737 lost them through insolvency and other causes within a decade, and in general small tenants reverted to holding from year to year, at the landlord's will. There was a general and extreme instability in the occupancy of farms. In 1779 the rent of farms in five Kintyre parishes stood at about 250 per cent of the level of rents in 1720. In this period of half a century the surnames of the tenants, in all but seven of the fifty-five farms, changed.

Entry into a world of competition led to modifications in the social structure which differed from one district to another. In the extensive grazing areas of Mull and Morvern, as in the more purely arable district of Tiree, society remained clearly divided between small, usually poor, tenants and gentlemen-farmers, paying on average ten times the rent.[11] In Kintyre, on the other hand, where the existence of the busy port of Campbeltown produced an interpenetration of trade and agriculture, and greater prosperity than was common in the highlands, the new social structure was characterized by a class of middling tenant-farmers who bridged the gap between the impoverished small tenantry and the gentlemen-farmers.

A rising population, combined with agrarian changes, tended to create a large landless class unknown before in the highlands. Emigration overseas or to the new lowland industrial towns drained off large numbers, but war conditions and the movement of prices in the last two decades of the eighteenth century and the first two of the nineteenth created new incentives to expand the fishing industry and the production of kelp from sea-weed. Lairds sought to discourage emigration in these circumstances. Farms were divided into individual crofts for fishermen and kelp-burners. It is in this period that the crofter emerges in coastal areas, taking the place of the traditional 'common tenant' and inheriting many of his characteristics.

v

Competition had come to stay, and its long-term effects were revolutionary. But it would be mistaken to think of clanship as irrelevant to the Argyll estate after 1737. Reference has been made to the instability of tenancies. Thus of sixty-one farms in Mull and Morvern for which information is available, thirty-nine changed hands wholly or in part between 1744 and 1779. But of the other twenty-two, where the tenant's surname did not change, twenty-one were in the hands of tenants of the name of Campbell. Could free competition produce such a remarkable result, or are other influences at work?

Ironically the clan Campbell had never been more vitally important to their chief than in the years following 1737. Jacobitism was rife and a rising was preparing to overthrow the Hanoverians. Some of the native gentry had regained their old lands by outbidding the Campbells in the newly-established auction of leases and the disgruntled Campbell colonists were threatening to leave Mull and return to the mainland. The new landlordism of the ducal house was placing in peril the police and security of the estate, perhaps even the stability and safety of the government. Without the backing of his clan the Duke's traditional role as guarantor of peace and order in the west highlands could not be sustained.

The third Duke who succeeded his mercurial brother in 1743 showed a sound appreciation of the crisis. He answered the situation by making political loyalty a pre-condition of tenancy on his estate. The instructions to his various chamberlains in 1744 contained the following clauses:

'You are to treat with the tenants of that part of my estate under your management for tacks of the farms where the possessors are under bad character or are not affected to the Government or my interest, and in farms that are not now under tacks you are to use your endeavours to introduce tenants that are well-affected to the Government and my family, and as I am informed that my lands are rather too high-rented in these countrys, so that there may be a necessity of some abatement of rent, I do approve that those abatements be chiefly given in those farms where you can bring in people well disposed to my interest.'[12]

In another instruction the Duke wrote : 'I would have it made a condition of the tacks that every tenant should take the oath of allegiance and a promissory oath never to raise or encourage any rising in rebellion against the present Government.'[13]

These measures and the elimination of numbers of the MacLeans and nearly all the Camerons from holding tacks for their participation in the '45 restored the Campbells to their holdings and made sound politics in future an essential condition of tenancy. Conversely, it turned the large tenants into collaborators with the Dukes in schemes of improvement. Their shaken loyalty to the Family was restored. They began to apply themselves to fulfilling the conditions contained in their leases concerning the enclosure of the land, the planting of trees, the draining of mosses, the building of slated houses. The Campbell tacksmen of the late eighteenth century were developing from chieftains into gentlemen-farmers, but in spite of innovation, clanship and estate management clearly were not yet divorced in the Argyll lands.

The cohesion of the clan Campbell under the third Duke showed itself not only in the relations between Duke and tenants but in the close alliance that the Duke maintained with that numerous body of Campbell lairds who were his vassals in Argyll. For about a generation after 1743 they enjoyed a halcyon time. Under the aegis of their powerful protector and patron they had no rivals to fear in the west highlands after 1746. They dominated Argyll politically by their near-monopoly of magistracies and commissionerships of supply (their Achilles' heel was their lack of freehold voting rights, since most of the property in Argyll was held of the Duke, not of the Crown). A web of intermarriage linked together branches of the Campbells into closer unions and maintained the integrity of their properties. Their solidarity is evident, too, in business partnerships and in mutual guarantees of credit. Their style of life was increasingly influenced by the ducal house. One notes the spread of a fashion for new country houses, parks and other embellishments; for town houses, carriages and servants in livery; for English and lowland ways and often ruinous expense.

In return for their solid political support (no more than a handful of Campbell lairds ever went over to the Jacobites), the Duke rewarded them amply out of the enormous store of his patronage, though he diplomatically kept open a channel of army promotion for the MacLeans and other highlanders, as a means of converting them into loyal subjects of the King. The alliance of the Duke and vassals went beyond politics into economics. Enterprising Campbells initiated and promoted ducal improvements at Inveraray and in the estate at large. The almost hereditary positions which several ancient families occupied in the estate administration gave them influence over it. Innovations in animal breeding, agricultural practice and tree-planting at Inveraray spread quickly to other estates in Argyll. New enterprises, underwritten by the Duke, for developing the economic potential of the highlands offered the Campbell lairds opportunities of participating: timber contracts for the iron furnace established on Loch Fyne in 1754; a spinning school and factory set up at Inveraray, and later a woollen factory at the Bridge of Douglas with all the shareholders Campbells; a whaling company at Campbeltown, and other ventures.

The third Duke played a dual role, half traditional chief, half modern landlord and entrepreneur. An estate management based on dispassionate economies was still impossible. Competition for land operated within limits set by political security and family alliance, and new enterprises mainly benefited the Duke's kinsmen and friends. In spite of the benevolent intentions of the Duke, circumstances still forbade the neglect of political connections. For the inhabitants of the former MacLean lands the Duke's policy was still 'daunting of the isles' and dividing the spoils among his clan.

VI

Inevitably the close identification of the Argylls' programme of economic expansion and the interests of a loyal élite provoked the resentment of the islanders. The history of the island of Tiree may be cited as a case-study in ducal intentions, often frustrated by native resistance. It is a small, flat, windswept Hebridean island, lying open to the gales of the Minch, destitute of shelter or a single tree, but favoured with good light soil and a long growing season. After being acquired from the MacLeans of Duart in the 1680s the whole island had been set in tack to a succession of Campbell tacksmen, who had sub-let to kinsmen and friends. In 1737, in the reorganization of the estate, Ardkinglas lost his tack but several Campbells gained leases of farms and continued to hold them, usually as absentees. Tacks of several farms were also gained (or regained) by cadet houses of the MacLeans resident in Tiree. Roughly half of the farms were in the hands of common tenants and continued to be so even after they had lost their short-lived leases.

In this isolated island, cut off for months on end from the outside world, the authority of a handful of resident Campbell colonists was limited by the influence which the MacLean gentry continued to have over the mass of small tenants. The Duke's chamberlain of Tiree, arriving in 1745 to recruit soldiers for the Government, had to retreat in alarm before menacing crowds of islanders. The ring-leaders were arrested after the rising and gaoled for a time at Inveraray, and on their return to Tiree were excluded from land-holding. Disaffection, however, persisted.

Between 1737 and the end of the century the instructions of successive Dukes to their chamberlains in Tiree range over a wide variety of 'improvements'; the construction of a harbour and roads and the provision of wheeled transport (unknown in Tiree at that date, as in most of the highlands); the drainage of peat-mosses and the building of sea-walls to preserve the land from inundation; the division and enclosure of farms and commons; the improvement of blood-stock and seed-grain, and the introduction of new crops; new domestic industries, schemes for training craftsmen, encouragement for fishermen, and much else.

Some elements of this ambitious programme were achieved; others

C

failed. Success and failure were unpredictable. There was a modest improvement in communications, some progress in land-reclamation and activity in the building of march-dykes, and a revolutionary change in crops with the introduction of hay and potatoes. A long-standing handicap to the export of cattle – their liability to the disease, red-water, when moved to other districts – was overcome by establishing an export trade in salt barrelled beef. In the third Duke's time, the domestic spinning of linen yarn employed over a hundred women and girls, and under the fifth Duke, marble was being exported from the Balephetrish quarry.

There was something doctrinaire, and often transitory, about much that was attempted. None of the new industries was long-lived. Projects for new fishing villages were disappointing in their outcome. Agricultural reform barely affected the island's basic technology or changed the structure of the run-rig farms with their joint tenants and shared arable and grazing land. In part they failed because of deficiencies in the islanders' resources of raw materials and skill, because of remoteness and poor communications, and because of inimical government policies, which, for example, by their legislation destroyed the domestic distilling industry which was Tiree's main export trade and which paid the landlord's rents – rents which, incidentally, though moderate by contemporary standards, absorbed half of the island's gross revenue.

Other, non-economic, factors played a decisive part too. The islanders were extremely reluctant to give up traditional ways and to accept what they considered to be lowland innovations. Nor must the effects of clan sentiment be under-estimated. 'The small tenants of Tiry are disaffected to the family. In this disposition it is thought that long leases might render them too much independent...and encourage them to that sort of insolence and outrage to which they are naturally prone and much incited by their chieftains of the MacLean gentry.' This was written by one of the chamberlains, not in the late seventeenth century, when it might be expected, but as late as 1771.[14] The islanders frequently obstructed improvements for no other reason than that they were regarded as Campbell tricks to deprive them once again, as another yet more wily manœuvre in the 'daunting of the isles'. There could be no radical reform of agriculture without long leases for the smaller tenants, and there could be no long leases so long as distrust lingered on. The attitude of the islanders was summed up in a popular saying still current in Tiree : '*Mur b'e eagal an dà mhàil, bheireadh Tiridhe an dà bharr.*' (But for the fear of double rent, Tiree would yield a double crop.)[15]

The fifth Duke (1770–1806) attempted a wholesale solution of the economic and demographic problems in Tiree. Like all his contemporaries he had no use for the run-rig farm and joint tenancy. In his sweeping scheme of reform he planned to give compact individual farms to the more prosperous joint tenants. The surplus tenants and the cottars, the 'supernumeraries' as he called them, were to be removed and settled in new fishing villages, receiving small crofts and other assistance provided they fished. Impeccable in theory, the scheme was a total failure in practice. It embodied many of the defects of doctrinaire planning and was highly unpopular. With the spirit of resistance spreading through the island and giving rise to plans of emigration, the Duke seized the first pretext to withdraw his plan.

In fact the joint farm represented a very practical adaptation to circumstances of material poverty and extremely low technology. Jointly the 'fellowship' of the farm could survive where isolated tenants would be at a disadvantage. Further, it lent itself to the maintenance of a kinship system in which all near relatives enjoyed rights to a share in land – rights which continued to be exercised and recognized even when it led to the utmost fragmentation of farms. The Duke's plan would have involved the abolition of joint run-rig farms and threatened basic elements in the traditional system. Run-rig was to survive for many years to come.

In his last years the Duke saw a gleam of hope in events in Tiree. To solve the problem of increasing population (around 1,500 in c. 1750, it was 2,776 in 1802 and would soar to 4,453 by 1831) the Duke took over the farms of the large tenants, including the absentee Campbells, and divided them into crofts and individual farms for the small tenants and cottars, offering long leases to those who undertook improvements. For the first time for a hundred and twenty years, the islanders' hostility to the house of Argyll began to wane. Presented with the prospect of a stake in the land they reacted with unaccustomed vigour, adopted new systems of cropping and new techniques, and even began to divide up the run-rig farms into individual holdings.[16]

VII

By the end of the eighteenth century the role of the house of Argyll had undergone a complete transformation. Jacobitism was no longer a live issue and so the government no longer needed a watchdog to overawe the west highlands. The fifth Duke was the first of his house to be free from a political role and so, under him, the house of Argyll was able to emerge as head of a more purely economic organization and as spokesman of a general highland interest distinct from that of the clan Campbell. Little was left of its character as a tribal and feudal congerie. Important changes took place in the make-up of the tenant body, in the composition of the feuars and in the character of the estate administration. All reflected the decline of kinship ties and political motivation, and the growing dominance of economic stimuli.

Economic considerations determined the choice of tenants much more than under the third Duke, but this is not to say that the largest rents always carried the day. Rents might be reduced for tenants of the right calibre, and stability of occupancy was given an important place. Nevertheless the position of the Campbell tenants decayed in this period. In particular they suffered through the creation of small holdings in coastal areas.

Dramatic changes were also taking place in the composition of the Duke's feudatories, that deeply entrenched body of Campbell proprietors whose alliance with the house of Argyll had long been of crucial importance in enabling the Dukes to fulfil their traditional role in the highlands. The ranks of these ancient families were being thinned by bankruptcy. The Duke's agent wrote to him in 1797 of 'the bankruptcy of so many of the old familys in Argyllshire whom your own goodness has led you to regard as so many parts of yourself – Dunstaffnage, Glenfeochan, Gallanoch, Inverliver, Ederline, are all irretrievable, and this day I have had a meeting with the creditors of Comby, who by an injudicious interference with his credit for the support of the others has brought himself into very great pecuniary difficulties....In my last letter I noticed some good is to be expected from ill. Here your Grace is about to lose a number of hereditary captains, who were ready to attend you to the field...but in their place you are to expect persons of more placid dispositions whose study will be to introduce industry and manufactures into the country and to convert it from a warlike into a rich one.'

The involvement of Comby in an attempt to save the credit of his fellow Campbells is in keeping with the solidarity of this remarkable body of kinsmen-lairds. Like climbers roped together, the fall of one could bring a whole team down.

Their days of influence in the Argyll administration were numbered too. This had always been entrusted to leading Campbell families. With the increasing absence of the Dukes the chamberlains of Argyll, as the chief officials, enjoyed greater authority. Each October the Duke, with his Receiver-General, would meet the Chamberlain and his colleagues or deputies at Inveraray to audit their accounts, hear business and give instructions. Such instructions were usually fairly brief, and the Chamberlain retained a wide discretion in day-to-day administration. Though most of his business was concerned with the granting of tacks and the collection of rents and feu-duties, it also meant deep involvement in politics. Before and after the '45 the

Chamberlain of Mull and Morvern maintained a regular correspondence about the state of the country and the progress of disaffection with the Duke's Edinburgh agent, Lord Milton, who was also the effective head of government in Scotland.

After the abolition of the system of tacksmen in 1737, the administration had to be expanded in order to deal with matters that had previously been part of the tacksmen's duties. A great many small tenants were now directly under the chamberlains. By the mid-eighteenth century there were separate chamberlains for each major district of the estate. As schemes of economic development and agricultural reform got under way, their duties became more multifarious and exacting. The instructions given to them were increasingly long and detailed, their content was more and more economic. The fifth Duke's agent, James Ferrier, who was a paragon of business efficiency, carried out a drastic reform of the financial system. Under a steady fusillade of criticism the older chamberlains retired. Their places were taken by a new type of official, men with greater skill in accountancy, law and practical farming, without pretensions to landed estates, and without clan and family ties with the Argylls. After 1800 only one Campbell remained in the five chamberlainries.

The Duke had no obligation now except to make the estate profitable, and it would seem that the evolution of the house of Argyll from power to profit was complete. But this was not the end of the story. The fifth Duke, for all his love of economy and efficiency, was a man of broad humanity. Whilst running his own highland estate, he was very conscious of the crisis in which the whole region was becoming involved. He saw that if the future of the highlands was to be other than that of a colonial territory, supplying raw materials and labour to the lowland industries, there had to be a master-plan to channel the benefits of the Industrial Revolution into the highlands. He discouraged emigration as a solution, advocating instead the fullest exploitation of highland resources.

There was scarcely a single enterprise in the highlands in which he did not take a leading part. His sanguine hopes included new industries, roads, canals, fishing villages and a score of other schemes. The new sheep farms would be linked with wool factories and would employ the displaced population. He was elected first president of the newly formed Highland Society, and was recognized as one of the great exponents of highland affairs.

The new role of the house of Argyll was that of protector and leader to the whole area. But in this role the fifth Duke enjoyed little success. He found himself struggling against the tide of events, a situation in which no member of his house had ever been for very long. The

Argylls had been leaders, successively, of political, religious and economic revolution, and had drawn the west highlands out of isolation and independence into the mainstream of events. But their attempts 'to introduce industry and manufactures into the country and to convert it from a warlike into a rich one' were doomed not to succeed. After the collapse of kelp and agricultural prices in the 1820s, the highlands, with a population perhaps double that of 1750, faced a future of dire poverty, famine and massive emigration. Their fate was to become sheep-walks and sporting estates, with a dwindling and aged population. Being in the mainstream was to men, in actual terms, economic decline and cultural decay.

NOTES

1. *Collectanea de Rebus Albanicis* (ed. Iona Club, 1847), 80–97, 196–208.
2. The Rev. William Matheson, Department of Celtic, University of Edinburgh, has drawn my attention to the fact that a chief's functionaries and men of skill were commonly not of the chief's name. The men of skill form a special category, but a chief might deliberately appoint his chief officials from other names in order to attach them and their friends to his person.
3. I.F. Grant, *The Macleods* (London 1959), 404–9.
4. Samuel Johnson, *A Journey to the Western Islands of Scotland* (London 1775), 216–17.
5. James Boswell, *Journal of a Tour to the Hebrides*, Thursday 2 September (Boston 1965), 208.
6. Inveraray MSS, Instructions 1756.
7. Inveraray MSS, v65.
8. S. Johnson, *Western Islands*, 197–203. His remarks on the tacksmen form an eloquent plea for the preservation of this class. 'If the tacksmen be banished, who will be left to impart knowledge or impress civility?' He notes that a growing burden of hospitality was falling on the ministers, as the tacksmen disappeared. In the nineteenth century the tacksman's role as social leader and educator was largely taken over by the ministers.
9. *Statistical Account of Scotland*, IV (1792), 575 and note.
10. In his instructions to the Chamberlain of Argyll in 1729 (Inveraray MSS), the second Duke wrote: 'You are to enquire into the condition of the sub-tennents of Glenary and Glenshyra, and particularly to examine what rent each pays for his possession to my tacksmen... and if they complain of any abuses, you are to protect and redress them as far as lawfully you can.'
11. B.H. Slicher van Bath, *The Agrarian History of Western Europe A.D. 50–1850* (London 1963), 129–30.
12. Inveraray MSS, loose papers.
13. Inveraray MSS, v65.
14. Inveraray MSS, v65 'Remarks on the Island of Tyree'.

15. I am indebted to members of my Extra-Mural class in Tiree for this information, and in particular to Mr Allan MacDougall, Cornaig-more.

16. Eric R. Cregeen (ed.), *Argyll Estate Instructions in Mull, Morvern, Tiree, 1771–1865* (SHS 1964), 73–8, 87, 92–4.

2. The Government and the Highlands, 1707–1745

ROSALIND MITCHISON

From 1689 onwards Scotland was ruled by a set of monarchs chosen by English politicians for English political purposes, and by a series of ministries thrown up in the changes of political power in England who were usually ignorant of and indifferent to the problem of government in Scotland. Only on the rare occasions that Scottish government presented major problems or caused trouble that could not be ignored, as it did just before the Act of Union, and during the jacobite rebellions and the Shawfield riots, was this system suspended. Otherwise government in Scotland was ramshackle and confused in structure, improvised and halting in execution. An example of this system is the destruction of the Scottish Privy Council in 1708 for purely partisan reasons, a move which left the functions it had discharged either to lapse or to be disputed between the Secretary of State for Scotland, the Lord Advocate, the judges, and those politicians who had wangled a position on the Commission of Police. No thought was given to the relation between these officers and institutions, let alone to the crucial problem of contacts between them and the Cabinet, or how far they could in practice replace the Privy Council. How the system would in fact operate, given the realities of Scottish problems and English needs, and what would be the real channels of power and influence, were left to be found out in practice.

The special Scottish problems of government which came into the range of the politicians in this haphazard way were the related ones of strong jacobite feeling, particularly in the north-east, and the general control of the Highlands. But in 1707 the Highlands did not offer any immediate threat. The massacre of Glencoe had been successful as a piece of terrorism : it had forced the jacobite chiefs to acknowledge William III. After that event the fort at Inverlochy and the payment of subsidies to the chiefs persuaded the Highlanders to preserve the appearance of tranquillity so long as the rest of Scotland was tranquil. Politicians were able to forget that in the summer of 1689 it had looked as if a jacobite army would oust the government of the 'Glorious Revolution' entirely from Scotland. For all that, the Highlands had not really been settled or incorporated into the political life of the country as a whole. As Eric Cregeen shows in his essay, the revolution settlement was identified with the house of Argyll, and therefore it was impossible for those clans which had lost lands, power or over-lordship and superiorities to the Campbells in the dirty work of the 1680s to rest satisfied.

This situation produced a hard core of non-cooperation in the southern Highlands, among the Camerons, Macleans, Macdonalds and Appin Stewarts. Their jacobitism was motivated by hatred of the Campbells much more than by personal affection for the Stewarts or appreciation of any merits they might have as kings. To this territorial embitterment was added catholic and episcopalian discontent in these and other parts of the Highlands. But episcopal loyalty was strong also in the north-east, an area richer, more populous and politically more important than the Highlands. Because the north-east wanted an episcopal church and was denied it under the new regime, it was jacobite.

'Government' as a word applied to Scotland in the eighteenth century is anything but self-explanatory, and includes several distinct manifestations. The ultimate resource of power was of course the Cabinet in London. In this body there might or might not be someone of influence who paid serious attention to Scottish affairs, or knew anything about them. Subordinate to this was the machinery in Edinburgh : the legal officers of the Scottish administration, chosen by the London ministry of the day and dismissable by it. If there was a Secretary of State for Scotland, as there was till 1725 and again from 1742–6, these were part of his empire. If there was not they would be given instructions by whoever inside the Cabinet took over Scottish business, for instance by Townshend during the earlier part of the Walpole era. In addition to the law officers were the judges. In the eighteenth century much of what we would call government in both England and Scotland was done by the courts. The judges of the Court of Session, especially the Lord Justice-Clerk and the Lord President of the Session, had a lot to do with the running of the country and were not dismissable by the government in London however much it might dislike them. It was the sympathy of many of the judges for the Shawfield rioters in 1725 that at first paralysed the government in Scotland. Any recently established ministry could count on the sup-port only of that part of the Scotch administration which it had itself appointed, and was consequently bound to be weak. Weakness or instability in London would thus be magnified in disagreement or indecision in Edinburgh.

Over and above this more or less formal structure stood the Dukes of Argyll. For a while the second Duke, and later and for much longer his brother and successor, the Earl of Islay, were managers for Scotland, controlling the patronage with a minuteness that led to constant complaints about dictatorship. By the late 1730s almost all the judges owed their position to one or other of the Dukes. They have a further importance because their estate was the greatest and most prosperous unit in the Highlands, and the one to which the most comprehensive heritable jurisdictions adhered. The Duke was hereditary sheriff and Lieutenant of Argyll. He controlled its Commissioners of Supply and Justices of the Peace, who would be members of clan Campbell. As Mr Cregeen shows, the Dukes of Argyll had not yet abandoned their political role as the leaders of the anti-Stewart movement in Scotland. They had also as individuals a particularly close personal bond with members of the judicial system. The second Duke used the Lord President, Forbes of Culloden, as his estate adviser and agent and the third Duke used the Lord Justice-Clerk, Lord Milton, for the same purpose. So no decisions made by them on estate policy can be divorced from questions of government.

The model of government in eighteenth-century England, which was being copied in Scotland, was one of almost negligible central executive power. The country was expected to administer itself through Justices of the Peace. On these lay the burden of carrying out the criminal law, maintaining highways and caring for the poor. Taxes were raised by separate machinery. The whole system was bound together by common assumptions, by patronage and by influence. It was a comfortable one for the increasing number of families that in one way or another were connected with the legal establishment : as these families provided the growth points of eighteenth-century Scotland in intellectual and economic affairs, it did much to develop the country. It was indeed a system which worked well enough provided its assumptions were accepted, but it was not capable of being the vehicle of a particular policy. Under it, new ideas or institutions might grow, but they could not be forced into a special mould. A line of action could not be pushed through.

However well this model of government worked for the lowlands, and even in the north-east, it cannot be regarded as suited to the Highlands, where long-standing habits of feuding, cattle theft and blackmail survived, and where clan chiefs or feudal superiors had authority much greater than the government. Such an area needed to be controlled by law backed by force, and also to be cajoled or coerced by political pressures. Neither could be done by this system in any adequate way. In any case, outside the area under Argyll the refusal of leaders and chiefs of jacobite sympathies to take the Oath of Allegiance meant that there were hardly any Justices of the Peace.[1] According to the Duke of Atholl there were only ten in Perthshire when the 1715 rising opened.[2] The prevailing opinion in legal circles, the families that provided the advocates and judges, was that the freedom of the English system of government would be fully extended to Scotland. Lawyers called this 'compleating the Union'. It would mean that the ordinary citizen, by which was meant the landed gentleman, was neither under the orders of government nor responsible to a great noble or clan chief. He would be answerable only to the law. Lawyers disliked the heritable jurisdictions, and the fact that the feudal law of Scotland still gave a real meaning to the rights of the superior. There was little opposition from them when, after the Revolution, the government dropped the habit of making clan chiefs stand surety for one another and for their clans. Here again there showed the problem created by the abolition of the Privy Council. It was the Council that had kept an eye on the clans, had used one chief against another in special commissions. It was in the Privy Council too that the right to call up the militia lay.

The pattern of power as it existed in 1707 was to be frozen. This meant that the two great imperialist clans of the preceding two centuries, the Campbells and the MacKenzies, remained in possession of vast areas of the Highlands, surrounded by a network of smaller, hostile clans, who wanted to regain these lands. In the Campbell case this was complicated by the fact that the Duke of Argyll had acquired the superiority of a good deal of the lands still occupied by their neighbours and opponents, by the Camerons of Lochiel and the Stewarts of Appin for instance.

This was not a situation likely to remain stable. But there were elements in the structure of clanship that gave advantages to government, as was shown in both rebellions. Clanship and superiority were weapons that both sides in politics, jacobite and Hanoverian, could use, provided only some attention was paid to their working. This was shown during the 1715 when the government allowed Simon Fraser, claimant to the lands, leadership and title of his clan, to go north and swing the Frasers to the Hanoverian side. There was a similar instance when Campbell of Fonab, by merely appearing, took the castles of Kilchurn and Finlarig from the Breadalbane men. They would not fight against him. (It is of course possible that they would not have fought against anyone : we do not know with what instructions the old Campbell Earl of Breadalbane sent his men into the rebellion when he at last decided which side he would back.) In short, clans could be gained by personal and territorial leaders, and could be manœuvred against other clans. The word 'manœuvred' is used with deliberation : in both rebellions, when Highlanders came up against each other there was very little actual fighting. The campaigns were like those of the Italian condottieri of the fifteenth century. Simon Fraser, Lord Lovat as he became, recaptured Inverness for the government at the cost of one casualty. But government circles, where legal opinion was dominant, came to dislike the idea of using one clan to control another even without bloodshed. It was distasteful to the concepts of the legal establishment. This dislike of threat and force as acknowledged weapons of government extended gradually to the society which used such a system. People began to apply to the Highlanders the sort of language that sixteenth-century government had used about the people of the Border. 'Even from their cradells bredd and brought up in theft, spoyle and bloode' was a comment of James VI about the Borderers. It could have been used by many in the lowlands of eighteenth-century Highlanders. But such a sentiment was late in growing: it did not appear until the pacification of the other jacobite areas had isolated the Highlands as a problem.

The government at first hoped that the Highlands would quieten down without drastic action. There was a general optimism that treating the chiefs like lowland gentry would transform them into such people. Such a view was not entirely misplaced; in 1711 when Macdonnell of Glengarry's men were caught out driving other people's cattle and gaoled the chief was prepared and able to use political pressure against Colonel Grant of the Independent Highland Company who had caught them.[3] In 1716 when the Hanoverian Garrison quartered in his house accidentally burnt it down, Glengarry claimed damages as an injured civilian as if the garrison had had no particular military reason to be there; and the Justice-Clerk recommended that he be at least partly satisfied because he had made himself unpopular with his neighbours by surrendering relatively early.[4] The chiefs of Glengarry were unusually double-faced, but there was another leader equally anxious to get the best of both worlds. After 1715 Simon Fraser, Lord Lovat, turned from rape and raiding to election politics, and treated his clan and its lands as a private estate. With 'I am resolved that the Lord Lovat shall be always Master of the shire of Inverness'[5] he created a system of faggot votes that would have been the envy of any lowland peer. With the best of both worlds available, there was always a hint of violence if he did not get his way. Lovat, not surprisingly, was a leading supplicant for government patronage.

The trouble was that the English system of government needed patronage to make it work, and in Scotland there was not enough of this available for chiefs and leaders who were thinking of abandoning jacobitism. At certain times there were the Highland Companies, ownership of which enhanced the position of a chief and his clan, and also brought in money. There was the bait of membership of Parliament. There were the sheriffships of Ross and Inverness in the crown's gift. But apart from a few trifling customs posts and sheriff clerkships, that was all. In 1738 Forbes of Culloden, the Lord President, suggested the formation of several Highland regiments. It was a proposal that would have done much to relieve the shortage of patronage, but nothing came of it. In 1740 Islay was trying to get a commission for young Stewart of Appin : it 'would be of service to the Government', he wrote, since it would help the young man to become a 'sincere convert'.[6] But prizes of this kind needed a good deal of asking, and it was widely felt, particularly by the Squadrone, that the Whig clans had the first claim on those spoils that were available.

Control and influence in the Highlands were weakened by the divided nature of the government in Edinburgh and the party structure of Scottish politics. The constitution wished on Scotland in the Act of Union provided that the Scottish peerage was only partly represented in London. When the Hamilton case of 1711 made it clear that there was no easy way by an English peerage to the House of Lords for peers of Scotland, the election of the sixteen representative peers, already important, became an occasion for a major show of strength. Only a party strong enough to contend for several of these seats could hope to be of weight. No aspiring Scottish lord could hope to have political advantages except by winning in this election. So the rival Whig parties in Scotland held together with much greater coherence than did their allies in London. Thus while groups in London grew, changed and dissolved in the forty years after 1707, those in Scotland remained remarkably static – the followers of the house of Argyll and of the Squadrone. The latter party had played an important part in the passing of the Act of Union, and though never numerically very strong, continued to hold a large part of the Scottish aristocracy who resented or opposed the Argylls. It was powerful enough to get political reward. The two Whig groups shared power and profit grudgingly. The third party in Scotland, the jacobites, had also to be taken seriously, even if only to the extent of keeping it out of preferment. Unlike English Jacobitism, which tended to be a disgruntled refuge for those who disliked the system of politics but had little positive to offer in exchange, in Scotland, it was a real political alternative to a large section of the country.

The groupings in Scotland thus accentuated the divided nature of the Whig coalition in London of George I's early years. With a good deal of ambiguity in the relationship between Argyll and the Secretary of State, Roxburghe, a Squadrone representative, as well as a completely unambiguous feud between the Lord Advocate and the Lord Justice-Clerk, it is not surprising that relatively little was done to stave off trouble in the Highlands. Government circles were not particularly worried by the Highland threat, because they were much more concerned about the active jacobitism of lowland areas. In the invasion scare of 1708 it had been for the most part lowland leaders, Erroll, Gordon, Aberdeen, who had been preventively gaoled, and this selection did not arise solely from the relative ease of laying hands on them. The military force of the north-east was much more to be feared than that of the Highlands. The 1715 was a rebellion well advertised in advance. There were conspicuous instances of packages of arms being ordered by chiefs : one for 500 of all kinds of arms had caused concern to the Commander-in-Chief[7]. Indications of trouble became more frequent until by the summer of 1715 it was clear that something was under way. Well-known agents were entering the country. Even the totally inadequate intelligence system of the government (two self-appointed correspondents behind the Highland line) could hardly fail to notice them. The Duke of Atholl, the Lord Justice-Clerk, and various other lawyers were all recommending the renewal of the old system of sureties for the chiefs, but nothing was done.[8]

Even though the Scotch administration was riven by the feud between the Lord Justice-Clerk, Cockburn of Ormiston, and the Lord Advocate, Sir David Dalrymple, it was in agreement over one fundamental throughout the 1715 and the pacification afterwards, that the rebels should be treated as leniently as possible once military action had ceased. Jacobitism was too widespread an opinion for there to be drastic action against it. There are 'not 200 Gentlemen in the whole Kingdom who are not very nearly related to some one or other of the Rebels' wrote Duncan Forbes.[9] The general attitude to rebel leaders was one of 'boys will be boys'. The only exceptions to this seem to have been among the Highland chiefs on the government side. Lovat and Munro of Foulis both urged strong action against Lovat's rival for land and leadership among the Frasers, Mackenzie of Fraserdale, and Munro was hot against Seaforth too. The Edinburgh administration was aware that 'loyalty' for chiefs and landowners was a question of prejudice and personal advantage, and that for the ordinary clansman the word was irrelevant. In both rebellions the ordinary Highlander only fought because he was forced 'out'; his own political opinions did not matter a damn. So every effort was made to pardon the rank and file as quickly as possible after the '15, and to send them home. A lot had already deserted before the campaign ended. General Carpenter, hearing that a group of prisoners had escaped from the Tolbooth of Stirling before they had been formally pardoned, wrote gloomily that these would probably now become bandits, whereas prompt pardon would have turned them 'loyal'.[10] The problem worrying government circles was the question of punishment or leniency for lesser landowners and chiefs, or for those strangely placed figures such as MacDonald of Keppoch who had a noticeable following but were not actually landowners. The Justice-Clerk repeatedly urged that Argyll, as Commander-in-Chief, be given power to treat with individuals and obtain surrenders. This would have smoothed and speeded up settlement and not involved much basic change. Leniency was inevitable, but the government in London managed to delay acknowledging this until the rebellion was over, and so lost any military advantage from it. Those forfeitures which did take place were mostly prevented from being effective by the connivance of the judges.

Though most of those inside government wished to get back to normalcy as soon as possible, there was some pressure from informed opinion to change the existing system. Islay was its main advocate. 'Nothing is a greater obstruction to us', he wrote early on in the rebellion, 'than that all the Highlanders have a notion (and I hope a just one) that when this Rebellion is over the Government will put an end to Highland troubles, they are the only source of any real danger that can attend the disaffection of the Enemies to the Protestant Succession. Several thousand men armed and used to arms, ready upon a few weeks call, is what might disturb any government. The Captain of Clanranald...has not £500 a year and yet has 600 men with him...'.[11] Another advocate of change was Captain Munro of Foulis, who wanted to see feudal superiorities abolished. But nothing positive was done. As soon as possible the whole military machinery that had helped to discipline the Highlands was broken up. The Highland Companies, the means by which the government both used and disciplined the well-affected clans, were disbanded in 1717, in spite of the fact that regular troops had had very little success in winkling out the rebels in the mountains, the expeditions against Rob Roy in particular being complete failures. Barracks were planned at Ruthven and Fort Augustus, Inverness and in Glenelg, but the government was dilatory and made difficulties over paying for the land and construction barely got under way. It was universally admitted that the Disarming Act of 1716, if it disarmed anyone at all, affected only the reliable clans. The gentlemen who had raised troops for the Hanoverian side appealed in vain for payment.[12] A small outbreak of papers telling the London government what to do about the Highlands was ignored. These papers put the usual case. The Highlanders needed education in habits of industry and in the Protestant religion. The General Assembly therefore asked for a subsidy for schools. Another paper pointed out that the Union should be completed by abolishing superiorities, which it was felt would end clanship and make the citizens of Scotland as 'free' as those of England. A third paper urged a Highland militia, to be paid when actively employed, and to have a regular and paid officer in command. The papers lay about.[13]

The minor rebellion of 1719 never created much stir in government circles. It was produced largely by foreign influence and localized in effect. The only importance it had was to undo completely any result of the Disarming Act, and flood the north-west with Spanish arms. Wade was later to report that these, easily identified, were to be found in bulk. This time nobody seems to have bothered the government with recommendations about the Highlands and nothing was done. But there were other Jacobite scares. In England there was the Atterbury plot in 1722. There were rumours of a plot in the same year between Mackintosh of Borlum, Lochiel and the young Glengarry. There was evidence that letters from Mar were circulating in the Highlands. In 1723 there was a story of the enemy landing in Ross-shire, but the ships thought to be bringing back the forfeited Earl of Seaforth turned out to be herring boats.

By 1724 the government had become sufficiently worried about jacobitism in the Highlands to give the area real attention. It was at last a body unified enough to be effective if it wished. Walpole's dominance was now established and he was pushing out the last important survivor of the old Stanhope–Sunderland bloc that had been in power, Carteret, the later Lord Granville. Roxburghe, Squadrone representative, remained as Secretary of State for Scotland for the present, but he need not be the main channel of communication. Opinions on the Highland problem were canvassed. Information was welcome. Townshend spoke to Lord Grange, the Lord Justice-Clerk, and Islay also urged him to give his opinion. The result was a sheaf of long-winded papers.[14] Lovat heard that something was in the wind and sent in a memorandum. This is a well-known document, and shares many of its ideas with Grange's. Probably the two men got together about it : they were after all to be found together later in the discreditable issue of the kidnapping of Lady Grange, and were already friends. Fortunately there is less similarity in the wording than in the content of the papers, for Lovat was a stylist. Lovat's points were the regular ones, and are now generally accepted as sound. Blackmail was systematic in all the lowland areas near to the Highlands, disturbances were on the increase; the well-affected areas were the only ones disarmed; known Jacobites (who also happened to be personal enemies of Lovat's) had been getting into positions of trust as deputy-lieutenants and Justices, and some of the Justices were not in fact landowners. In fact the system of Justices of the Peace was functioning no better than before the '15. Blame for most of this was laid by Lovat on the disbanding of the Highland Companies. Regular troops could not get about as they had been able to do and were useless for dealing with small troubles before they grew into big ones. The big Lieutenancy of eight shires held together by the Earl of Sutherland meant that there was too much power in the hands of a man who could not hope to know local issues and men well except in part of it. The Companies should be revived, Lieutenancies distributed, and with discretion, roads should be built up into the Highlands. It is true that much of this programme would be of advantage to Lovat himself, but this does not mean that the recommendations were not sound, and they may have been meant with as much sincerity as Lovat was ever capable of. 'Whatever tends in any degree to the civilizing these people and enforcing the authority of the law in these parts, does in so far really strengthen the present government. The use of arms in the Highlands will hardly ever be laid aside till, by degrees, they begin to find they have nothing to do with them.' These points were true, if obvious.[15]

Grange's papers went further. In one of them he started off by explaining, as many papers about the Highlands, then and now, have explained, that feudalism and clanship were not the same thing. But he could see that the system of military attachment and superiority did enhance the strength of some clans, and gave the whole clan system a favourable soil. This led him to discuss whether superiorities should be abolished, and in page after page he showed the inconveniences they caused. But he did this entirely from the point of view of the lowland gentlemen. He criticized not only the heritable jurisdictions but also the habit of giving the crown's sheriffdoms to great lords who were certainly not going to carry on the business of their offices. He wanted mobile sheriff courts in the bigger shires, run by sheriffs and clerks who had a real knowledge of law. From this he passed to the need to reorganize the shire system of Scotland. Inverness-shire and Perthshire were too big, while Clackmannanshire and Cromarty were obviously too small. A new shire was needed, made out of the western parts of Inverness-shire and the south of Ross, electing a member of Parliament at every election. Nairnshire and Cromarty could then be welded into the rest of Inverness-shire, and so

D

on. Then the Justiciary circuits should be remodelled into bigger groups, and a special spring circuit should bring the judges of all three of these into the Highlands. Judges and sheriffs should be made to report back regularly on the state of the Highlands. Grange did not recommend the old system of sureties. He preferred to use the judges rather than the chiefs as a form of control, to avoid encouraging and emphasizing the clan unit and the 'slavish dependence' of the old system. A wedge of foolscap on the need for education and industry in the Highlands rounded off his ideas for the time being.

The trouble with these proposals was, of course, that they went too far. No eighteenth-century government unless absolutely forced to was going to recast the land law, the criminal courts, the local government system and the distribution of seats in Scotland. By emphasizing the scale of the problem he succeeded in frightening the ministry off. But Lovat's proposals were feasible; and whether or not it took its ideas from him, the government decided to go ahead on the lines that he had laid down. Wade received a broad commission, to investigate the whole state of the Highlands, the need for Highland Companies, roads, more and better barracks, to consider the question of the Lieutenancies and the Justices of the Peace, to see how operative was the Disarming Act, and to report. How were divisions and feuds to be ended and the law enforced? In particular what was to be done about the scandal of the forfeited Seaforth estate, where the rents were still going to the exiled Earl, and the agents of the Government Commission being terrorized? Secrecy in all this was essential, so Wade was given, as cover, the job of inspecting the regular troops in the Highlands.[16]

As luck would have it Wade arrived in Scotland with this commission in 1725 just at the time of the Shawfield riots, when the urban classes all over Scotland were near to rebellion and the movement against the government showed signs of becoming national. These riots were the violent side of Scottish resentment at the new malt tax, and the tax had been imposed because Scotland was contributing very little to the central government. Glasgow was the only town in which the feeling exploded in violence, but in all the towns of Scotland it ran high. The Edinburgh brewers tried to stop business altogether, and messages ran from town to town urging similar resistance. The ex-Lord Advocate, Dundas of Arniston, was fanning the flames, and the country was near to rebellion. For once London paid real attention to Scotland. Forbes, as Lord Advocate, was asked to send frequent reports to the Duke of Newcastle. Islay was to bring the Scotch judges to order. Walpole used the crisis to force out the last remaining rival element in his Cabinet, the Duke of Roxburghe, Squadrone member and Secretary of State for Scotland. Walpole was master in London, and Islay his invaluable lieutenant.

So for a time Scotland had the attention of government and things went well. Wade made his report and started to put his proposals into practice, building roads and barracks. Six Highland Companies were created, and one went to Lovat. Wade made terms with the Seaforth tenants, so that rent paying to the Commission instead of the Earl's illegal agent should start, in return for oblivion about the past. There was a new Disarming Act, and with ceremony and dignity arms came in, over 2,000 stand. This surprised Wade, for there was no financial inducement in the Act, and metal could be put to many uses in the Highlands. On Wade's recommendation various Jacobites still in the country were granted pardons in return for expressing the right sentiments of contrition, and, also on Wade's recommendation, Mackintosh of Borlum, who was too honest to oblige with the right turn of phrase, was not.[17] Jacobite agents avoided the Highlands, and if they did not, Rob Roy had agreed, for a small subsidy, to let Wade know what was going on.[18] The Crown gave £1,000 a year for schools in the Highlands. Naturally this intense interest in London in what was going on did not last. It died out in about a year, but things still looked good. Government appeared to be winning.

Jurisdictions and clanship remained as unsolved problems. The device of the Highland Companies was a compromise between allowing the well-affected clans to remain in arms and being without defence. They were also a favour to the clans given them. Jurisdictions were a bigger advantage and one outside government control. Islay was fussing about the Earl of Cromarty who was bankrupt and had retreated home from his creditors. No effective action could be taken by them against him except with the aid of the sheriff of the county, and as he was hereditary sheriff, that was that. 'The Highlands can never be civilized so long as any person is tolerated in the giving publick defiance to the courts of the Law, and the difficultys that attends the execution of the processes of the Law in the Highlands seems to be the very essence of their barbarity', wrote Islay,[19] and suggested that Wade should take action. Wade refused: it was not his business to act as bailiff. Islay was a good enough lawyer to dislike the whole set-up of heritable jurisdictions even though his own family did well by them. Private justice was inferior to public, he thought, and he wished to see the end of both them and clanship. The Seaforth estate continued to give trouble. It was put up for sale, and clan pressure kept the bids so low that it finally went for three years' purchase to members of the clan who passed it back to the family.[20] The Earl was let off the terms of his attainder and came back. Eventually the heir was won for the government side, but a lot of the important cadet families in the clan remained influential and hostile. All the same things still looked tranquil at the end of the 1720s. They began to crumble in the 1730s.

One clear sign of the weakening of government's purpose and power is found in the behaviour of Lovat. This chief is one of the most remarkable figures of eighteenth-century Scottish politics, who would well requite a full-scale biography. He was highly intelligent, totally selfish and unscrupulous, and his charm still shows in his letters. After a scandalous early career he had become a government supporter in the '15 and so dominated the Frasers, to whom he claimed to be chief, that they had changed to the government side at his insistence in the middle of the rebellion. Then he had entered on the task of reclaiming the Fraser estates from Mackenzie of Fraserdale, who had stayed on the other side. He also set out to rule his clan as an old-style chief. In 1730 he had finished most of the long-drawn lawsuits for the estates, and by 1733 his whole claim was settled. Hanoverian government had little more to offer him except the sheriffship of Inverness-shire. This he obtained in 1733, and used to rig elections. In 1737 he was the first to fall in with a new Jacobite intrigue, and was angling for a Dukedom from James VIII. In some way this became known, and in 1739 on Wade's recommendation his sheriffship and his Highland Company were taken away.

Another thing that was both a sign and a cause of the weakening of government was the breach between the second Duke of Argyll and Walpole over the Excise scheme. Walpole transferred his friendship fully to Islay, but Islay, though a much better man than his brother for the performance of business and a far greater political intelligence, had not the standing in the Highlands of actual chieftainship. Argyll linked up with the Squadrone, and in 1741 swung the Scottish seats away from Walpole. Almost as serious as this from the point of view of the Highlands was his policy after 1737 of running down his position as chief and attempting to become a mere landowner. Rents on the Argyll estate were to be raised, and tacks were to go to the highest bidder, regardless of clan and family. The plan proved over-optimistic economically: more serious, it weakened the loyalty of the cadet branches of clan Campbell. His clan was a big unit, and one by no means homogeneously under the chief at the best of times. The judges might talk about the 'slavish dependence' of the clan system, but this was not what the chiefs of the big clans, Campbell or Mackenzie, found in practice. Their cadet houses were always liable to take a line of their own, and had to be consulted and humoured if the clan was to function as a unit. In 1740 cattle raiders were attacking

Inveraray itself,[21] and it is difficult to see how they got there without Campbell connivance. Blackmail, even if Wade had really managed to put a stop to it, was now re-established systematically, and the Argyll estate was paying regularly to the Camerons.[22] Islay could see the dangers of his brother's policy, but was powerless to interfere.

The regime of Walpole had already suffered a blow when the prime minister split with Townshend in 1730 : the crisis over the excise bill in 1733 had weakened it further. It was obviously crumbling at the end of the 1730s, while Britain slid into a series of wars. Weakness at home and war abroad made possible renewed jacobite activity in the Highlands. Murray of Broughton reported a shortage of arms, at least not enough for a major campaign, in the early 1740s, and tried to remedy this. But from the government's point of view there were more arms than it liked in disaffected hands, though it did nothing to get hold of them. Then in 1742 came the end of Walpole's rule and the start of a coalition government. Pelham and Newcastle, survivors from Walpole's imperium, allied uncomfortably with Granville and Chesterfield. Islay represented the Pelhams in Scotland and Tweeddale was put in as Secretary of State to satisfy the Squadrone supporters of the others.

If any one single event can be seen as the cause of the '45 rebellion it was this appointment. This is not a judgement based solely on the personal qualities of the Marquis of Tweeddale. Admittedly these were not up to a crisis. Through a large part of the critical November, when the rebel army was marching south, Tweeddale was unable to get to Cabinet meetings because of his gout. His knowledge of Highland geography was poor : when writing to him about the landing of the Prince his more intelligent correspondents took care to explain to him where Moidart was. Either from disinclination or inability he failed to insist on any point against the opinion of the English members of the Cabinet. He had the temperament that fusses, fails to take action all the same and later on notes with relief that the opportunity for action has passed. But the main significance of Tweeddale's appointment is that it split the forces of government in Scotland. Further, he represented the group in London that wished to pare down home commitments to concentrate on the war abroad.

He came in full of the wish to reform. Something must be done about the two main problems of Scotland, the courts of law and the disorder in the Highlands. But a brief correspondence with Forbes showed that reform would not be easy. It would require both skill and money.[23] Neither would be forthcoming under Tweeddale. The Cabinet at war was cheeseparing on the Highlands. Forbes had a plan for raising regiments in the Highlands for foreign service. Nothing was done about it : instead the Highland Companies, which had been expanded and drafted into a regiment, were taken away from their police duties and sent south. Tweeddale agreed with Forbes that this was unwise, but made no real move to stop it. Blackmail and the Watch system were now the only security for property in the Highlands. On top of it all the Highland regiment mutinied at the prospect of being sent abroad, making it clear that even for its immediate object cheeseparing was not a sound policy.

In October 1743 Islay succeeded his brother as third Duke, and immediately put into reverse the new estate policy. 'You are to use your Endeavours to Introduce tennants well dispos'd to the Government and my family', was his order to his factor, even if this meant lower rents.[24] All tenants were to take the Oath of Allegiance. Meanwhile the Duke tried to pacify the Jacobite chiefs under his superiority. The old forfeitures of 1715 had brought some of their lands to him as superior, and these were to be given back, but with reservations of forest and mineral rights. These reservations may have related to the systematic extortion the Camerons had been practising in Strontian. Lord Milton thought that the Duke's concessions would not be enough to win friendship – 'what is given will be of no use but to raise an Ennemy'[25] – but it was on the Duke's lines that charters were drawn up and ready for issue at the end of July 1745.

The '45 did not come out of the blue, though it was not as well advertised before as the '15. From early in 1744 government circles had been fussing about the risk, chasing Jacobite agents, catching some of them, watching out for recruiting agents for the Jacobite regiments abroad, and retailing stories about French fleets on their way to Scotland. One group of Highlanders, caught at the port on their way to enlist in a Jacobite regiment, were persuaded instead to join the government forces. It was a comment on the nature of Highland loyalism and an indication that a little money spent in the Highlands might have been a sound economy.[26] But Granville was an optimist, and determined to do things on the cheap, and Tweeddale was his follower. 'There is little ground to be alarmed for any Insurrection', Tweeddale was writing in July 1745,[27] with the Prince already at sea. Even when the first news of the landing had belatedly come through, his second in command, Sir Andrew Mitchell, was writing to Scotland, 'How any body with you where the truth may be easier known than it can be here, can be alarmed, is to me astonishing.'[28] The Scottish administration was too deeply split to be effective. Argyll and Tweeddale opposed each other, Argyll supported by most of the judges, who had been made by him, Tweeddale by the political side of the administration. When Cope had been appointed to Scotland, Argyll told the Lord Justice-Clerk and Tweeddale told the Solicitor-General Dundas, to maintain tolerable but cool relations with him.[29] Tweeddale was soon complaining that Cope and the Lord Justice-Clerk were keeping company together too much, in spite of the fact that Cope's appointment had been opposed by Argyll.[30] Both sides complained bitterly that the other passed them no information, though again the principals had issued instructions for minimal cooperation. The Earl of Marchmont was to remark after Prestonpans that Scotland 'was undone in the dispute between two men who should be viceroy'; Tweeddale, he added 'from resentment to the Duke of Argyll...had neglected the common and necessary precautions to defend the Kingdom.'[31] This judgement is the more telling in that Marchmont like Tweeddale was a Squadrone man.

The neglect of precautions was not simply a short-term affair. Forbes, on hearing of the Prince's landing, wrote an analysis of the Highlands situation that is well known. It begins

'First the government has many more friends in the Highlands than it had in 1715, yet I do not know that there is at present any Lawful Authority that can call them forth to Action, even should occasion require it. In 1715 Lieutenancies were established in all the Counties. If any such thing now subsists it is more than I know.'[32]

Forbes had every reason to be uncertain as to the state of Lieutenancies. Those of 1715 had never been revoked. In 1727 names had been selected for new Lieutenancies for the reign of George II. Instead of the old big Lieutenancy of the Earl of Sutherland they were mostly to be on a single shire basis. There was to be Hugh Rose of Kilravock for Nairn and Cromarty, Charles Ross for Ross, Brodie of Brodie for Moray, the Earl of Sutherland for Sutherland and Caithness, and as a climax to twelve years of political climbing, Lovat for Inverness-shire. The commissions were drawn up : expressly they included the duty of raising the militia. Then doubts took over in Whitehall. Perhaps Caithness should go to its own Earl instead of the Earl of Sutherland? Were Hugh Rose and Charles Ross prepared to act? Was it really a good idea to hand over Aberdeenshire to the Earl of Rothes? Charles Ross changed his mind and refused. And then, in the middle of this discussion the whole business comes to a halt. There is no further trace of it in the government correspondence[33] and no sign that the commissions, already made out, were ever issued, whether to Highland or Lowland landowners. Some Lieutenants from 1715 were still alive in 1745, the Earl of Buchan for instance (though he was under the impression that his Lieutenancy had lapsed), but none of those held for the Highlands.

The failure to go ahead with Lieutenancies for Scotland was

probably caused by dislike of putting power into the hands of the heads of clans. All the same, as the political situation deteriorated in the 1740s various people pointed out the need for them. But already some legal mind had raised the question, had the crown the legal right to call up and arm a militia? There survives a printed pamphlet arguing that it had. But it was general legal opinion that a militia could not be raised without Lieutenancies, and a general legal dislike of a Highland militia, which would mean putting the clans in arms. By the beginning of 1744 Tweeddale had come round to seeing that Lieutenancies were needed. He had made out the commissions but had not yet passed them to the King. Doubts had seized him : as he wrote 'the best schemes if nott putt in the right hands for execution, they will doe more harm than good.'[34] He dithered. Perhaps Forbes of Culloden would take Inverness-shire? What about the young Duke of Gordon, recently salvaged from Roman Catholicism, instead? But then there was Sir James Grant 'who thinks himself entitled to itt as also to the sheriffship which the Earl of Moray enjoys at present'. The Duke of Montrose was havering about taking Stirlingshire : 'I can never bring him to tell me his mind if he knows itt himself.' (Coming from Tweeddale this judgement has a boomerang quality.) Lord Aberdeen turned down Aberdeenshire, and there were difficulties about Ross. Lord Fortrose, the Seaforth heir, expected to get it, but he, as Robert Dundas, Lord Arniston, wrote, was a young man who had not 'hitherto shown great Constancy'.

February 1744, a month later, saw Tweeddale again asking for suggestions. He felt that the European war was at a crisis and that he must act. In March he was writing in the same strain : he was being pressed to get on with the Lieutenancies. Arniston and his son, the Solicitor General, urged him to appoint Forbes for Inverness-shire. Forbes, who wanted to reward the Duke of Gordon for his protestantism, refused and recommended the Duke. Lord Reay was a possibility for Caithness, and probably knew more about the county than its Earl. Then there was the question of Argyll. 'The Duke is Heretable Lieutenant by his Rights', but 'several are of opinion' that this 'was not altogether a regular Grant'. Still, it was very unlikely that he could accept nomination by his political rival to a post he thought his already by inheritance. The hardest problem was Ross. As young Dundas wrote, 'The persons best affected to His Majesty's Government are the Rosses and Munroes, but at the same time the Mackenzies are rather more numerous, and bear no good will to the others.' He suggested Lord Cromarty, or the office could be left vacant. This latter would have been a poor solution since Mackenzie territory was an area of great political uncertainty.

Forbes refused when asked : 'and indeed', wrote Tweeddale, 'it would appear odd here to see the President of the Court of Justice named to such an Employment.' In any case, since Forbes had been an adherent of the second Duke of Argyll and was now trying to heal the breach between the two factions, Tweeddale seemed relieved to have him out of the list. By now, April 1744, the Marquis had a new plan. The Duke of Gordon would be sheriff and Lieutenant for Aberdeenshire, and Inverness-shire and Ross should be divided. After all, Yorkshire was divided in the same way. This would solve all problems of precedence and 'might in some measure tend to reconcile the different competing interests'.

Dundas jibbed at this. The solution might be legal but 'I can't find any precedent. But the truth is the office of Lieutenant is new in Scotland and only lately introduced after the example of England, and will be governed by the same rules as it is there.' He left it to Tweeddale, who was in London, to find out what these were, but pointed out that Yorkshire, with its separate Ridings, was not likely to be a good precedent. In any case 'the Remedy will not remove the Evil. If a Munroe or a Ross is named with Seaforth...Cromarty will take it amiss and thereby divide the Mackenzies.' The trouble was that young 'Seaforth' had a large and disaffected clan, and his conversion to protestantism and Hanover had been both sudden and unpopular. The change from Highland chief into landed gentleman had been too successful. There was a real risk that political stress might split the clan, and the disorder that would follow would be worse than simple disaffection of the whole clan. However much London might ignore the realities of clanship, the Edinburgh administration could not.

A fortnight later Tweeddale was still trying to plan his Lieutenancies. Perhaps Ross should be left vacant, 'tho' from the situation of that county it seems to require the naming of a Lord Lieutenant as much as any'. Perhaps Sir James Grant would do for Inverness-shire : he had been at odds with Forbes in election matters, so Tweeddale added that he could be particularly instructed to submit his recommendations to Forbes. It must not go to the Duke of Gordon since he was to have Aberdeenshire and 'some peculiarities of his character' would make him unacceptable for a double office. Tweeddale had failed to see that what mattered was to give authority to the men whose military support would be needed in a crisis, and wallowed instead in problems of who was, or was not, acceptable to his own political gang. And so he did nothing, in spite of the invasion scare of 1744, and the topic lapsed until September 1745.

By then the '45 was well away. English politicians and Sir John

Cope had been astonished at the failure of the Whig clans to stop the rebel army. Historians have commented on it too. The Lord Justice-Clerk and Argyll agreed with Forbes that authority to call out the Whig clans did not exist. At first Tweeddale's advisers took the view that this was 'an opinion invented and published on purpose to justify the Lethargy into which the Whig Clans seem to have fallen'[35] and Sir Andrew Mitchell mocked the Justice-Clerk for asking for authority to arm without saying what the authority could be. By the end of the month Tweeddale is reported as saying that Lieutenants would now be too late :[36] by mid-October Mitchell was arguing that there had been no time, once the rebellion had started, to appoint them. In November the question had ceased to be a Highland one. The Squadrone peers, Montrose, Marchmont, Rothes and Queensberry, impatient with Tweeddale's dallying, were urging the raising of Lowland regiments without bothering about Lieutenancies.[37] Argyll at last persuaded the King to accept him as Lieutenant for Argyll, not on a royal commission but as a hereditary office. He took the oath and sent his cousin at once to raise the Campbell militia. All that Tweeddale's hesitations had done was to ensure that the only Scottish Lieutenancy was that of his greatest political enemy.

Legalism had by now gone on from niceties about Yorkshire precedents to a refusal to allow any action at all. The Lord Advocate was informing the Solicitor-General that the only legal power to raise the militia had been in the Scottish Privy Council, and had disappeared with that body. 'How you or I as Lawyers should advise the Nameing Lord Lieutenants to raise the Militia…Passes my Skill. I know they were named in the 1715 And had Instructions Given them, but I own Even at that Time I could not find out by What Rule they were to…Obey their Instructions.'[38]

The combination of Tweeddale's indecision and the lawyers' dislike of clanship had effectively dealt with one of the traditional forms of defence. Over the other, the Highland Companies, delay had been as serious if not as total. From the end of 1743 pressure had built up in London for refounding these. The King was known to dislike the idea. Tweeddale was nervous that it would mean more influence to Argyll. Forbes was in favour, but recommended also a system of cautions, to prevent the favoured clans making too much advantage out of their Companies. But in April 1744 Tweeddale wrote that a system of Lieutenants and well-chosen deputies would be less militaristic, and then neglected to create it.[39] Eventually it was agreed that there should be three new Companies. By February 1745 the commissions were on the way. In July the men were just raised, but the arms for the third Company had not come. The Companies were not trained or stationed when the rebellion broke out, and this explained the forced enlistment on the rebel side of Cluny Macpherson, who was to have captained one of them. The later Companies, raised by Forbes by special powers once the rebellion had begun, were only useful as distractions to the rebel forces.

This lamentable story of how the government created a power vacuum in the Highlands should not be taken as proof that it was impossible to govern the area on the lines attempted. It might have been possible to make a success of treating the Highland chiefs like English country gentlemen, but it would have had to be attempted with more benefits to offer. As it was, most of the small amount of spoils available went to the Whig clans, though for the few years just before the '45 there was an attempt to modify this. Kindnesses were shown to Seaforth, and the Mackintoshes and Macphersons were eventually offered Companies. If the Squadrone had been in sole power this would not have been government policy, for that party was much more severe than Argyll or Forbes on ex-Jacobites. Marchmont did not believe that there could be a sincere Whig north of the Tay,[40] and said 'once a Jacobite, always a Jacobite'. There had been some successes, conspicuous among these the fact that Cromarty managed to bring out only some of the Mackenzies. The Duke of Gordon, in spite of the 'peculiarities of his character', at least preserved neutrality, and may well have been unable to do more. But the pacification of the Border in the seventeenth century had needed more power than this system allowed. There had had to be Commissions appointed by the Privy Council, with special disciplinary powers, and even then in an area surrounded by relative law and order, the system had shown signs of breaking down in Charles I's reign, and during the war with Cromwell the whole area had reverted to banditry. There was another difficulty in the eighteenth century. The belated Jacobitism of the bankrupt Earl of Cromarty reminds us that bringing the chiefs into the orbit of other landed society was apt to increase their expenses, and that there was a marked correlation between bankruptcy and rebellion. 'Every Petty head of a Tribe who was in any Degree tinged with Jacobitism, or Desperate in his Circumstances, Assembled his Kindred and made use of the most Mutinous, to Drag the Most Possible out of their Beds and to Force others to List', wrote Forbes.[41] Even with important individuals won over there would still be a need for a Highland police force run by men who knew the area well, to protect the disarmed and peaceful clans. But it was a possible theory that with the Highland Companies, a stable government, and a few rewards to the clans in the southern Highlands, the main difficulties might have passed. There would be no guarantee of good justice so long as the Heritable Jurisdictions survived, but in a peaceful country the royal courts might have been able to supervise these. There are instances of Islay attempting to provide this supervision. Another generation without a rebellion might have ensured peace.

But in practice the necessary conditions were lacking. The central government was divided, it economized on Scotland and took away the Companies, and there were never enough rewards. Even so, the trouble when it occurred might have been localized, as both Cope and Forbes hoped, if it had not been for the work of the lawyers. Their doubts about the right of Scots to defend themselves had a paralysing effect. First of all they insisted that the Disarming Acts must be observed by their own side. Then they doubted whether there could be defence without a special commission from the King. Later they wondered whether even the Crown could issue such a commission. The result bears a resemblance to the later English muddle over the meaning of the Riot Act. Could magistrates act to quell a riot if they had not first read the proclamation? The eighteenth-century dislike of military action and authority was enhanced in the Scottish case. Tweeddale had a personal unwillingness to use the clans, for that would enhance Argyll's position. The lawyers disliked clanship still more. It reminded them of the bad old days, it was incompatible with 'compleating the Union'. There were several cases in the eighteenth century of soldiers being sentenced for murder in putting down riots, usually excise or customs riots, of which the best known is the Porteous affair. This legal climate made it easy for anarchy in the Highlands to get legal blessing. Islay at least, though he shared the legal dislike of the jurisdictions, was aware that tranquillity in the Highlands could not yet be achieved by running down clanship. Yet in the end tranquillity itself would run down the clans. The anonymous survey of the Highlands in 1750 commented that if the Campbell clan was called out on the scale that the Camerons used when they mustered, there would be 10,000 men in arms, but in practice it was possible to expect only 3,000.[42] Farming and other activities, if encouraged, as all advisers urged they should be, did prevent effective use of manpower for war. As Dr Johnson said 'there are few ways in which a man can be more innocently employed than in getting money.'

In 1746 the spate of papers on what is to be done about the Highlands begins again, and this time something is going to be done. The climate of opinion had hardened : there was to be no more of the 'boys will be boys' attitude. When Lovat, while he was still sitting on the fence, suggested to Forbes that he might be able to expect leniency whatever happened, he was answered 'no weight of interest whatsoever could prevail with the Government to act gently with such as, contrary to their expectations took Arms against them on this occasion'.[43] He was right. Besides extremely tough action against individuals at all levels of society who could be suspected of aiding the rebels, the government massed a major attack on clanship. It was three-fold in its impact; the jurisdictions and the military side of feudalism went, whether they were connected with clan loyalty or not; the carrying of arms and the dress, both real if not vital parts of Highland culture, were forbidden; and the living presence of the chiefs of the disaffected clans was prevented by the long exile of most of them. At last the government had taken a sledge hammer to crack its nut.

NOTES

1. Hew Dalrymple and the Lord Justice-Clerk, August 1715 (SRO Photostats of State Papers, hereinafter S.P., 54/7, ff. 22, 84, 164).
2. The Duke of Atholl, 5 Sept. 1715 (S.P. 54/8, f. 70).
3. David Dalrymple, 7 Aug. 1711 (S.P. 54/3, f. 67).
4. 8 Sept. 1716 (S.P. 54/12, part 1, f. 393).
5. Lovat to Fraser of Inverallochy, 3 Jan. 1741, Spalding Club *Miscellany*, ii (Aberdeen 1842), 10.
6. 30 May 1740 (NLS, Saltoun MSS, Box 400).
7. Earl of Leven, 8 Sept. 1711 (S.P. 54/4, f. 81).
8. 2 and 3 Aug. 1715 (S.P. 54/7, ff. 21, 22, 25). The Justice-Clerk thought that Mar should be summoned as a Highland chief to give surety, 23 Aug. 1715 (ibid. f. 152).
9. Forbes to Walpole, Aug. 1716, *Culloden Papers* (London 1912), i, 62.
10. 11 Sept. 1716 (S.P. 54/12, part 2, f. 407).
11. Islay, 7 Oct. 1715 (S.P. 54/9, part 1, f. 65).
12. Duncan Forbes, 8 Aug. 1745 (S.P. 54/25, part 2, f. 170).
13. 1717 (S.P. 54/13, part 1, ff. 180–195).
14. Mar and Kellie MSS at present uncatalogued in SRO. The papers are referred to in HMC *Mar and Kellie*, i (London 1904), 528.
15. S.P. 54/18, part 2, f. 220. Printed as an appendix to E. Burt, *Letters from a Gentleman in the North of Scotland* (London 1822), ii, 254–67.
16. 'Private Instructions to General Wade', 1724 (S.P. 54/14, f. 326).
17. Wade, 2 Oct. 1727 (S.P. 54/16, part 1, f. 152).
18. Wade, 20 Oct. 1725 and 13 Nov. 1725 (S.P. 54/16, part 1, f. 152 and part 3, f. 351). (NLS, Saltoun MSS, Box 402.)
19. 21 Oct. 1725 (S.P. 54/16, part 2, f. 237).
20. Anon. *The Highlands of Scotland in 1750*, ed. Andrew Lang (1898), 27.
21. NLS, Saltoun MSS, Box 402.
22. G.H.Rose, *The Marchmont Papers* (London 1831), i, 141.
23. *Culloden Papers*, i, 175–88.
24. NLS, Saltoun MSS, Box 402.
25. Ibid.

26. Deposition by James Drummond, 2 Aug. 1745 (S.P. 54/25, part 1, f. 137).
27. Tweeddale to Harrington, 12 July 1745 (S.P. 54/25, part 1, f. 85).
28. 20 Aug. 1745 (Arniston MSS, microfilm in SRO iii, f. 34).
29. April 1744 (Saltoun MSS, Box 402) : 6 March (Arniston MSS ii, f. 106).
30. 19 April 1745 (Arniston MSS ii, f. 135).
31. G. H. Rose, *Marchmont Papers*, i, 106–7.
32. 8 Aug. 1745, *Culloden Papers*, i, 205.
33. The correspondence and commissions are in S.P. 54/18 and 19.
34. The correspondence is all in the Arniston MSS ii, f. 77 onwards.
35. Sir Andrew Mitchell, 19 Sept. 1745 (Arniston MSS iii).
36. 29 Sept. 1745, G. H. Rose, *Marchmont Papers*, i, 110.
37. 19 Nov. 1745 (Arniston MSS iv, f. 105) : (S.P. 54/25, part 3, f. 432) : G. H. Rose, *Marchmont Papers*, i, 149–53.
38. 26 Nov. 1745 (Arniston MSS iv, f. 114).
39. 14 April 1744 (Arniston MSS ii, f. 134).
40. G. H. Rose, *Marchmont Papers*, i, 251.
41. 13 Nov. 1745 (S.P. 54/26, part 2, f. 211).
42. *Highlands in 1750*, 135.
43. 30 Oct. and 4 Nov. 1745, *Culloden Papers*, i, 238, 240.

3. Who Steered the Gravy Train, 1707–1766?

JOHN M. SIMPSON

Since 1707, Scotsmen have had to look outside Scotland, to West-minster, for the ultimate source of political patronage. This is clearly a fact of some importance, whether or not we grant that there are any political questions other than questions of patronage. And in this context the first half-century or so of the Union has a peculiar interest. What was for ambitious Scots the period of initial adjustment to the Westminster spoils system was, at the same time, for many politicans throughout Britain the era *par excellence* of the naked and unashamed pursuit of patronage. Not only was patronage the 'political cement' that helped make governments out of disparate factions : it also served to bind Scotland into the novel political construction styled Great Britain.

I believe that, however fashions change,[1] the work of Sir Lewis Namier will remain crucial to an understanding of eighteenth-century politics. Partly at least under the inspiration of Namier's work, several scholars have recently told us much that is new about the structure of Scottish politics in our key half-century. Lady Haden-Guest and other writers in the *History of Parliament* are supplying the biographical and local electoral groundwork. William Ferguson has charted the maze of legal rules for playing the great electoral game, and shown the game in progress.[2] P. W. J. Riley's *English Ministers and Scotland, 1707–1727* (1964) not only shows how politics and admini-stration were interwoven – a considerable achievement in itself – but supplies brilliant insights on individual politicians. An exciting range of tasks remains. There is room for innumerable studies of the countless areas of political life, such as Jeremy Cater's discussion of the election of William Robertson as principal of Edinburgh Univer-sity in 1762, in the *Scottish Historical Review* Volume XLIX Pt I. Rosalind Mitchison's essay in this volume raises in a pioneering way the question of how far the normal government patronage policies were applied in, or were indeed applicable to, the Gaidhealtachd. Behind this lies the still larger problem of how far early eighteenth-century society in Scotland as a whole remained so distinctively Celtic in structure that political rules evolved for a Westminster Parliament were inappropriate. Above all, future historians must relate the tiny political nation of early eighteenth-century Scotland and their electoral high-jinks to the broad development of Scottish society. The minutiae of patronage and intrigue seem sometimes to have happened in a vacuum, and, incredibly, we seem to see a landed society that was basically static. Yet the changes immediately ante-cedent to the Industrial Revolution were taking place at that time, and we require a model that will incorporate the underlying dynamic elements in the situation, even if the activities on the political surface of society continue to seem to us like a formal dance. Perhaps the ulti-mate historian of early eighteenth-century Scottish politics will re-quire to be a Mozart, and his work a *Così fan tutte*.

This essay avoids all these cruxes. It seeks to answer a dogged, basic, old question which has as yet refused to lie down, namely how far there was at all a distinctively Scottish patronage system, and hence a distinctive Scottish politics in the early eighteenth century. That grandest of questions, how far Scotland has had her own history since 1707, admits of no ultimate agreed answer. But the technicalities of political management comprise a relatively tangible topic. And the question was, and is, could an eighteenth-century British government afford to let their Scots supporters manage their own political patronage, or should delegation of authority be always partial, and under strict supervision? How far could native hands be trusted on the controls of the Scots gravy train? Historians have normally agreed that, for some parts of the period at least, the Scots enjoyed a fair degree of control. The venerableness of this belief is shown by the following comments on the Walpole era. John Ramsay of Ochtertyre, who had been born in 1736, wrote during the last quarter of the eighteenth century that Lord Milton 'was for many years the confidential friend and deputy of Lord Ilay, afterwards Duke of Argyll, who had long the entire direction of Scottish affairs'.[3] John Hill Burton in the mid-nineteenth century described how 'it became the policy of Walpole to hand over the administration of Scotland to the house of Argyle; and when the duke himself happened to be dis-contented with the Court, it seems to have served all purposes effectively to accept of the services of his brother, Lord Ilay. This viceroyalty, in effect though not in name, was in harmony with the peace minister's method of seizing the shortest way of ruling effec-tively and beneficially, without a thought about constitutional results...[this] saved the statesmen of Whitehall from much anxiety and perplexity in the management of a people whose peculiarities they could never comprehend.'[4]...In the 1960s, William Ferguson describes how, from August 1725 'working closely with Duncan

Forbes, Islay thereafter enjoyed a general oversight of Scottish affairs and long before Henry Dundas was born became known as "king of Scotland"....His lieutenants, Forbes and Andrew Fletcher of Milton, dispensed patronage, blatantly influenced elections, and in general supervised administration....For eleven years Walpole, by these means, achieved his aim of bringing Scotland into "a position of quiet subordination".'[5]

Perhaps none of these writers meant to imply that Walpole gave his Scottish managers an entirely free hand, still less that other ministries at other times did so. But in Hill Burton's words at least these broader assumptions do seem to lurk, and I believe that many averagely cautious readers of Scottish history books have over the years arrived at some such conclusions. But it needs to be asked, who was to benefit by such a complete delegation of patronage powers? All Scots not directly connected with the managers might hope for a relatively more impartial handout from London than from Edinburgh. This is the essence of Duncan Forbes's well-known whoop of delight, in a letter of August 1725 to Baron Scrope, at the news that Roxburghe was to have no successor as Scottish secretary:

'...for some time at least, we shall not be troubled by that nuisance, which we have so long complained of, a Scots Secretary, either at full length or in miniature; if any one Scotsman has absolute power, we are in the same slavery as ever, whether that person be a fair man or a black man, a peer or a commoner, 6 foot or 5 foot high, and the dependence of the country will be on that man, and not on those that made him.'[6]

From the London angle, the same objection to an over-mighty Scots manager held good. If the difficult art of the manager was 'to find pasture enough for the beasts that they must feed',[7] a Scot in the role required watching, lest he display over-narrow familial and other preferences within the herd, and thus ineptly provoke dispeace. The opposite danger existed too. A viceroy might come either genuinely to prefer the applause of his subjects to the approval of his London masters, or calculatedly to use the support of these subjects as a lever to prise more power for himself from those masters. Thus a bloc of votes in the Commons might be created by and for the government with its patronage powers, and then turned against it. That English ministers could not fully comprehend Scots peculiarities was perhaps not a total impediment to their retaining patronage management in their own hands. Legal and ecclesiastical appointments were the less tricky to make from a distance, and by those unfamiliar with Scottish institutions, the less they were made on grounds of pure, disembodied merit. And if English ministers had the motive for keeping control

E

over Scots patronage, did not the ever-busy 'galley-slave' Newcastle, for instance, a member of cabinet for over forty years, have the will and energy to do so?[8] Could the Scottish manager and his team not be kept under the same sort of surveillance as, say, John Roberts, m.p., Henry Pelham's secretary and a borough manager and dispenser of secret service money?[9] A survey of the half-century after the Union may show how often the Scottish manager existed as a free-standing monolith, and how often one sees in bas-relief merely the unimpressive figures of Scottish administrators executing London orders. If we study the personalities of the various Scottish statesmen, and their relations with London politicians, we may better understand what the Scots made of the system within which they were operating.

Might-have-beens are never profitable : but it does seem likely that the Squadrone did more than merely create a Scottish administrative vacuum in 1708 when by their factious proceedings they caused the end of the Scottish Privy Council.[10] They probably also damaged the long-term prospect of Scots retention of control over Scots patronage. Godolphin wished to preserve the Council, and it is possible that he and his successors would have acquired the knack of making it a rubber-stamp for ministerial decisions and appointments. But it seems more likely that, had it remained, it would have afforded for Scots statesmen a school in self-sufficiency and cohesion. It is true that in the short run, Godolphin sought to preserve powers of patronage in the hands of the Scottish Court Party, first through Mar as keeper of the Signet for Scotland, later (in February 1709) by making Queensberry a third secretary of state for Great Britain. But the context of this is the ebbing of power from Godolphin, throwing him into the arms of the Scots and of his other remaining supporters. On Godolphin's fall in August 1710, a new situation, at once more significant and more ominous for the future, obtained. Harley sought to establish the new ministry on as broad a bottom as possible. 'I dread the thought of running from the extreme of one faction to another, which is the natural consequence of party tyranny, and renders the government like a door which turns both ways upon its hinges to let in each party as it grows triumphant.'[11] This statement of Harley's seems to represent his deeply-held beliefs. Amid the bitter factions of Anne's last years, these were beliefs both particularly impractical and peculiarly admirable. But in the calmer waters after 1714 the Harleian tactics, deployed by men more amoral than Harley, provided the shortest route to political success, by way of a broad-bottomed ministry, drawn from throughout the whole gamut of Whiggery at least.

It is therefore important to see what Harley's views entailed for the conduct of Scottish patronage. Queensberry was kept in office till his death in July 1711, but by-passed : Mar and Argyll were the pivots of the regime, but were not given their heads : the Scots Tories were kept loyal, but as cheaply as possible : and the key-stone of the whole Scottish administration, with Baron Scrope as his intermediary, was Harley himself.[12] No single set of crabbed Scots was to be invited to tyrannize over the rest. The Scots were not as well attuned to this situation as, arguably, they were in later years to be. As Riley says, 'under Oxford's system they did not know where they stood when obvious control was given to no one'.[13] In 1713 Harley (who had become Earl of Oxford in May 1711) was led to revive the third or Scottish secretaryship, as part of his assertion of authority against the challenge of Bolingbroke. But Mar who was given the post received it very much as a Harley nominee. He was not a political magnate as Queensberry had been, or as the brothers Argyll and Islay now were. His lack of a great family behind him underlined the extent of his subordination within the ministry. Mar managed Scotland, but no one needed to ask for whom.

(Argyll and Islay will often be mentioned again : Islay of course succeeded his brother in 1743 and thus became 'Argyll', but for simplicity's sake I shall throughout call the younger brother 'Islay' or 'Duke Archibald' and reserve 'Argyll' [as well as 'Duke John'] for the elder.)

After the accession of George I, English ministers saw the continuing value of keeping the Scottish part of the ministry on a broad bottom; and this had become more feasible than in Harley's day. The rival Whig factions, the Argathelians and the Squadrone, competed for favours, and splitting the favours evenly between them served also to keep the Scottish Tories out. In parallel to this, until the Walpole break-through in 1721–2 the ministry as a whole was, for at least part of the time, a finely-balanced mechanism of the different Whig factions. Arbitrary changes in the Scottish balance of power were sometimes effected by the English Whigs as a part of accommodations among themselves. The name 'Argathelians' is characteristic of the political style of the period in Scotland. The imperious John, second Duke of Argyll, led an exclusivist group in politics, bound to him by ties of family and clientage, and thus directly comparable with the Squadrone. Argyll had clearly abandoned the old concept of a Scottish Court Party, whereby in Queensberry's day there was at least the pretence that favour would be impartially extended to all men of political good will.

The initial share-out of offices in 1714 reflected the balance held between Scottish factions. Montrose as secretary and Roxburghe as keeper of the Great Seal led the Squadrone contingent, while Argyll became commander-in-chief in Scotland and groom of the Stole to the Prince of Wales, and Islay added the role of lord clerk register to his previous post of lord justice general.[14] It was clear that there could be no single exclusive source of Scottish patronage. Robert Munro, younger of Foulis, was in December 1714 apprehensive about the lack of Whig cohesion: 'Our Scots great men don't own that they differ about the imployments but this I know that all the affairs for Scotland go on sloly, however when once the places are given they I hope will all agree in opposeing the torrys.'[15] The Scottish Tories under Mar simplified matters for everyone in 1715 by opting for fruitless armed rebellion rather than patient politicking. Thereafter the ministry showed, as often as was necessary, how well *divide et impera* worked as a method of controlling the Scottish Whigs. Montrose was permitted to resign his Scottish secretaryship in August 1715, and his Squadrone colleague Roxburghe was prevented from succeeding him. But then Argyll and Islay fell foul of King George and lost their offices in the summer of 1716. And as part of the process by which the Stanhope–Sunderland faction gradually ejected the Townshend–Walpole faction from the ministry, the Squadrone were fully rehabilitated. In late 1716 Roxburghe received the vacant secretaryship, and Montrose succeeded him as keeper of the Great Seal.[16] In addition, the lord advocate, Sir David Dalrymple, a political maverick who urged some clemency towards Jacobite rebels, found himself not dismissed but plainly ostracized in London. The ministers, he complained, did not 'speak one word of business to me, nor have they to this hour, though the character I serve in, one should think, made it decent to have done so.'[17]

Such kaleidoscopic changes, usually occasioned by a shift of power within the English part of the ministry, characterized the whole decade 1715–25. The ministry, facing in 1718 the full blast of opposition from Walpole, strengthened itself by permitting Argyll to crawl back to favour. He was to be steward of the Household, but without any say in Scottish affairs. Two years later Walpole and Townshend composed their differences with the court, and one of the conditions was another sacking for Argyll. In two further dramatic years, Walpole rose to a supreme, if not unchallenged, place within the ministry. Two of his consolidating measures before it was clear how far he was to rise were to reintroduce Islay to the ministry as keeper of the Scottish Privy Seal in April 1721, and to follow this by making Argyll master of the Household in July of the same year.[18] Duke John's dash and disappointing volatility, and his brother's cunning are well known, as are their broad acres and powerful clan.

The mutability of human fortune is even better known. But even all these do not add up to a complete explanation of the house of Argyll's remarkable yo-yo progress in politics as I have described it. We must add that it simply did not suit the English politicians' game to leave either section of the Scottish Whigs in undisturbed possession of the Scottish patronage for very long. The English ministers of the first Hanoverians, like those of Anne, 'were concerned with Scotland as a field of tactical manœuvre in which success could improve their respective positions at Westminster'.[19] To maintain themselves they had all to be like Newcastle, in office 'for the service of those friends, in whose cause I am, and have ever been embarked'.[20] While English groups were in contention, each thrust forward its particular Scottish friends. When one English group prevailed, it did not invite an unfettered Scottish manager to choose its Scots friends for it. (The dismissal of lord advocate Dalrymple came in 1720 but as a rather detached figure in politics he was not hounded, and was an auditor of Scottish revenue for the remaining year of his life.)[21]

1725 marked a new departure. This new disposition of Scottish affairs may be described as originating in the basic long-term miscalculation inbuilt into Sir Robert Walpole's political strategy. As soon as, with the death of Sunderland in 1722, Walpole had manifestly got his nose in front of all rivals in the race to dominate the ministry, he began to prove that he would always place the elimination of any strong runner in the race as a priority higher than that of preserving the equilibrium of the ministry itself. To say that Walpole in 1722 entered a political cul-de-sac along which his consummate ability enabled him to travel for two decades may not seem the most promising way to explain his career. But, as with Trevelyan's famous aphorism about Marlborough, – 'Abnormal only in his genius, he may have been guided by motives very much like those that sway commoner folk'[22] – the straightest way to explanation may be through paradox. In seeking to subordinate all to himself, Walpole broke all the rules of the age of patch-work quilt ministries. As George Grenville recalled in 1761 : 'What had been the constant charge against Sir Robert Walpole, but his acting as sole Minister? Yet his modesty had declined the appellation. Prime Minister was an odious title'.[23] But however modest Sir Robert sought to appear, his contemporaries had known their man.

Let us see how Walpole's basic misconception, if such it was, expressed itself in Scottish terms. Roxburghe, the secretary of state and prominent Squadrone politician, was in 1722 working with Carteret and Cadogan, Walpole's remaining rivals within the ministry. It was therefore logical for Walpole to work, as he did over the next year or two, to reduce Roxburghe's influence and even to oust him. But merely to weaken Roxburghe was simultaneously to exalt Argyll. Walpole probably intended the programme attributed to him by George Baillie of Jerviswood in March 1723 : 'I think the whole points at taking the management of Scots affairs into their [the ministry's] own hands without regard to either side.'[24] But Riley's contention that Walpole laid the foundation of this programme 'in a masterly fashion' is open to question.[25] Walpole had been quietly dropping Squadrone supporters from their posts when in 1725 events developed a momentum beyond his control. The government's Malt Tax proposals for Scotland provoked conflict. Within the ministry the trouble expressed itself in backstairs intrigues : in Glasgow it took the form of extensive rioting. The Squadrone lord advocate Robert Dundas, known to have framed an anti-government resolution at a meeting of Scottish members,[26] was dismissed early enough in the crisis for him to have time to concert popular opposition in Scotland. Roxburghe dug his heels in and made the maximum trouble out of the crisis for Walpole. In late August, as the crisis petered out, Roxburghe was at last dismissed as third secretary.[27] No successor was appointed. The brothers Argyll and Islay were now clearly the Scotsmen most likely to enjoy government favour. But how nearly does this approximate to saying that they ran Scotland?

With the two secretaries in theory now sharing Scottish business between them, and Newcastle transacting it the more often in practice,[28] the way was apparently open for direct control of Scottish patronage from London. Duncan Forbes, in the letter previously quoted, rejoiced that access to the fountain-head of patronage was open at last. Riley argues that, at least until the excise bill crisis year of 1733, matters in Scotland worked out as the ministry had intended. He documents impressively his statement that Argyll and Islay were not their own political masters. Islay had to keep Newcastle informed of developments, whereas appointments might be made from London without, or even against, Islay's advice.[29] But the brothers, with their strong inherited power base, and with the younger's native wit added to it, were hard to bridle. One feels that Walpole had really been forced in 1725 to go further than was desirable in weakening the rivals of the Argathelians, and that the only feasible system of checks and balances thereafter was to be sought in letting these rivals recoup their losses. Without the creation of countervailing forces within Scotland itself, strict control from London was not quite enough to fetter the managers, at any rate at this stage. It is true that the ministry had before them, at the commencement of the new deal in 1725, a promise by Islay not to be too partial to the name of Campbell when recommending persons for places.[30] Yet such a promise, coming from such a grand seignior of deviousness, amounted to a declaration that there were broader means by which to encompass his essential ends. Riley is surely right to insist, in contradiction to the long-established consensus, that Walpole did not intend to, and to some extent never needed to, hand Scotland's patronage unreservedly to Argyll and Islay. Yet paradoxically, the strongest-handed administration of its epoch, simply because its Scottish strategy ignored the need for a balance of forces, suffered a slow draining away of its patronage powers into the greedy maw of Clan Diarmid.

The process was gradual, but the dramatic events of 1733–4 serve to show how far it had advanced. The way that the excise crisis added to the ranks of Walpole's opponents shows in general how hard he made it for able men to remain in contented subordination to him. In particular, the Scottish opponents of the Argathelians worked with the opposition, and were at last thrown root and branch from their offices. The way that men like Marchmont, Montrose and Stair committed themselves irrecoverably to opposition and dismissal certainly suggests that they had abandoned hope of engrossing their due share of the spoils. Islay remained a steady Walpole man, but Argyll took the chance to establish successfully the fact that by their joint control of Scottish patronage the brothers had made themselves indispensable. Argyll voted against the government in a division in the Lords on 24 May 1733, and compelled Walpole to win him back with offers of fresh preferment before the decisive vote on 2 June. Plumb succinctly demonstrates the significance of the episode in indicating where the power in Scotland lay : 'In the end Walpole had to accept [Argyll's] abstension and be grateful for it. There were few men in 1733 who could treat Walpole with such a lofty display of independence and not only retain but increase their honours and dignities.'[31]

1734 and its general election seemed to offer hopes of revenge to the Squadrone, 'that motley phalanx which, with very different views, assailed Sir Robert Walpole, whom they represented as a second Sejanus, whilst they assumed to themselves the name of patriots'.[32] Of the 45 Scots Commons' seats, however, they captured very few, while Islay and the government list swept the board in the peers' election. Islay was accused of corruption by his opponents, but the contrast between him and them was simply that between successful government-backed corruption and failure. The chagrin of the Squadrone is manifest in their correspondence at this time. Andrew Mitchell complained to Robert Dundas that 'the whole nomination [of sheriffs] seems to be little more than a list of the sons, sons-in-law, and alliances of those gentlemen whom the D[uke] of A[rgyll] has thought fit to place upon the bench'.[33] Dundas in turn evinced contempt for the newly elected representative peers : 'if [God] hath destined us for destruction, to be sure we must fall into it. For the other house, nothing can be expected from them; such a sixteen as we have. God pity them....'[34] The intelligent Martian, once assured that these writers really knew the rules of the eighteenth-century political game, could conclude only that they were on the losing side.

On Scotland, as on Cornwall, there hinged the crucial swing against Walpole in the election of 1741.[35] It is therefore particularly disappointing that we cannot be sure of the motives, or indeed of all the actions themselves, of Argyll and Islay in the previous years. In 1736 they both opposed the government-backed bill that proposed to humble Edinburgh for having been the scene of the Porteous riot[36]: I do not think we need accuse ourselves of starry-eyed or of anachronistic thinking if we regard them as Scottish patriots in doing so. The stages by which Duke John moved into opposition thereafter, so that he was eventually deprived of his posts in 1740, are not entirely clear. Neither are his motives. Had the mercurial peer served Walpole till he could bear him no longer? Did vaulting ambition get the better of him, or was he merely bored, since, as Lady Louisa Stuart argued, political parties in opposition are apt to be more socially amusing than a party in power?[37] Or did the Porteous affair lead him belatedly to feel that he and his brother had been duped into 'bringing Scotland to direct slavery and dependance' on England, as others had alleged against them as early as 1727?[38] (The Rev. Robert Wodrow had recorded these accusations then, considered that they would reveal 'a bold push' and 'a plot very deeply laid' if true, but himself reserved judgement.) Did Argyll perhaps genuinely believe the ideas he himself expressed about the desirability of a broad-bottomed administration, so that the fall of Sir Robert would be the prelude to a change not merely of men but of measures?[39] Betty Kemp has argued that not all eighteenth-century 'patriot' programmes should be dismissed as the respectable cover for the naked desire of the 'outs' to get in.[40] And it would be a bold historian indeed who denied the possibility of altruism in Duke John's nature.

The Squadrone, with Argyll as their vigorous new recruit, took just over half the Scottish seats from the government in 1741. Of course, it has sometimes been argued that this was less Argyll's doing than Islay's, and that the latter betrayed Walpole by allowing Scottish seats under his management to fall to the opposition. But John Owen does seem to have disposed of this idea by citing the evidence of the Rev. Henry Etough.[41] There is a convincing ring to Etough's story of Walpole, always a sound judge of men, dining at the very end of his life with an old Northamptonshire man, a lifelong Tory:

'After dinner Sir R. said, "Mr Tryon, you and I have acted upon very different principles all our lives, but now party considerations are over with both of us, you must indulge me; let me drink two toasts." His first was the Duke of Devonshire, his second the Duke of Argyll [i.e. the former Islay] : "Now," says he, "toast whom you please. All the rest of the world are equal to me." This shows the opinion Sir R. had of his steadiness and friendship to the last hour of his life.'

Islay's ability to keep his feet on the shifting ground of eighteenth-century politics was developed to an uncommon degree. The Rev. Mr Etough's story gives, then, all the more pleasing impression of Islay's 'steadiness and friendship' towards his old political chief.

Walpole's resignation took place in January 1742. The consequences for Scotland were complex and perhaps unforeseeable. For John, Duke of Argyll, they may certainly be described as tragic. A new administration was concocted with the 'old corps' of Walpole men as a base, and a judicious admixture of Carteret and Pulteney supporters. Opposition elements who awoke from their dreams of a 'broad bottom' to find the mixture much as before and themselves excluded, created a great but ineffectual stir. At the Fountain Tavern meeting of 12 February, Argyll took the lead in urging that the boundaries of the ministry should be extended even to include the Tories. Though prevailed on a few days later to accept office in the ministry for himself, he so despaired of affecting the general line of policy that he favoured, that on 10 March he hurled in his resignation and rushed off again to the political wilderness. His conduct thereafter bears the signs of mental collapse, perhaps the result of despair at his own miscalculations. And on 4 October 1743 he died.[42] Eighteenth-century caricature is distinguished by its unselfconscious brutality. A print appearing on 1 March 1743, 'The claims of the Broad Bottom',[43] depicts a meeting of those politicians lately disappointed in their plans and disappointed of office. Argyll, paralytically hunched, is shown prophetically as 'The Ghost of a penitent Duke at the Head of the Board'. Beside him his erstwhile follower George Bubb Doddington mutters : 'I doubt we are out; in our politics I will never trust a Scot again; oh, damned Argyll; his daughter's title rot him!' (The Duke's eldest daughter Caroline married, on 2 October 1742, Francis, Earl of Dalkeith, eldest son of the second Duke of Buccleuch : this greatly angered Lord Quarendon, Tory M.P. for Oxfordshire and a rising Opposition politician, who had fancied her pledged to him.)[44] We today are not obliged to substitute sentimentality for the brutality of

Duke John's contemporaries. But it is hard not to sympathize with a man so evidently designed for a brilliant part, yet eternally at odds with the script, with his fellow players, and with himself. And if any consistent pattern is to be detected in the activities of his last years, it may be that of a sustained attempt by him to end the system whereby Scottish patronage was monopolized, regardless of the monopolist's identity.

Of course, if anyone was going to monopolize the Scottish patronage in the 1740s, it was most likely to be someone antipathetic to the Campbells, namely John Hay, fourth Marquis of Tweeddale. A Squadrone leader and a friend of Carteret, Tweeddale was given the Scottish secretaryship in the new Administration. It must have been Tweeddale whom Duke John most wished to offset in the ministry: and it fell now to the more stable Islay (third Duke of Argyll by his brother's death) to contain him. Tweeddale's own inclination was clearly to be the manager in Scotland in much the same way as Islay had been in the previous ministry. He regarded the Rev. Robert Wallace, for instance, as his ecclesiastical adviser in the way that Islay had employed the Rev. Patrick Cumming.[45] But power shifts in the ministry as a whole once more prevented the emergence of a stable Scottish system. Tweeddale's chief, Carteret, was elbowed out of the ministry in November 1744. By February 1746 Henry Pelham and Newcastle, the political heirs of Walpole, felt strong enough to purge the ministry of all remaining Carteret influence. This they did by the mass resignation of 10–11 February, leaving George III no option but to beg them to return. One minor result of this spectacular and successful manœuvre was the sacking of the Squadrone lord advocate. Tweeddale would certainly have gone then too, had he not in fact chucked the sponge in even earlier.[46]

It is important to stress how once again power struggles in London determined the fate of Scottish patronage. Otherwise one might be tempted to ascribe too much credit for the turn of events to the ineptitude of John, fourth Marquis of Tweeddale. This factor should certainly not be overlooked, as Mrs Mitchison has shown. It was Tweeddale's misfortune, just as it was Islay's good luck, that the Forty-five took place at a time when it served to expose Tweeddale's administrative shortcomings to the full. But Islay, utilizing the power struggle in the ministry, might well have supplanted Tweeddale in any case. Over the centuries it is most instructive to study the tactics of the Campbells during periods immediately after they appear to have been knocked out of the game. Islay's tactics were to help to suppress the Rebellion as actively as possible without actually aiding Secretary Tweeddale to do so. John W. Wilkes's remark that Duke

Archibald was 'not of much use during the rebellion'[47] would no doubt have pleased the Duke himself mightily. Mindful of the false position his brother had been jockeyed into during the Fifteen,[47A] Islay was careful, as it were to 'take instruments' in canny lawyerly style, that he was not responsible for the government's lack of military preparedness. In September 1744 Pelham wrote to him that he had discussed with the king 'the other subject, which your Grace has so often mentioned to the king's servants, the want of arms in the hands of friends of government, and the little care there has been to disarm the enemies'.[48] During the Forty-five, as Mrs Mitchison's account suggests, Islay cut a far better figure than Tweeddale, whom Islay indeed by-passed. To the sheriff of Argyll the Duke wrote on 2 November 1745 : 'All the correspondence from Argyllshire is to be sent to me, or the Duke of Newcastle, or General Wade, and not to the Marquis of Tweeddale. This is so settled.'[49] Horace Walpole's version of all this, especially of the affair of the lieutenancies, is demonstrably unfair to Islay : Horace may never have been fully convinced that Islay had not proved disloyal to his father in 1741. But Horace Walpole's version and syntax convey something as near to the true spirit of Duke Archibald, a captiousness so consistent that it attains to a kind of nobility, that quotation is mandatory:

'By a succession of these intrigues, the Duke of Argyle had risen to supreme authority in Scotland : the only instance wherein he declined the full exertion of it was, when it might have been of service to the master who delegated it; in the time of the Rebellion : at that juncture he posted to London : the King was to see that he was not in Rebellion; the Rebels that he was not in arms. But when this double conduct was too gross not to be censured, he urged a Scotch law in force against taking up arms without legal authority; so scrupulously attached did he pretend to be to the constitution of his country, that he would not arm in defence of the essence of its law against the letter of them.'[50]

The hapless Tweeddale resigned in January 1746, just anticipating, as we have seen, his inevitable dismissal. The Scottish secretaryship itself may be termed a casualty of his tenure of office.[51] If the ministers really wanted a Scottish manager, he could be accommodated somewhere else within the machine. If, as was more likely, they did not, it was tempting providence to confer the prestigious title of secretary on some noble place-seeker who might misunderstand their purpose. It was too much to hope for that they would turn up a Tweeddale every time. The next secretary for Scotland was Charles Henry, sixth Duke of Richmond and Lennox, and first Duke of Gordon : he accepted office on 9 August 1885.

Again without stressing Tweeddale's personal responsibility we may wonder if his secretaryship helped to kill off the Squadrone. Since the days of Tweeddale's grandfather, before the Union, family ties had helped bind the tight little group together. But the basic *raison d'être* of the continuing 'Argathelian–Squadrone' balance in Scottish politics was simply the relationship of Scotland to England. The predominant interest in the ministry normally found it expedient to pair the groups in office, or to alternate them, and a spirit of healthy competition prevailed. The Squadrone nourished its hopes of office throughout the 1730s, and these hopes sustained in particular its great pushes against the ministry of 1734 and 1741. They might have survived the swift dashing of their hopes, so soon after they had been realised in 1742, but the world no longer seemed to have a place for the Squadrone. Thereafter there were times when a strong personality, first Islay's, then Dundas's, impressed itself on Scottish politics. But they did so partly by refraining from trying to create an exclusivist faction. During their ascendancy, just as much as in the intervening period when place-seekers could go straight to the fountain-head in London, no talented and accommodating political outsider need feel initially abashed about currying favour. In this climate the Squadrone would appear simply to have withered away. The concept of a 'formed opposition' persisted in Britain, of course, in the day-to-day actions of the sturdy political practitioners. Hardwicke and Mansfield might in April 1757 convince Newcastle that oppositions were 'the most wicked combinations that men can enter into' but at the same time Mansfield warned King George that if Newcastle went into opposition the Whigs would follow him.[52] But while the idea of 'government' and 'opposition' lived in its limbo, awaiting its birth into political scientific respectability through the gentle midwifery of Burke, it was ironically dropping out of the political practice of Scotland, where since 1714 the two Whig factions had given perhaps the neatest text-book demonstration of it in the Britain of that day.

Whoever lost out in the 1740s, Duke Archibald was clearly among those who triumphed. Horace Walpole, commenting on his father's fall, wrote that 'Lord Isla's power received a little shock by Lord Tweeddale's and Lord Stair's return to Court on that minister's retreat; but like other of Lord Orford's chief associates, Lord Isla soon recovered his share of the spoils of that Administration'.[53] In retrospect how little was the shock delivered to Islay's power in 1742! But his return was not really altogether like that of Henry Pelham, Newcastle and the rest of the 'Old Corps'. They showed dexterity in their recovery, but, with the over-mighty Walpole gone, the Epigoni did offer an institutional stability and continuity attractive to both

King and Parliament. Islay's disadvantage was that his former colleagues had seen him at work, building on his natural power-base in Scotland a superstructure that made him alarmingly strong. His return was scarcely at the invitation of the Pelham brothers. The easy-going Henry Pelham may have fretted less about Duke Archibald than did the ever-fussing Newcastle, or perhaps Henry, without his brother's passion for minutiae, never really reckoned up exactly how much in Scotland turned upon the word of Islay. By 1747, as John Owen says, Pelham 'had assumed the fallen mantle of Sir Robert Walpole'.[54] One especially gratifying feature of the general election of that year was the way that Scotland sent only ten hostile members to the Commons, as opposed to twenty-three six years earlier.[55] Pelham either did not realise, or was unconcerned at realising, how much of this part of the triumph belonged to Islay rather than to him.

1747 was also the year of the Heritable Jurisdictions (Scotland) Act. Islay spoke for the bill, but in an 'exotic' way. 'Had I not been informed before', complained Andrew Mitchell, 'that he was to speak for the bill I should have thought from his facts and reasonings that he intended to vote ag't it.'[56] With Islay's character in mind, one may suppose that Mitchell was nearest to seeing the orator's motive in the observation that 'the dreadful description he made of Scottish policy and government, set in contrast to the wise policy and just laws of England, must give a high idea of the candour and capacity of the Speaker to an English audience, who generally think every other nation their inferiors'.[56] But with regard to Islay's current standing in Scottish affairs, the relevant piece of information one requires is that in compensation for giving up his own jurisdictions Islay received £21,000,[57] more than an eighth of the entire sum allotted for compensation, and more than three times as much as anyone else got.[58]

The Pelhams had a ministry to run, and it would be foolish to assert that then, or at any other period of his career, Islay had matters entirely his own way. In 1747–8 for instance, Islay backed Charles Erskine for the Lord Presidency, but succeeded only in blocking the appointment for nine months. In a compromise effected by Pelham, the elder Robert Dundas at last got the job, and Erskine the Lord Justice Clerkship.[59] In 1753 Islay again ran Erskine for the Lord Presidency, and again was defeated, this time by Lord Hardwicke and his candidate Robert Craigie.[60]

In the election year of 1754 one item of secret service expenditure was a lump payment of £1,000 to Islay for Scotland. This shows that Islay was doing the government's Scottish electioneering for it. That the same amount was given to a single candidate at Reading,[61] who subsequently lost, does not mean that Scotland or Islay were lightly esteemed. Rather it means that secret service money was not the great feature of elections that historians once believed it to be, that 'by 1754 there was no real opposition' anyway,[61] and that people were brought to the government side not by the quick bribe but by steady patronage, in which field again Islay was the government's man in Scotland.

But Islay's place in this sphere was called in question by another event of 1754, namely the death of Henry Pelham in March of that year. Islay and Pelham had reached an accommodation, but Henry's brother Newcastle ' "hubble-bubble", busy and unsteady' could never convince himself that it was safe to leave Duke Archibald undisturbed. The following year found Newcastle intriguing against Islay, and uneasily aware he had lost control of the Scottish members as a result. Once, however, Newcastle had received Henry Fox into the administration, he changed his tactics in order to woo Fox's ally Islay once more. In reply to an assurance from Newcastle about a troublesome election petition, Islay wrote in a vein that showed he knew exactly how to hit the sensitive Newcastle in a tender spot:

'I am much obliged to your Grace for your declaring for Captain Campbell, Member for Stirlingshire; that will heal a sore place I have felt for some time, and which while Mr. Pelham lived did not want a cure.'[62]

In July 1756 Islay was the trusted emissary of the ministry in the delicate negotiations with his nephew, the Earl of Bute.[63] But, amid the bewildering permutations of the following year, one of Newcastle's many objects was again the exclusion from influence of Islay. Perhaps Newcastle's fears became lively again at Fox's suggestion, in March 1757, that 'the D. of Newcastle should be minister for England, the Duke of Argyll for Scotland, professedly and independently'.[64] This set Newcastle to computing how many Scots Members might be expected to follow Islay if he were dropped from the ministry.[65] Newcastle even handed over the administration of Scottish patronage to Mansfield for a time,[66] though presumably rather in the spirit of 'he only does it to annoy, because he knows it teases', than from any real hope that the redoubtable legal *émigré* could prise loose Duke Archibald's grasp upon Scotland.

For many years the houses of Argyll and of Bute had been closely related both by marriage and in politics. Duke Archibald had for many years sought, without success, to bring his willing nephew Bute into the administration. As George II's death seemed to become imminent, the fact that Bute was the favourite of the king's grandson and heir seemed to presage a possible adjustment of roles between

Duke Archibald and his nephew, but no great adjustment in the power structure of Scotland. John Dalrymple's prophecy of October 1759 seemed reasonable:

'The relation betwixt the Duke of Argyll and Lord Bute, and the partiality of the future sovereign to this last, makes the transition (I speak of Scotland) of power from the one to the other almost imperceptible.'[67]

But William Mure, M.P. for Renfrewshire, had in the previous year provided the spark for a possible conflagration. He had led Bute to consider attempting to secure the Ayr Burghs seat, for which Islay had other plans. This caused a quarrel between uncle and nephew, which widened to include other pieces of patronage such as the Renfrewshire seat and the governorship of Dumbarton Castle.[68] Mure had now perforce to work to undo the mischief he had caused. The quarrel was still being patched up early in the election year of 1761, but patched up it was, and the elections proceeded according to the well-tried Islay formula.

By the death of George II on 25 October 1760, Bute had already become the key figure among the new king's ministers, a role for which he was temperamentally unsuited. Death was now to remove Bute's most trusted confidant, for his uncle Duke Archibald died on 15 April 1761. The brevity of Bute's subsequent ministerial career was attributed by a friend to Bute's not being guided by his uncle's bequeathed advice. In September 1763 Alexander Forrester observed that

'Had his Lordship [Bute] taken the sound advice given him, to my knowledge, by one who was a sort of parent, and who knew men and things much better than he, of *keeping behind the curtain whereby he might make and unmake ministers*, much of the mischief would have been prevented...'[69]

Bad advice indeed, as Namier suggested, for a king's closest adviser, in the constitutional context of 1760–1! But we are at liberty to suppose that Forrester was writing his own gloss on the advice, in the light of the events and controversies of the years that had elapsed since it was given. Within the particular context of Scottish politics, there is no doubt that it was by the steady pursuit of unobtrusive power that Islay himself had prospered. And a further remark of Forrester's shows that Bute had a just appreciation of his uncle's political stature : 'Indeed, he [Bute] told me himself the very night of the Duke of Argyll's death, that he had by that event lost more than any man in Britain.'[69]

In Scotland as elsewhere, the complex politics of the early 1760s have their own fascination. For Scotland, Frank Brady's analysis is recent, and is likely to remain convincing.[70] During the Bute ascendancy, the management of Scotland was in the hands of his brother James Stuart Mackenzie. This scrupulous and able administrator was continued in office on Bute's fall in 1763, and indeed had the office of keeper of the Privy Seal conferred on him. Ferguson's remark that 'Stuart Mackenzie had neither experience nor talent' for patronage is too harsh :[71] that he was too honest and impartial may be nearer the mark, and that he had no vast family interest behind him, particularly after 1763, is also relevant. Grenville marked him down for slaughter and he was sacked in 1765. Though he was in 1766 given the Privy Seal again for life, he never returned officially to the field of Scottish patronage. Conditions had to be very propitious for the emergence of an Islay or Dundas, and historians have been ungenerous to the talented Stuart Mackenzie in not conceding that he remained an underling through his stars' fault, not his own.

In the first Rockingham ministry of 1765, Newcastle's final spritely initiative in the sphere of Scottish patronage was to offer its management to Lord President Dundas.[72] Unquestionably the latter was right to decline the offer (though at the same time coyly hinting that he could give useful general advice), and thus prevent the Scottish bench from being plunged back into politics. One may still remark how lord presidents and other Scottish judges, creeping politically to the top as they have done for so long, have always shown little aptitude for pulling apolitical faces thereafter. For a decade after Dundas's *démarche*, no personality strong or weak thrust itself between the Scottish place-seeker and the fountain-head in London. In 1766, though, a portent for the future was supplied : Henry Dundas, the lord president's younger half-brother, not content with having married 'a very genteel Girl with £10.000 fortune' took a step towards political immortality by becoming solicitor-general.

The foregoing summary of the doings of men long dead may convince us merely how hard it is to encompass these doings within the scope of any enlightening generalizations whatever. But perhaps we can do a little better than that. Sometimes one has a misty impression of a line of substantial managers running eighteenth-century Scottish politics. Who then can we cast for this exalted role? Perhaps Queensberry, in the brief period before Harley circumscribed him, and death foreclosed on him. Then, in the period before Dundas emerged, and with the mighty exception of Archibald, Earl of Islay and third Duke of Argyll, there is no one. Duke John had no stomach for the role, and no one else the opportunity. Mar, Montrose, Roxburghe, Tweeddale, Stuart Mackenzie – English political exigencies determined that the share these men had in the running of Scotland should be partial, subordinate and brief.

Given that eighteenth-century politics was a politics of balance – between king and ministry, between minister and minister, between ministry and parliament – and given that Scotland was run from Westminster, with the Scottish balance a product of the other balances – given all this, the emergence of an Islay was an even greater prodigy than the emergence of a Walpole. From few houses other than that of Argyll can one imagine such a man coming. Elsewhere in this volume Eric Cregeen's invaluable article shows exactly where the economic and social strength of Clan Campbell lay, ready to the hand of its ambitious chiefs. But there was no certainty, even among Campbells, that every chief would have the capacity to fulfil his ambitions. Good character contrasts between Duke John and Duke Archibald have often been drawn, perhaps best by Lady Louisa Stuart.[73] Lord Hervey's famous explanation of how two such contrasting men ever collaborated at all may be accepted, if only on the hypothesis that the truth tends to be stranger than fiction : the brothers were for years not on speaking terms 'yet were always in the same interest and perpetually convened to the same political meetings, and by the means of a Mr Stewart (who went between them), a Scotch gentleman, an adroit fellow and a common friend to them both, they acted as much in concert as if they had been the most intimate and most cordial friends.'[74] ('Mr Stewart' was the M.P. William Steuart, of Weyland and Seatter in Orkney.) Duke John, 'Red John of the Battles', was certainly better at shaking fields and senates than at wheedling favours from ministries, and the patient minor arts of management were further still from the areas where his undoubted talents lay. As Ferguson says, he 'was too much the monarch in the west Highlands to make a good courtier in London'.[75] A paradox here is that Duke John the old-style clan chief was also the vigorous estate improver, even to the detriment of the established social pattern : perhaps the element of paradox may be reduced by giving Duncan Forbes his due place in the work of improvement. At the same time Duke Archibald, the pliable, the modern, knew when to back-pedal to the security of the old clan loyalties, when faced with the disaffection his brother's policies had produced. References in Duke Archibald's correspondence to 'our neighbours the clans' perhaps illustrate his equivocal outlook in this respect. If, given an otherwise favourable background, children may profit intellectually from living in a bilingual situation, Duke Archibald may have gained insight in an analagous way from his observation of the social systems of the Gaidhealtachd and of the rest of Scotland, at a point in time and space of maximum interaction.

F

The construction of a detailed model of the spoils system under Islay must await another day, but a few misconceptions may be cleared up here. A manager like Islay (though there was no other such, till Dundas) did not require a title like third secretary of state, and would indeed have been hindered by it. Islay was in fact in charge of the Scottish Privy Seal from 1721 to 1733, and was keeper of the Scottish Great Seal from 1733 till his death. There is evidence that Islay himself did not in 1725 appreciate how holding the secretary-ship might make a politician too conspicuous. On 24 August of that year Baron Scrope reported to Duncan Forbes that 'D. of Roxburghe hath at last obtained leave to retire : of this Mr Delafay will give you a more particular accot & how that office is to be managed, which don't please a friend of ours.'[76] But if Islay really wanted a new secretary, presumably himself, appointed in 1725, at least he did not let disappointment cloud or check his subsequent career.

A point related to this one has been well taken by Nicholas Phillipson.[77] Islay as manager was usually in London, and Scottish business was done through a *sous-ministre*. And once more, the system worked the better for being informal. Just as the one outstanding manager of the period was never Scottish secretary, so his *sous-ministre* was a lawyer resident in Edinburgh, but not the government's chief legal officer, the lord advocate. Islay's *sous-ministre* was in fact Andrew Fletcher, Lord Milton, lord justice clerk from 1735 till 1748. One may discern other *sous-ministres* in our period. Baron Scrope may arguably be described as such from Harley's day till 1724. Baron William Mure may be described as *sous-ministre* to James Stuart Mackenzie in the early 1760s. 'Jupiter' Carlyle speaks of Stuart Mackenzie himself in terms suggesting he was but a *sous-ministre* to his London bosses, and of Mure as succeeding him in that capacity after only a year.[78] This is unfair to Stuart Mackenzie, but does illustrate the imprecise nature of the terms involved. In other words, we must beware as much of describing too precisely the office of *sous-ministre*, using Milton, the one undoubted example in our period, as we must be chary of generalizing about managers from the single great example of Islay. Individual personality was almost all, constitutional precedent for them almost nil.

Milton was a lawyer of marked ability, and his work for Islay extended from the field of patronage into other useful administrative areas. Milton's son Andrew was Islay's private secretary, and travelled with him. 'Jupiter' Carlyle's account of Milton gives us an idea of how, as Islay's man in Edinburgh, he was sedulously courted by the ambitious:

'The Duke had early made choice of Fletcher for his coadjuter, and

had proved his sagacity by making so good a choice; for Lord
Milton was a man of great ability in business, a man of good sense,
and of excellent talents for managing men; and though his conversation was on a limited scale, because his knowledge was very
much so, yet being possessed of indefeasible power at that time in
Scotland, and keeping an excellent table, his defects were overlooked, and he was held to be as agreeable as he was able.'[79]

Writers scrutinizing the office of lord advocate have sometimes
reached the correct conclusion, that eighteenth-century governments
frequently avoided employing a Scottish manager, but they have done
so for the wrong reasons. As Phillipson shows, lord advocates before
Henry Dundas were neither managers nor *sous-ministres*. G. W. T.
Omond's *The Lord Advocates of Scotland* (1883) contains the classic
statement of this misleading view of lord advocates, and George
Menary's valuable *Duncan Forbes of Culloden* (1936) caused the office
to continue to bulk too large in our minds. Forbes was a formidable
and admirable lord advocate, who deserved well of his country. But
if Milton's patronage duties overflowed into the field of administration, Forbes's administrative achievements rarely, except in his own
Inverness-shire, took him directly into the field of patronage.

The unavailability of Duke Archibald's own papers is a barrier to
studying his system in action, but we may see parts of the system in
Milton's papers,[80] and observe the communication with the Pelhams
from the other end.[81] Sometimes Milton and Islay discussed great
matters : 'The scheme of abolishing ward holdings seems in itself to
be a very reasonable thing as it is a great discouragement to improving
our grounds and is much more hurtfull to the vassall than it can be
beneficiall to the superior...'[82] Frequently, though, we find them concerned with the small change of Scottish patronage : 'The cess collec-
tor of Aberdeenshire is a very troublesome business, both sides have
used my name too much, and I think I had better not meddle in it at
all.'[83] Among the Pelham papers, there is the spare outline of the 1747
Scottish election plan. Pelham himself may well have taken the credit
for it, but it was clearly a masterwork of political horsetrading on
Islay's part. The allotting of competing interests each to its seat or to
the promise of the reversion of one was particularly complex in the
north-east, and one is bound to compare this with Henry Dundas's
similar exercise in the same area in the late 1780s. An extended comparison between Islay and Dundas as patronage managers would be
splendid but inconclusive. My own judgement is that Islay's achievement was the greater : he pioneered the way, he did so without benefit
of the East India patronage, and no minister ever trusted him as Pitt
was to trust Dundas.

The tone of Islay's official letters is always instructive. In mid-career he could sound obsequious : 'I beg leave to tell your Grace that no clerk in your office can be more ready to make your business easy than I shall be in any capacity that I can be any ways useful.'[84] As Riley says, Mar had addressed Oxford as Islay here addressed Newcastle.[85] It may be fair to say that the difference was that Mar meant it. Later in life, Islay normally modulated his tone from the obsequious to the straightforwardly punctilious, as in his comment to Henry Pelham in 1747 : 'Lord Galloway told me that he puts this gentleman [the m.p. for Wigtownshire] into my hands and upon my telling him that I at present did not deal in Members of Parliament but if he would let me put him into your hands I would accept of his offer, to which he answered that he meant it in that sense...'[86] But consistently throughout, there is an undertone of someone smilingly keeping his own counsel.

A last glimpse of the system in action is provided by Professor W. L. Burn's account of the 1761 Ayr Burghs election.[87] Although the Islay-Bute rift was now healed, local interests working under cover of it had stirred up opposition to Islay's candidate before Bute's endorsement of him had been obtained. John, fourth Earl of Loudoun and an Islay protégé, was Islay's local agent in the matter. Eventually Loudoun got Sir Adam Fergusson, the other candidate, to withdraw by producing a letter from Islay to the provost of Ayr, 'professing friendship for the burgh and asking the council, in the event of Fergusson's withdrawal, if they would be good enough to accept Bute's [and Islay's] nominee'.[88] In fact, Loudoun and the provost had written 'Islay's' letter themselves. Islay had really written, in the last week of his life, berating Ayr town council for not accepting his candidate at once, and saying that Ayr's behaviour reflected no credit on it.[89] What could more have offended the prickly sensibilities of the councillor-electors, had Loudoun been so misguided as to show them the letter? But Islay had built well. His system by its very nature could not survive his death : while he lived, however, it was structured to carry him through even his own momentary miscalculations.

In 1759 at Dalkeith, 'Jupiter' Carlyle read the cocky young Charles Townshend a lesson in Scottish politics. Of Islay he explained that 'without his viceroyalty in Scotland, His Grace was of no importance in the State'.[90] This was a lesson that Duke Archibald had learned thoroughly for himself. A Scottish manager was there on ministerial sufferance, and Islay was so circumspect as to be the only real manager suffered to arise, and to remain, before Dundas's day. Islay died 'the absolute Governor of one of His Majesty's Kingdoms'[91] to quote Newcastle, who must be accounted competent to judge. Riley's basic argument, that the ultimate outcome of Scottish political struggles in our period was determined in England, is so just, that it is all the greater pity that his book stops short of the period when Islay was in full cry. 'If the ministry was strong enough to control England it could also control Scotland'[92]: we must concede that this was so, and that such a state of affairs is inherent in the Union situation at all times, however much it may stick in our craws to do so. Islay, the wily Gael, was unique in lulling ministries into making over their powers to him. Since Riley's book, our view of Islay can never be quite the same as before. His tenure of power was always more precarious, yet his political stature is consequently the more awesome, than we had hitherto supposed.

Finally, a man is best viewed by his contemporaries. Horace Walpole in seeking to judge Islay so much lacks a Scottish perspective as to be grotesquely wrong, since he reckons him a man who 'had so little great either in himself or in his views, and consequently contributed so little to any great events, that posterity will probably interest themselves very slightly in the history of his fortunes'.[93] But when Walpole merely looks at Islay, we see him too, and more clearly than in any other way: he 'was slovenly in his person, mysterious, not to say with an air of guilt, in his deportment, slow, steady, where suppleness did not better answer his purpose, revengeful, and, if artful, at least, not ingratiating. He loved power too well to hazard it by ostentation, and money so little, that he neither spared it to gain friends or to serve them.'[93]

In contrast, Ramsay of Ochtertyre may be accused of offering us a lay figure. But Ramsay is generally accounted a sincere man, and is as entitled to his opinions as the rest of us:

'Though both that noble lord and his deputy Milton were for a great while the objects of much envy and obloquy, it is now understood that the former was not only the wisest and greatest Minister, but also the most enlightened patriot, Scotland has produced.'[94]

NOTES

1. J. H. Plumb in the *New Statesman* of 1 Aug. 1969 argues persuasively why Namier was fashionable in the 1950s and is less so today. But Plumb himself seems to me markedly to underestimate Namier's achievement.

2. W. Ferguson, 'Electoral law and procedure in eighteenth and early nineteenth century Scotland' (unpublished Glasgow PH.D thesis, 1957): also his article, 'Dingwall Burgh Politics and the

parliamentary Franchise in the Eighteenth Century', *Scottish Historical Review*, XXXVIII (1959) 89–108.

3. J.Ramsay, *Scotland and Scotsmen in the Eighteenth Century* (1888), i, 87.
4. J.H.Burton, *The History of Scotland* (1874 edn), viii, 346.
5. W.Ferguson, *Scotland : 1689 to the Present* (1968), 143. (Referred to below as *Scotland*).
6. Duncan Forbes to John Scrope, 31 Aug. 1725, *More Culloden Papers*, ed. D.Warrand (Inverness, 1923–30), ii, 322. (Referred to below as *MCP*).
7. Lord Chesterfield to S.Dayrolles, 16 Nov. 1753, in L.B.Namier, *England in the Age of the American Revolution* (London 1961 edn), 65. (Referred to below as *England*).
8. The best description of Newcastle occurs in L.B.Namier, *England* 67–83.
9. For Roberts see L.B.Namier, *The Structure of Politics at the Accession of George III* (London 1957 edn), passim.
10. P.W.J.Riley, *The English Ministers and Scotland, 1707–1727* (London, 1964), ch. 7 : R.Walcott, *English Politics in the Early Eighteenth Century* (Oxford 1956), ch. 7 : W.Ferguson, *Scotland* 54–6.
11. Quoted by A.McInnes, 'The Political Ideas of Robert Harley', *History*, 50 (1965), 309–22.
12. P.W.J.Riley, *English Ministers*, chs. 10–11 : J.Scrope to R.Harley, 7 July 1711, BM Loan 29/156.
13. P.W.J.Riley, *English Ministers*, 238.
14. P.W.J.Riley, *English Ministers*, 258 : A.Grant to J.Forbes, and R.Munro yr to J.Forbes. both 20 Nov. 1714, *MCP*, ii, 48 both illustrate the share-out proceeding at the local level.
15. R.Munro yr to J.Forbes, 4 Dec. 1714, *MCP*, ii, 50–1.
16. P.W.J.Riley, *English Ministers*, 262–5 : *HMC Polwarth*, i, 23 : *HMC Laing*, ii, 188–9.
17. Sir D.Dalrymple to Stair, 23 June 1716, Stair MSS, in G.W.T.Omond, *The Lord Advocates of Scotland* (1883), i, 305.
18. P.W.J.Riley *English Ministers*, 265–72 : J.H.Plumb, *Sir Robert Walpole : The Making of a Statesman* (London, 1956), 268–70, 289.
19. P.W.J.Riley, *English Ministers*, 290.
20. Newcastle's Memorandum of 10 Aug. 1761, BM Add. MSS 32926, ff. 348–51.
21. P.W.J.Riley, *English Ministers*, 270 : G.W.T.Omond, *Lord Advocates*, i, 308–10.
22. G.M.Trevelyan, *England under Queen Anne : Blenheim* (London 1930), 182.
23. Horace Walpole, *Memoirs of the Reign of King George the Third* (London 1845 edn), i, 113.
24. G.Baillie to Lord Polwarth, 1 Mar. 1723, *HMC Polwarth*, iii, 248.
25. P.W.J.Riley, *English Ministers*, 273.
26. Roxburghe to R.Dundas, 4 June 1725, in G.W.T.Omond, *The Arniston Memoirs* (1887), 69–70.
27. P.W.J.Riley, *English Ministers*, 284–5 : J.H.Plumb, *Sir Robert Walpole : The King's Minister* (London 1960), 105–6.
28. P.W.J.Riley, *English Ministers*, 287–8.
29. P.W.J.Riley, *English Ministers*, 287 : J.Scrope to D.Forbes, 24 Nov. 1726, in *Culloden Papers*, ed. H.R.Duff (London 1815), 355.

30. Newcastle to Townshend, 3 Sept. 1725, BM Add. MSS 32687, f. 153.
31. J.H.Plumb, *Sir Robert Walpole, The King's Minister*, ch. 7, esp. pp. 276–81.
32. J. Ramsay, *Scotland and Scotsmen*, i, 83. There is material on Squadrone activities then in *HMC Polwarth*, v (London 1961).
33. G.W.T.Omond, *Arniston Memoirs*, 89.
34. R.Dundas to R.Dundas yr, 6 Feb. 1735, in *ibid.* 81.
35. J.B.Owen, *The Rise of the Pelhams* (London 1957), 4–9.
36. For the context of this see P.Hume Brown, *History of Scotland* (Cambridge 1909), iii, 218–26 : G.Menary, *Duncan Forbes of Culloden* (London 1936), ch. 6.
37. *Lady Louisa Stuart : Selections from her Manuscripts*, ed. J.A.Home (1899), 17.
38. Rev. R.Wodrow, *Analecta* (Maitland Club, 1842–3), iii, 436–7.
39. A.S.Foord, *His Majesty's Opposition, 1714–1830* (Oxford 1964), esp. pp 226–9.
40. Betty Kemp, 'Frederick, Prince of Wales', in A. Natan ed., *Silver Renaissance* (London 1961), 38–56.
41. Rev. Henry Etough in BM Add. MSS 9200, ff. 125, 211, quoted in J.B.Owen, *Pelhams*, 8.
42. J.B.Owen, *Pelhams*, 82–3, 97–100, 102, 110–12.
43. Reproduced in Lloyd Sanders, *Patron and Place-Hunter : A Study of George Bubb Dodington* (London 1919), opposite p. 128.
44. J.A.Home, *Lady Louisa Stuart*, 26–35.
45. J.Ramsay, *Scotland and Scotsmen*, i, 239–40, 252–3.
46. J.B.Owen, *Pelhams*, 295–301.
47. John W.Wilkes, *A Whig in Power : The Political Career of Henry Pelham* (Evanston, Illinois, 1964), 94.
47A. H. Tayler, 'John, Duke of Argyll and Greenwich', *Scottish Historical Review*, XXVI (1947), 64–74.
48. Pelham to Islay, 22 Sept. 1744, in William Coxe, *Memoirs of the Administration of the Right Honourable Henry Pelham* (London 1829), i, 252.
49. Islay to A.Campbell of Stonefield, 2 Nov. 1745, SRO, Campbell of Stonefield MSS, S.42.
50. H.Walpole, *Memoirs of the Reign of King George the Second* (London, 1846 edn), i, 277. (Referred to below as *George II*).
51. W.Ferguson, *Scotland*, 154.
52. L.B.Namier, *England*, VOL 50–1 : P.C.Yorke, *The Life and Correspondence of Philip Yorke, Earl of Hardwicke* (Cambridge 1913), ii, 389–94.
53. H.Walpole, *George II*, i, 276.
54. J.B.Owen, *Pelhams*, 318.
55. Ibid. 5, 314. The correct initial Scottish election returns for 1741 are given on p. 5 : 19 Administration supporters, 23 opponents, 3 double returns.
56. A.Mitchell to D.Forbes, 22 May 1747, *MCP*, v, 180–3.
57. J.H.Burton, *History of Scotland*, viii, 504.
58. G.Menary, *Duncan Forbes*, 320.
59. G.W.T.Omond, *Arniston Memoirs*, 99–105 : G.W.T.Omond, *Lord Advocates*, ii, 24–5.
60. J.Ramsay, *Scotland and Scotsmen*, i, 101.
61. L.B.Namier, *Structure*, 199–204.
62. Islay to Newcastle, Oct. 1755, BM Add. MSS 32860, f. 262.

63. L.B.Namier, *England*, 87n.
64. H.Fox to Ilchester, 4 Mar. 1757 in Lord Ilchester, *Henry Fox, 1st Lord Holland* (London 1920), ii, 36.
65. BM Add MSS 32995, f. 383.
66. See 'William Murray' in *DNB*, xiii, 1306–12.
67. Quoted in L.B.Namier and J.Brooke, *Charles Townshend* (London 1964), 58.
68. L.B.Namier, *England*, 117–18.
69. A.Forrester to Sir A.Mitchell, 12 Sept. 1763, in L.B.Namier, *England*, 161–2.
70. F.Brady, *Boswell's Political Career* (New Haven 1965), 7–10.
71. W.Ferguson, *Scotland*, 236.
72. G.W.T.Omond, *Arniston Memoirs*, 176–7.
73. J.A.Home ed., *Lady Louisa Stuart*, esp. pp. 13–14.
74. John, Baron Hervey, *Memoirs of the Reign of George the Second* (London 1848 edn), i, 336.
75. W.Ferguson, *Scotland*, 145.
76. *MCP*, ii, 321.
77. N.T.Phillipson, 'The Scottish Whigs and the Reform of the Court of Session, 1785–1830' (unpublished Cambridge PH.D thesis, 1967), 29–32.
78. Alexander Carlyle, *Autobiography* (London 1910 edn), 482.
79. Ibid. 272.
80. Saltoun Papers in NLS.
81. Newcastle MSS in Nottingham University Library : Newcastle Papers in BM Add MSS 32689–33201.
82. Milton to Islay, 17 May 1746, in NLS Saltoun Papers, Box 49.
83. Islay to Milton, 1 Apr. 1756, in NLS Saltoun Papers, Box 85.
84. Islay to Newcastle, 11 Nov. 1725, Public Record Office, S.P. 54/16, 344.
85. P.W.J.Riley, *English Ministers*, 287.
86. Argyll (Argyll is the former Islay) to H.Pelham, 6 Aug. 1747, Nottingham University Library, Newcastle MSS No. Ne C 1950.
87. W.L.Burn, 'The General Election of 1761 at Ayr', *English Historical Review*, lii (1937), 103–9.
88. Loudoun to Bute (copy), 11 Apr. 1761 (LO 10619) : Loudoun to Islay (copy), 11 Apr. 1761 (LO 10708) : both in the Loudoun Papers, Huntington Library, San Marino, California.
89. Islay to Loudoun, 11 Apr. 1761 (LO 7555).
90. A.Carlyle, *Autobiography*, 405–13.
91. Add MSS 32922, f. 5, quoted in L.B.Namier, *England*, 173.
92. P.W.J.Riley, *English Ministers*, 291.
93. H.Walpole, *George II*, i, 276–8.
94. J.Ramsay, *Scotland and Scotsmen*, i, 87.

4. The Landowner and the Planned Village in Scotland, 1730-1830

T. C. SMOUT

In the early eighteenth century the typical English village was a nucleated settlement of some size focussing on a green or a street, with a church, perhaps a manor house, and certain other accepted institutions such as a smithy and one or more hostelries.[1] In Scotland, by contrast, the typical unit of settlement was a hamlet, known as a farm-toun in the Lowlands and a baile in the Highlands,[2] a cluster of turf and stone dwellings that might be arranged contiguously under one long roof (as in Kintyre)[3] or separately scattered as impermanent huts, housing a small number of peasants whose livelihood was to cultivate as 'joint-tenants', an area known as the farm. This remained the normal unit of rural life until the agricultural changes of the late eighteenth century broke the system on which it was based.

Nevertheless Scotland was not, even at an early date, quite devoid of larger and more sophisticated rural settlements. There were, for instance, some places in the south-east that had been under the occupation or the influence of Anglian settlement, and looked exactly like green-villages in Northumberland : Dirleton and Stenton in East Lothian and Ceres in Fife are examples. Then, some of the farm-touns had already begun to develop from a hamlet to a village. Since all but the most primitive and stagnant of agricultural economies must at some stage feel the need to exchange their surplus commodities for essentials obtainable from otside, and to appreciate the convenience of craft specialists who devote their skills entirely to satisfying one particular requirement of the community, there must therefore be a tendency for something like a village to emerge at favoured geographical sites where retail traders and craftsmen begin to live among the farmers and cottars.

There is no telling when this first became evident, but between the middle of the fifteenth century and the end of the seventeenth there was a proliferation of burghs of barony which to some degree appears to foreshadow the developments in village planning in the eighteenth century.[4] We know the landowner was closely involved in some of these, doing more than merely obtaining a grant of charter to a settlement that had already grown of its own accord. In 1527, for instance,

the Earl of Glencairn feued out forty lots of six acres each, and pro-
cured a charter for a burgh of barony at Kilmaurs in Ayrshire. He
compelled the smallholders to live together in the village centre, with
all the craftsmen and merchants found within the barony.[5] In 1628
the Earl of Nithsdale feued out ten lots to create what was perhaps
scarcely more than a new farmtoun at Langholm, Dumfriesshire, on
the main west road from England to Edinburgh : but he took the
trouble to endow it with both charter and hostelry.[6] In 1677 Walter
Stewart founded a very successful burgh of barony that was to become
Newton Stewart in Kirkcudbrightshire : he built houses, gave feus
on generous terms and established the right to a market – a century
later, the growth of the village from this base was described in the
Statistical Account as 'amazing'.[7] Stornoway was a fishing burgh
planted in Lewis in the seventeenth century by the Earl of Seaforth,[8]
and Campbeltown a royal burgh planted in Kintyre at the same period
by the Earl of Argyll[9] – both settlements had strategic and cultural as
well as economic purposes, being intended as a help to hold down
and civilize wild country in a manner similar to the intentions of
several enthusiasts for Highland village settlement after 1745.

These examples are sufficient to establish that the planned rural
settlement was not itself a novelty in the eighteenth century. This earlier movement differed, however, from that of the eighteenth century in several respects. Firstly, fewer settlements are known to have
been planned, and these lie within a much more restricted area – apart
from Stornoway, Campbeltown and Inveraray,[10] there was nothing
at all done within the Highlands where so much of eighteenth-century
interest focussed. Secondly, it was in no sense an aesthetic and social
movement like that of the eighteenth century, when the appearance
of the village was usually considered street by street, house by house
and garden by garden with certain social, economic and architectural
considerations always in view. Eighteenth-century improvers were
indeed scornful of the failure of their predecessors:

'Nothing could be more detestable than the method in which villages
were originally constructed in Scotland. The houses were not built
according to any regular plan, but scattered in every direction. The
roads and alleys were inconceivably bad, especially in wet weather,
as few of them were paved; and what added greatly to their miserable state was the abominable practice of placing the dunghill, in
which every species of filth was accumulated, before their doors, a
practice highly injurious to the health of the inhabitants.'[11]

Thirdly, and most importantly, the transformation of the village was
not ever seen (at least as far as our evidence permits us to be dogmatic)
as part of an overall plan to change and develop the estate, let alone as

part of a still larger ideal of promoting economic growth in the kingdom. The seventeenth-century village existed within the context of the traditional peasant farming all around it: it was not expected to change it. The eighteenth-century village was developed in response to and also to assist a revolution in the economy of the estate and of the nation: it was expected to provide a completely new framework for human life in the countryside. This is what makes it so rewarding to study.

1. *The Ideal of the Village*

When the eighteenth-century writers consdered the advantages of building or developing a village on the estate, there were certain principal gains they saw arising from it : a village would provide a point of consumption for the produce of the surrounding lands, it would provide employment for tenants and sub-tenants who might otherwise find themselves cast out of the district by enclosure, and the presence of industrious villagers in a purely rural society would provide an example and an inspiration to the tenantry without diminishing the landowner's hold over the countryside.

Almost invariably the first advantage that landowners saw in developing a village was that it would form a market for the food their tenants grew. The century between 1730 and 1830 saw a total re-organization of the methods of husbandry practised in Scotland : the old runrig farms and joint-tenancy disappeared, enclosure was undertaken, capitalist farmers emerged : the net result was that a relatively smaller proportion of the population occupied farms, but that this contracted farming class produced a relatively larger quanitity of agricultural produce. The disposal of the surplus over and above what they and their servants could eat remained a serious problem of estate management until the arrival of the railway in the mid-nineteenth century. To this problem the construction of a village housing country traders, shopkeepers and non-agricultural craftsmen and artisans offered at least a partial solution : it was, for instance, in the mind of the tutor of the Grant estates in the north-east when, around 1763, he considered where the first tentative moves in agricultural reorganization were likely to lead:

'I don't wonder that the present tenants complain of the improvements of the hills : 'tis a new thing to them. They have not so much room for pasture, their present ideas are confined to feeding cattle, but in a few years when they are obliged to till more ground and to till it better, less ground will maintain their cattle... Necessity will first make them apply to the raising of corne, and by degrees they'll find the advantage of it preferable to pasture and do it of choice. Hence it is probable the tenant will not be hurt and the master will have more rent or more tenants. And an increase of tenants will give opportunity to form a town and raise manufactures'.[12]

The writers in the first *Statistical Account* were full of instances where plans like those of the Grant factor had been carried to completion, with beneficial results to all from the establishment of a rural market. It is worth giving two instances from the same area of Scotland (Aberdeenshire) where contemporaries tell the story. The first relates to the parish of Montquhitter, where Joseph Cumine of Auchry had begun to enclose land and to lay out new farms shortly after his succession to the estate in 1739. He appears to have been the epitome of the best eighteenth-century improver – astute, careful, far-sighted, successful and paternalist:

'Observing that his tenants were frequently at a loss for a market, he determined to establish a permanent one on his own estate. For this purpose, he planned a regular village, contiguous to the church, upon the moorish part of a farm which in whole yielded only £11 a year. For a while, he felt in silence the sneers of his neighbours, who reprobated this scheme as wild and impracticable; but these temporary sneers soon gave way to lasting esteem. He prevailed upon a few to take feus; he assisted the industrious with money; – obtained premiums for the manufacturer; – decided every difference by his arbitration, and animated all to their utmost exertion by his countenance and counsel. Settlers annually flocked to Cumines town ...and the village, built of freestone, soon assumed a flourishing appearance... and instead of £11 sterling, the original rent, produce him annually from £120 to £150 a year.'[13]

Cuminestown, like the almost exactly contemporary villages of Crieff in the southern Highlands and Ormiston in East Lothian, produced a crop of imitations : one was certainly Newbyth in Aberdeenshire, feued out in 1764 by James Urquhart.[14] It was probably also the original model for the Duke of Gordon's reconstructed village of Huntly in the same county, begun about the same time : this nobleman was particularly anxious to attract industrial employers, and Huntly was only one of several of his new villages.

'The village...has surprisingly increased within these fifty years, in population and industry, in so much that where all around it for some distance was formerly barren heath, swamps or marsh there is now scarcely one uncultivated spot to be seen; and barley, oats, lint and potatoes, and turnips are produced in abundance where nothing grew before. This spirit of improvement and manufacture was first introduced by a few who dealt in the yarn trade. From their laudable example and from observing the profits arising from industry, others were encouraged ; and now it is become one of the

first villages in the North… Being situated in the midst of a large and fertile country the industrious inhabitants have a ready sale for what they bring to market by which many poor cottagers and sub-tenants are enabled to pay for their scanty possessions.'[15]
A ready sale and rising standard of living for the tenants, a swelling rent roll for the landowner : these seemed the first benefits that a village properly placed and encouraged would bestow upon the rural classes.

Very closely allied to the conception of the village as a market was the idea of a village as a place of employment, thereby acting as a sponge that would suck up the superfluous population and prevent emigration. A Scottish landowner of the eighteenth century was fre-quently very conscious of the social disruption his agricultural chan-ges were bringing about, and the best and most responsible among them were as anxious to mitigate this dislocation as they were con-vinced that the changes they were intitating were economically and even morally desirable. They were not in an easy ethical situation. On the one hand, reorganization of the farms involved them in weeding out many small tenants and subtenants, not all of whom were willing or able to take work as landless labourers. On the other, popula-tion in the countryside of Highlands and Lowlands alike was rising steeply, to complicate the problem of finding rural employment. By tradition, no landowners were more deeply and sincerely paternalist than the Scots, treasuring the old values that a laird's worth was still to be measured as much by the abundance of the dependent popula-tion around him as by the weight of his rent roll. They regarded towns as sinks of iniquity, and foreign emigration as a waste of manpower. If, by planning villages on their estates, they could rehouse the popula-tion whose life on the land they had disorganized, they would then enjoy the best of the old world of heavy population and paternalism and of the new world of efficient farming and larger rent rolls. What was more, they might even do those they displaced more of a favour than they realised when they got the first notice to quit:

'No man will venture to say that a farm of fifty-acres in the hands of four tenants who have each a horse in the plough and their grounds mixed in run-rig will produce the quantity of subsistence which has both money and industry to cultivate the ground. With respect to population, where is the difference whether the other three farmers live on the farm or in an adjoining village? But with respect to industry the difference is great : on the farm they are three-fourths of the year idle; in the villages they are skilful artists and able to rear their families without begging their bread.'[16]

Just what employment were the villagers supposed to take up in their settlements? We shall discuss in the next section some of the different types of village that developed from different answers to this problem, but it is relevant here to indicate the development of land-owners' opinions on the matter. Before 1790 there was a school which believed that villages could be composed mainly of agricultural small-holders, who, by intensive cultivation of their lots, could learn to com-pete with the big capitalist farmer and (in some mysterious way) live by exchanging produce with them. To do them justice, they believed that no settlers would come to a village unless they were promised feus of several acres as holdings, and therefore it would be impossible to attract industrial employment as the second stage in the growth of the community without starting off with small-holders : 'I should humbly propose to erect villages in the most convenient situations in each barony', said the General Inspector to the Forfeited Estates in 1767, 'however I humbly apprehend for the genius of the people nothing will go further to induce them to breed their children to trades than the idea of their commencing proprietors.'[17]

The trouble with this theory was that so frequently industrial employment failed to arrive : the villages accordingly became rural slums like the crofters' settlements in the Highlands, where those displaced by agricultural change found a plot on which they could just survive alongside the farmers in the wider countryside, living more or less as squatters off a potato patch. In the north and south-west these shortcomings became obvious first. The minister of Borgue in Kirkcudbrightshire put the position in immoderate language:

> 'In villages the most worthless and wretched part of society is commonly to be found. Thither the dregs of the community from all quarters are poured in. Every incentive to vice is presented and no proper police is established to give a check to the growing evil. Where villages are founded manufacturers ought invariably to be established as the best means to give encouragement to industry, which will operate as a more effectual check to the progress of vice and contribute more to the felicity of the inhabitants than the best code of municipal laws or the most rigid exercise of that power which is vested in baron bailies.'[18]

This latter view of the essential importance of bringing non-agricul-tural occupations to the village, as a *sine qua non* of making them function efficiently, carried all before it. Robert Rennie put it well in his prize-winning essay on village foundation presented to the High-land Society in 1803 :

> 'The great *desideratum* for the original establishment, the steady support of a village...is trade or manufactures. Without this men

will not feu; or if they do they cannot build; or if they build it must soon prove a deserted village.'[19]

The problem remained, what trade and what manufacture was most suitable to bring into a village in order to promote rural industriousness? Different landowners in different situations came up with different answers, but most villages were established either on a basis of fishing, on a basis of small rural textile manufacture, such as linen or stocking weaving, or on a basis of factory employment. It was quickly realised that the plans for laying down villages would be no use at all for stemming emigration out of the estate unless the kind of opportunity that the industrial revolution was presenting to emigrants to the towns could itself be reproduced in the villages. How successfully or otherwise this was done is a problem for our consideration in the next sections.

Nevertheless, the idea of bringing industry into the villages was by no means anything the landowners found alien to their preconceptions about society. It tied in with their third motive, the belief that a village community, properly conducted, offered the ideal moral environment in which to keep a working population virtuous and respectful – the perfect mean between the indolence of the deep rural peasantry and the profligacy of unregulated life in the big towns. The dwellers in rural hamlets, said Sinclair, 'are generally more ignorant, duller and more uncouth than those who are assembled in villages', while in towns 'human nature is liable to temptation, corruption, infirmity of body and depravity of mind'.[20] Well-regulated villages where the reins of government had been 'held by a steady hand', said Robertson, produced workers who were steadier, more intelligent 'and certainly more hardy than the deformed spawn and jail-sweepings of great towns'.[21]

'It is from the temperate and healthy family of the country labourer or tradesman and not from the alleys and garrets of a town that the race is to be sought who are best calculated to cultivate our fields or defend our properties from danger...villagers are in general contented and unambitious'.[22]

These revealing sentiments account for much of the enthusiasm felt for village life by reformers of all kinds. When the Commissioners of the Forfeited Estates wished to introduce Highlanders to Lowland values after the '45 they could think of nothing more likely to promote industriousness and civilization than the plantation of villages with linen works, English schools, post-offices, markets and prisons : 'all this would have a good effect towards civilizing the inhabitants of the Highland parts of Aberdeen and Banff' said one of their surveyors after discussing the site for a settlement on Deeside.[23] Another spoke of Beauly in Inverness-shire, a clachan inhabited by 'a great collection of poor people who live in hutts and retail ale and spirituous liquors': 'a village properly encouraged here', he stressed 'could not miss to attract strangers of different professions from many corners, and would consequently soon diffuse a spirit of trade and industry, as well as promote agriculture, through all this extensive country'.[24] These were going to be settlements for a new morality, towns to bring respectability to the Celtic fringe.

An idealist of another type was the anonymous writer of the 'Considerations on the Interest of Scotland', a manuscript now in Edinburgh University Library.[25] In pursuit of his maxim that 'to encourage *industry* is the pinnacle of political maxims, to inspire and instill into a nation that commendable spirit is procuring wealth and power to the state and ease, affluence and plenty to every individual', he proposed the creation of villages of charity. These would house a thousand boys, teach them crafts from the example of resident artisans, book-learning from schoolmasters and farming from agricultural experts. The whole settlement was to be self-supporting from the sale of surplus agricultural produce and linen cloth.

This scheme (which was purely that of an armchair philosopher) has a lot in common with the ideas of Robert Owen – perhaps because both drew inspiration from the seventeenth-century English Quaker, John Bellers.[26] This is not the place to discuss in any depth the philosophy of Owen, but it is worth pointing out how his scheme for villages of cooperation, with their emphasis on a communal life, spade cultivation of the land, liberal education and a mutual sharing of the profits and possessions of the enterprise, fitted into the Scottish scene where he must have formulated them in the first place. He first experienced village life in Scotland at the factory village of New Lanark that had been formed in the first place by an arrangement between an industrialist and a landowner, and then transformed by the benevolent autocracy of Owen's own management.[27] His most highly-polished version of what he wanted his Utopian villages to be was addressed to a group of Scottish gentry, who knew what founding villages was about and who could appreciate the detail he went into with regard to the lay-out of the buildings and the type of employment envisaged.[28] It was one of them who provided the land on which the British Owenite communty was launched at Orbiston in Lanarkshire. Above all, the faith in village life and the optimism about its moral effects were completely shared by the generality of Scottish landowners. 'Mutual confidence betwixt landlord and villagers will take deep root; and industry cherished by benevolence will produce the happy fruits of prosperity and affluence' – thus James

Robertson on the ideal landowner's village.[29] 'The proposed villages will ever be the abode of abundance, active intelligence, correct conduct and happiness' – thus Robert Owen on the cooperative village.[30] The sentiment is interchangeable.

At root, of course, the vision of the Scottish landowners and that of Owen were perfectly incompatible. The landowners believed that the main point of planning a village that would incidentally make people happy and virtuous was that by doing so their own profits would be increased, and their own hold on the leadership of society thereby confirmed and strengthened. Owen believed that a village (on his plan) would make people so virtuous that a new social order could be built in which landowners, and indeed government itself, would eventually be unnecessary. It was as though Owen had taken the landed preconceptions, added a dash of relish of his own, and turned them into a menacing and idealistic parody of what the landowners themselves intended.

Where did this deviation end? The landowners saw the collapse of Orbiston with relief.[31] Kropotkin, the anarchist thinker, influenced by Owen and ignorant (or uncaring) about Orbiston, took up the idea when he was fighting the Social Darwinists' theory of the survival of the human fittest : in an article entitled 'The Industrial Village of the Future' he proposed restoring our 'senile, decrepit, crumbling society' by establishing 'free village communities' in which man's humanity could flower at last.[32] His ideas thus pointed forward to Ghandi's ideas on the organization of economic life in modern India and pointed back, through Owen, to the sort of thing Joseph Cumine of Auchry had been trying to do in Aberdeenshire in 1739. It is fascinating to think there is a small connection, however twisted and hard to discern among other threads, between the first and the last of these enthusiasts for the village life.

This, however, is something of a red-herring. Few landowners were philosophers, still fewer were conscious Utopians : most were practical men concerned, for reasons which seemed to them good and sufficient, with laying out and developing actual villages in the Scottish countryside. How did it work out when they stopped theorizing and started to build?

2. *The Planned Village on the Ground*

How many planned villages were built in Scotland between 1730 and 1830? In one sense the simplest question is the least answerable. Some landowners laid out new villges or reconstructed old ones, introduced new classes of inhabitants, new employment and new amenities, and thereby saw their ideas about villages through to their logical

G

conclusion on the ground. Others also wished to develop older villages, tried to bring new employment, encouraged settlers by new houses, easy feus or long leases, but did so without transforming the character of their settlements in any very basic way : thus for instance from about 1786 the Earl of Hopetoun repeatedly bothered himself with the problems of village life at Leadhills, trying to encourage supplementary employment and toying with plans for a complete reconstruction, but the character of the place as a very isolated mining village built on the hillside in a fairly haphazard way was not fundamentally changed, and it would be hard to justify placing Leadhills in any list of 'planned' villages.[33] A more notorious group of landowners had ideas of directing settlement when they compelled the inhabitants of Highland settlements to leave their dwellings and to live by kelping and crofting in new townships on the coast : however, since they generally provided no amenities, no secure leases or feus, no new houses, and made no other attempt to diversify employment, it would be a degradation of the term to include their efforts among the planned villages. Yet both the latter classes of landowners were influenced in their behaviour by contemporary ideas about villages, and the life of their communities was affected to a greater or lesser degree by these views. There was also a good deal of overlap between the three categories of landowner and their villages, making it difficult to know what precisely to count as 'planned' village and what to leave aside.

I have tried to overcome this problem mainly by shifting it onto others' shoulders. The appendix provides a list and a map of nearly one hundred villages that are mentioned by the authors of the *Shell Guide to Scotland* (considerable historians in their own right) as having been either founded or substantially rebuilt in the period we are considering.[34] To these I have added a short supplementary list of eighteenth-century planned villages mentioned in this text but not in the *Shell Guide*, and another short list based on work by J. M. Houston and John Dunbar which has added to our knowledge of the eighteenth-century village building movement.[35] The total here comes to over 130 : Mr Houston has independently calculated that there were (between 1745 and 1845) 'over 150 planned villages excluding coal-mining and urban development' started on the ground. The appendix cannot properly be regarded as exhaustive. It is possible to argue even over the inclusion of a few which are on it, and undoubtedly there are a number which were well qualified to be included but which have in fact been omitted. It ought, nevertheless, to be comprehensive enough to give an impression of the scale of the movement, and also to illustrate the regional distribution of the settlements within Scotland.

The uneven pattern of the settlements raises some questions. There are no examples on our list from Orkney, Shetland or the Outer Hebrides : if this does reflect an absence (or near absence) of planned villages on the islands it is not easy to see why. Perhaps it was because the problems of emigration did not seem acute in many of these isolated places until after the middle of the nineteenth century : perhaps lairds were discouraged by the difficulty of attracting any outside capital or employment-opportunity to the islands : perhaps they were merely out of touch with, or indifferent to, contemporary example.

The other main gap is in the south-east. There is only one example from Fife on our list and only two from the middle and eastern Border counties (including Galashiels, a slightly dubious example, in so far as only part of the village can be regarded as 'planned' by the Scotts of Gala); in the populous Lothians there is only a handful tucked up in one corner. The explanation here is not isolation : it must surely be that there were already enough large villages. The Anglian nucleated settlements did not need rebuilding on a different ground-plan, and late medieval or seventeenth-century burghs of barony, especially along both coasts of the Firth of Forth, were numerous and well-established. Nevertheless, contemporaries immediately recognized the difference it made to a county like Fife whether or not landowners looked after and encouraged development in their existing villages. Thus David Loch in 1778 criticized West Wemyss, East Wemyss and Methil as poor, neglected places owned by the same landlord (Mr Wemyss of Wemyss) while he praised neighbouring Elie, St Monance, Anstruther and Pittenweem as flourishing through the enterprise of their owner, Sir John Anstruther. Of Leuchars he said:

'In place of a village of smugglers, has become a manufacturing village, and the people industrious in spinning and weaving. The merchants buy up the yarn all over the county. Sir Robert Henderson the proprietor has great merit in bringing this Reformation about.'[36]

Thus even in areas where it was not necessary to build a new village there were plenty of village planners whose active interest in the economy of their settlements made the crucial difference to the quality of local life.

The villages on our map can be arranged into eight main geographical groups. The first consists almost entirely of coastal settlements along the shores of Caithness, Sutherland and Cromarty : apart from two villages on the Cromarty Firth, they all date from after 1780 and owe a great deal to the policy of two men, Sir John Sinclair of Ulbster and the first Duke of Sutherland. Most of them were meant to rehouse crofters who, having been displaced by the spread of sheep-farming in the interior, were being encouraged to settle as fishermen on the coast. Thurso (by Sir John Sinclair) and Helmsdale (by the Duke of Sutherland) are, from the point of view of planning, outstanding examples of their type :[37] the former is particularly ambitious and even splendid.

The second group is concentrated in the counties of Moray, Banff and north-western Aberdeenshire – planned villages are thicker on the ground here than anywhere else in Scotland. Some, particularly those built in the first quarter of the nineteenth century, occupy the coast and are primarily fishing settlements. More, including all the early ones like Cuminestown, Keith and Huntly, are situated inland and were associated in their early history with the linen trade. Part of the reason for the concentration here is undoubtedly the force of individual example and enthusiasm – Cuminestown influenced Newbyth and other places; Keith, laid out by the Earl of Findlater when he was one of the Board of Trustees for Manufactures, had an influence beyond local boundaries;[38] the Dukes of Gordon gave their immense local weight to the movement by constructing several planned villages of their own. Nevertheless, external circumstances favoured a concentration here : it was only within the previous century that much of the region had become safe from Highland raid – there were few old villages, and ample room for settlement on greenfield sites and re-development of farmtouns. The prospects for the country linen trade and for fishing did not seem unreasonable, yet the counties of Moray and Banff were threatened in the second half of the eighteenth century with a decline of population. It had been reversed, perhaps with the assistance of the new villages, by 1810.[39] Here was fertile ground for new plantations.

The third group, a small one, consists of inland villages in the Central Highlands, the earliest being the Duke of Perth's Crieff, laid out on a grid plan from 1731.[40] Most of them were inspired or influenced by the Commissioners of the Forfeited Estates after 1745, and had the moral purpose of civilizing the Highlanders even more to the fore in their creators' minds than any economic function. Two of them founded by private landowners, Grantown-on-Spey (Sir James Grant) and Tomintoul (The Duke of Gordon)[41] remain to this day among the best preserved and most interesting of all Scottish planned villages.

The fourth group also contained a small number of widely scattered settlements – those along the shore of the Western Highlands, almost all of them fishing villages founded after 1780. The British Fishery Society's Ullapool and the Duke of Argyll's Inveraray are both architecturally outstanding : the three villages on Islay testify to the exceptional qualities of the local Campbell lairds as Highland land-owners in the early nineteenth century.

The remaining groups all lie to the south of the Highland Fault. Of these, the fifth group in some ways resembles the second : it is stretched along the plain that bounds the southern end of the Highlands from Callander at one end to Stonehaven at the other, and like the villages of the Moray plain, their founders also saw them mainly as centres for the linen trade. Callander (the Duke of Perth) at one end and Laurencekirk (Lord Gardenstone) at the other, were perhaps the two most influential of the villages : almost all of them were completed before the end of the eighteenth century while the linen trade was still prosperous in rural areas, and they sent their supplies of yarn and cloth to the marketing centres at Perth and Dundee.

The sixth group lies within the orbit of Glasgow, and is dominated by factory villages like Balfron, Deanston, Catrine and New Lanark which, as we shall see, often owed their existence as much to the enterprise of thrusting middle-class entrepreneurs as it did to the initiative of the landowners themselves. The great majority of the settlements were founded in the last twenty years of the eighteenth century, when it was still regarded as highly advantageous to site a cotton-spinning mill on a fast-flowing stream in the countryside – after 1800 most factories were built in the towns.

The seventh group, in the Lothians, is quite small; it almost certainly owes most to the much-admired early planned village of Ormiston, laid out by John Cockburn about 1740,[42] but the other examples are diverse in origin – Athelstaneford, for instance, was a purely agricultural settlement, Grangemouth was Dundas's new port at the eastern terminal of the Forth-Clyde canal, and Tynninghame was founded by the Earl of Haddington for estate workers pensioned off from his service.[43]

The eighth and last group was on the plain along the northern shore of the Solway Firth, where a good many villages had been founded as burghs of barony in the middle and later decades of the seventh century. Here, indeed, the strongest initial incentive to eighteenth-century planning may have been the tradition of interest in the matter from the previous age. Certainly the economy of the whole area had begun to expand first in the seventeenth century with the growth of the cattle-rearing industry, and this development merely continued throughout the eighteenth. The villages were diverse in function, some being fishing or shipping centres like Glencapel and Port William, some with a cotton mill, like Kirkpatrick, Durham and some with linen and woollen weaving like Brydekirk and New Langholm. Some seem to have been founded twice. It is difficult to decide, for example, whether Newton Stewart and Castle Douglas are planned villages of the seventeenth century, of the eighteenth century, or of both.

How was the planned village built, populated, provided with employment and governed? The answers to some of these questions can be provided as generalisations, but ultimately we will have to deepen our analysis by looking in more detail at some of the different types of villages. The most meaningful division will prove to be by function, not by region. Life in Ullapool was different from life in New Lanark not because one lay in Wester Ross and one in the Clyde Valley but because in one the inhabitants hoped to live by dragging herring out of the sea in nets, and in the other they operated the most sophisticated machinery then known to man. One feature, however, that Ullapool, New Lanark and almost every other planned village shared in common was the basic essentials of its external appearance. In almost all the villages, the houses were built of free-stone, in most cases with tiled or slated roofs. Many, and occasionally all, of the houses had two (sometimes three) stories, and between three and five rooms. They were meant to look nice, and the landowners were proud of insisting on a better standard of housing than the one-room turf or rubble building with a thatched roof which was characteristic of the old farmtouns and bailes. As John Cockburn wrote about Ormiston in 1742:

'I can give my consent to no houses being built in the Main Street of the town but what are two storys high. None who thinks justly and wishes well to it can wish to have it disfigured in that particular, or any other that can be prevented. Every man concerned in the place has an interest in having the Main Street appear as handsome and to look as well as we can and not to have little paltry houses... I suppose you design little poor Windows and Doors that nobody can go in or out without breaking their heads except the (y) remember to duck like a goose. It is a common wise practice which proceeds from their wise heads and noble way of thinking in Scotland that if anything is made to look ugly, or if neat, is spoiled in dressing, it is thrift.'[44]

The details of the houses and the ground plan of the settlement were on occasion the work of a distinguished architect or his associate– thus John Baxter, mason to William Adam, laid out Fochabers; William Adam himself, with John Adam his son, Roger Morriss and Robert Mylne all had a hand in Inveraray; Thomas Telford designed Ullapool and Pultneytown at Wick.[45] In the simplest case the basic plan was two rows of houses facing each other across a wide road or a green: alternatively it was a cross, with one wide main street, bisected at right angles by a second street (rather less wide and long) and a green or marketplace laid out where they met. Narrower parallel streets might then branch off the two principal thoroughfares to complete an oblong grid, and this could occasionally be further elaborated as at Thurso, by more squares, and even by an obelisk or circuses.

Most landowners kept the ground-plan simple, favouring geometrical rigour in contrast to the haphazard arrangement of the farmtouns and bailes. In order that the inhabitants should not dump their middens in front of the house (as happened in the farmtouns) they made the front-doors open directly onto the pavement. This normal absence of front-garden is one feature that can make a Scottish village appear singularly forbidding to English eyes. Land was, however, provided in a long strip running at the back, in some villages of the eighteenth century as much as two or three acres, or even more, directly contiguous to the house.

Though the landowner thus exercised detailed control over the appearance and layout of the village, he did not normally build the houses himself : he left that to the tradesmen or smallholders who bought the feus, or to the employers he was able to attract to the site. Where he did expend money was on one or two amenities – the construction of an inn was the most usual. Lord Gardenstone's hostelry at Laurencekirk became a famous example, equipped with good accommodation for the gentry, a library and a gallery of portraits of the villagers themselves : both Dr Johnson and John Wesley stopped to admire it. A landowner might also build a church (this was, however, exceptional) and provide a court house or perhaps a school. Finally, he had land available for bleaching greens and drying grounds if these were appropriate, and sites for manufacturers to build along watercourses where they could construct weirs for their mills.

Having come so far, how did he attract settlers? All landowners were unanimous in the view that, just as they only permitted the construction of neat houses according to their own specifications, so they would only admit into their new villages settlers of good character, respectful and industrious.[46] At Tomintoul, for instance, newcomers had to find a local person of standing to attest that they were 'very honest, harmless men'.[47] Once over that moral hurdle, it was usual to give preference to local people displaced by agricultural changes, and to craftsmen with special skills. Both could hope to get feus on easy terms in the early days of the settlement. It was also possible to advertise : the tutor of Grant noticed two such advertisements in the north-east about 1763, and jotted down the contents. They give a vivid and precise idea of the conditions of settlement.

'Lord Macduff invites all well-qualified and sufficient manufacturers or artificers of any kind with or without families to come to his house of Down, where there is a safe harbour and there set up and carry on business. Artificers will have houses or feus to build upon, with materials necessary for that purpose, firing, yards and crofts of land at hand.'

'Lord Errol intends feuing out a town in the parish of Slains. As the grounds are at present unimproved he will give 'em their feu free for 7 years and after that period for 40/- per acre. He will also give them at the rate of 100 bolls limestone per acre, to assist 'em in improving their grounds. Town situated in plentiful country within half mile of sea, plenty of turf, close by a loch of fresh water, fit for bleeching. Manufactures will meet with encouragement. Any person inclining to feu on the above conditions may apply to...'[48]

It would not normally be difficult to get common settlers to fill the feus, at least if a small-holding was attached. It was much more difficult to get employers and highly skilled craftsmen to come, yet without external employment the village could not function properly as a market and a stop to emigration. Landowners faced this problem in various ways, sometimes by giving premiums or loans to manufacturers, sometimes by providing the buildings in a finished state, sometimes by practically giving away the land. Since the solution varied widely with different types of village, detailed consideration of this is better postponed.

Lastly there was the problem of government. Even a village of 'very honest, harmless men' was not expected to run by itself. Robertson warned that 'a watchful eye ought to be kept over villages no less than all other collections of men, and that the reins of government ought to be held by a steady hand'.[49] David Loch gave dire examples of what happened in villages where the hand was not steady, like Inverkeithing, a self-governing Royal Burgh where 'their politics and squabbles about the management of the town keep them poor and insignificant and almost totally idle', and North Queensferry, where 'there is no sort of industry...the M'Ritchies and the other boatmen are all indolent, insolent fellows under no sort of order, authority or government' : he contrasted them with villages like Cromarty which felt the smack of firm government and blossomed out in industry and profit to their superiors.[50]

In these circumstances it is not surprising that most landowners believed in absolute power, and controlled the villages through a baron bailie who was also their factor or their nominee. There were, however, certain exceptions to this rule. The most optimistic believed so much in the virtues of village life that they were happy (as many of their predecessors had been in previous centuries) to allow them to become self-governing bodies. George Dempster thus gave his village of Letham such powers, and Lord Gardenstone made Laurencekirk a free burgh of barony with as much solemnity as if he were the British Government conferring sovereign status on a former colony.[51] Landowners in factory villages seldom tried to keep the power of government in their own hands, but surrendered it to employers. This, however, raises again the problem of diversity of experience in different types of villages, to which we must now turn.

3. *Four Types of Village*

Almost all planned villages could be placed in one of four categories according to the employment intended to be their economic mainstay – almost all were either agricultural villages, fishing villages, villages based on small rural industries or factory villages.

Houston reasonably suggested a fifth category, 'inland spas, tourist and residential centres'.[52] I have not followed this lead since (before 1830 at least) only an insignificant number of settlements had this character. Ballater in Aberdeenshire (from 1808) with its spa, and Helensburgh on the Clyde with its residential villas, are justifiable examples, but some of the other settlements instanced by Houston, like Bridge of Earn, do not seem to have been initially planned with these ends in mind although after 1830 they turned towards them.

(i) *The Agricultural Villages*. The majority of planned villages began life as agricultural settlements, placed in a rural world and populated by smallholders who at first hardly looked beyond cultivation of their feu. Large numbers of planned villages also ended up as agricultural settlements, housing little more than farm workers and a sprinkling of tradesmen when attempts to bring industrial work to the village had failed. Nevertheless few were planned from the start to rely on no more than agricultural employment : such a thing was regarded as largely defeating the purposes for which they were built. Those that were genuine agricultural villages fell into two groups, Lowland villages on or close by the site of an older rural settlement, and Highland villages, laid out as a rule on greenfield sites, by the Committee of Forfeited Estates.

Athelstaneford in East Lothian is a remarkable example of the former type : its plan looks like a determined attempt to retain the social values of the old farmtoun in conjunction with the efficiency of modern farming. In these words Sir John Sinclair explained and commended it :

'The houses are built upon feu-tacks of 38 years, at the expense of the feuars, who pay the proprietor a trifle annually for the ground...

they have large gardens of an excellent soil...[and] besides this, the feuars hold, in a conjunct lease, about 100 acres of good land at a moderate rent. It is divided among them into small lots. Two of their number have each a pair of horses. With these they labour the land for the community at a reasonable hire, and drive coals and other articles necessary for the village. The produce of this land supplies the inhabitants with meal and potatoes, and many of them keep a cow. In this manner they live comfortably, clothe and educate their children decently and assist in setting them out in the world. There is no village where of late years the inhabitants have improved more in comfort and convenience than in Athelstaneford.'[53]

The latter type were of more miserable aspect. The Commissioners of the Forefeited Estates were obsessed by the thought that the Highlanders needed steadying and civilizing : they were also gentlemen well versed by their classical education in the civil and military habits of the Romans. They put two together, and determined upon plantations of old soldiers as *colonia* upon the estates of forfeited proprietors. Public advertisements of 1763 explained their plans : they had £3,000 available for settling discharged soldiers on the annexed estates, and they were going to build up to 300 houses (at £5 each) to be held rent-free for life. Each soldier would be given a premium of £3 to buy himself houshold furniture if he was married, and a plot of up to three acres 'for raising corn, hay, pot-herbs etc. to maintain his Family and to feed one Cow' : such holdings would be rent free for the first three years, and would then pay not over 5s. an acre. The Commissioners were also prepared to give a loan of £5 to each family in the first year to help stock the ground, and to pay a premium to unmarried soldiers of £1 for three years to retain them on the settlement. a further paper added that all soldiers 'shall cultivate their grounds by the spade only and not by plowing, and shall be subject to such orders and regulations as shall be laid down from time to time by the Commissioners'; they were commanded to behave 'honestly and industriously', as good neighbours with the country folk and with one another, 'under the pain of their being instantly dismissed'.[54]

Several settlements were laid out : one at each end of Loch Rannoch on the Robertson of Struan estate, for example, and others at Whiteley, Benniebeg, Borland Park, Strelitz and Callander on the Perth estate. Most of them, however, were very small – with two dozen houses they were more like hamlets than villages. The soldiers who occupied them in the first place were mainly Highlanders themselves, returning from the Seven Years War and taking the opportunity of getting land of their own on advantageous terms : some, however, appear to have been cashiered to the settlements against their own will.

Almost all the *colonia* also ended in failure. Several are represented on the map today by no more than a single building, a cottage or a farm. Very often the plantation turned out to have been made on highly unsuitable land – two acres of peat bog was no support for a retired soldier with a family, as a stream of petitions to the Commissioners in Edinburgh soon testified. Those settlers who had been seconded by their commanding officers sometimes appeared too ill to survive the rigours of colonization in the hills : the Commissioners received a pathetic request from one of them, Alexander Stewart, who was 'unable to work for his bread, much less that of his large family'. He asked if their Lordships would 'recommend him to the Commander-in-Chief to be appointed as a soldier in any of the Garrisons of North Britain, or to any other Charity your Honours shall think proper'. Then there were soldiers who took the bounty and ran away, 'without bidding goodnight', as one factor sadly observed.[55]

Perhaps the only *colonia* which made a permanent economic success of their settlement was that of Callander, which was in any case attached to a well-established planned village of another type, and that at Kinloch Rannoch. The latter was on the other hand a moral disaster – the Commissioners found that their soldiers, 'honest and industrious' though they were meant to be, had brought venereal disease to north Perthshire.[56] Altogether they cannot have been thrilled by the total outcome of their scheme to imitate the ancient Romans.

(ii) *The Fishing Villages*. The provision of non-agricultural employment was the chief problem for the promoters of planned villages in most of the country; the favourite solution along the seaboard of the Western Highlands, in Caithness, Sutherland and on parts of the southern shore of the Moray Firth was the establishment of a fishing centre. It owed its populartiy to a number of causes – the traditional belief in the inexhaustible riches of the Scottish seas and the wealth to be gained by exploiting them, the exceptionally pressing need in the west and north to find alternative employment for a population bursting at the seams, and the absence of any other practicable choice in areas of low natural endowment. It might also be added that any suggestion that the population would be materially better off on the coast was psychologically attractive to the lairds, wishing as they did to remove the peasants from the interior, so that they could lay the land down to sheep and pay off their mounting arrears of debt,[57] but not wishing to lay themselves open to the charge of inhumanity or of forcing emigration upon unwilling dependents.

The movement to found fishing villages had its roots before the

Union of 1707, as the seventeenth-century development of Stornoway testifies, and there were flashes of activity in this direction in the first three-quarters of the eighteenth century. It took on a new impetus, however, in 1786 when a group composed mainly of landed proprietors came together to form a semi-charitable joint-stock organization called the British Fisheries Society. Its mentor was John Knox, a 'political economist' who had lectured to the Highland Society on the desirability of founding fishing stations along the Scottish coast to tap the economic potential of the Minch.[58]

Knox proposed the construction of no less than forty villages, each containing 36 houses, of which twenty should be fishermen's houses with two rooms and half an acre of garden, 12 should be tradesmen's houses with four rooms and an acre of ground, and one each should be reserved for the general merchant, the surgeon, the schoolmaster and the innkeeper.[59] An English writer, John Smith, offered the society an alternative plan, more suitable, he believed, to 'a hive of labourers and not a cluster of pensioners':

'The more the working class are brought by close neighbourhood to be witnesses of each other's conduct, to be examples or reproofs to each other, the more they will be excited not to consume their hours in lazy basking or vain tattle.'[60]

In pursuit of this he proposed a much smaller number of much larger towns, each consisting of several score of one-storey, two-room houses with earth floors without any sort of contiguous garden, arranged on an unrelieved grid around a dockyard. It was the worst plan of the century, further blackened by his fatuous expectations that out of such nuclei a series of cities the size of Liverpool would emerge to adorn the west coast of Scotland.[61]

In the event, the British Fisheries Society built only four villages of its own, all nearer to Knox's conception than to Smith's : Tobermory in Mull, Loch Bay in Skye, Ullapool in Wester Ross and the Pultneytown suburb of the old Royal Burgh of Wick. All but the last failed as fishery centres, though Tobermory was to succeed as a market town and port : even the relatively striking success at Wick came too late to save the Society from bankruptcy in the nineteenth century. Nevertheless, private proprietors followed where the Society had blazed the first trail : Plockton in Inverness-shire, Jeantown (or Loch Carron) in Wester Ross, Sarclet in Caithness, Helmsdale, and a whole crop along the shores of the Moray Firth in the early nineteenth century were the outcome. Those in Moray and Banff particularly came into their own after the decline of the rural linen industry forced landowners to think again about what employment was feasible for the villagers.

Helmsdale may be selected as an example of what a landowner with plenty of capital might do to attract reliable employers to settle in a fishing village. The Duke of Sutherland, approached by a Moray firm in 1814, first built a complete curing installation at a cost of £1,200 and rented it to them at 6½ per cent per annum. He then came to a similar arrangement with a Berwick firm at a capital cost of a further £2,100, and attracted other firms to settle from Leven, Leith and Golspie. He constructed an Inn, and nine large houses on his own account, and employed Rennie to construct a harbour in 1818 for a further £1,600. Within five years the Duke had invested a total of over £14,000 and created a viable port and fishing community on what had formerly been a greenfield site.[62]

It has always been habitual to pour vituperation on the first Duke of Sutherland for his part in the clearances. It would only be just to recognize that the Duke was actually more lavish with capital to ameliorate social dislocation than any other landowner in the North of Scotland has ever been. Perhaps his only rival was Lord Leverhulme at Stornoway in the twentieth century, and like Lord Leverhulme, he got small thanks and less profit for his pains.

(iii) *Villages with Small Rural Industry*. The fishing villages form a relatively compact group, confined at least to the north and west. Those villages planned with the intention of introducing small-scale rural manufacturing industry are, by contrast, extremely widely diffused, stretching from Dumfriesshire to Cromarty, and from Argyll to East Lothian and Aberdeen. No type of village indeed is more numerous, or more typical of the eighteenth-century planners' intention.

Ormiston in East Lothian, founded by John Cockburn in 1738, was one of the first of this kind. Something of its impact on contemporaries may be gauged from this enthusiastic letter from Sir James Hall of Dunglas to his friend the Earl of Marchmont, written about 1740:

'His toun is riseing exceedingly he having 40 Linning lomes and wabsters, and to every 6 lomes has 60 spinsters and all others for cairding, and the wark so that thers not a boy or a girel of 7 years old but has something to doe that ye will not see ane in the toun except in ane hour of play. Blacksmiths, shoemakers, candlemakers and baikers, malsters, etc. make throng doeing... There is boths building for all their merchandise, and to be market days, and ther is 16 houses contracted for this nixt season... I shall, dear Marchmont, in a little time be better able to let you know more about it. I have sent for a duble of his tacks and fews.'[63]

In the next half-century there were to be many places built along similar lines, with a variety of different trades conjured up to support

them. Lord Gardenstone, for example, built his village of Laurencekirk in Kincardineshire and endowed it with bleachfields, a print-
field, linen workers, stocking-knitters, cabinet-makers, smiths and
other sorts of country tradesmen:[64]

> 'He surely succeeded in converting a paltry kirk town into a neat
> and flourishing village... It is a herculean task to think of establish-
> ing manufactures in a country ill provided with fuel and at some
> distance from the sea'.[65]

Not far off in Angus, George Dempster of Dunnichen, another of the
great improvers of his day, laid out Letham on a greenfield site. He
wrote excitedly of his own work in the *Statistical Account*:

> 'Streets have been marked out on a regular plan, and lots of any
> extent are let upon perpetual leases, at the rate of £2 an acre. It con-
> tains about 20 families, and new houses are rising in it daily...here
> a fair or market has lately begun to be held, once a fortnight, on
> Thursdays, for the sale of cloth, yarn, and flax.'[66]

Up in Inverness-shire, Sir James Grant laid out Grantown-on-Spey
with sawmills and a distillery. Still further north George Ross of
Pitkerie transformed Cromarty by bringing in a cloth manufactory,
a nail and spade works, a brewery and lace and sacking works. In
Moray and Banff the Dukes of Gordon and the Earls of Findlater were
leaders among those bringing the linen trade to the small new villages.
Away in the west, the Duke of Argyll had provided Inveraray with a
new site, and linen and woollen works to keep it busy. The Duke of
Buccleuch laid out Newcastleton on the Borders as an intended rival
in the woollen weaving trade to the independent burgh of Hawick;
a few miles away Sir William Maxwell built Springfield near the
boundary of England and Scotland.[67]

Despite the diversity, a certain pattern lies behind almost all the
examples: there was great faith in the domestic textile trades, especially
in the linen trade, and to a lesser extent reliance on brewing or distilling. Always the problem, the 'herculean task', was getting entrepreneurs interested in a village site, and once interested, getting them
to stay. It was tackled on similar principles to the Duke of Sutherland's
intervention at Helmsdale. The Duke of Argyll provided premises
for the manufacturers at Inveraray, and his neighbours supported the
works by taking shares.[68] The Earl of Findlater paid the expenses of
linen tradesmen to come from Edinburgh, built them a workshop and
gave them an interest-free loan for seven years.[69] George Ross built the
brewery at Cromarty with his own money, and drew up a deed of
co-partnership with other local gentry to finance the sacking works.[70]
Repeated a hundred times, in bits and pieces all over the country, this
represented an appreciable landed investment in the business of

encouraging industry in the countryside. Whether it was wise investment was another matter. Certainly the industries so carefully implanted had in too many cases a heart-breakingly short life in the
community they were meant to help.

(iv) *The Factory Village.* The factory village differed initially from
the group we have just been considering only in the scale of the
business unit the landowner succeeded in attracting to his lands. In
place of a small workshop with a country trader making or finishing
linen with the help of domestic workers who spun or wove in their
own homes, he got a cotton mill ruled by an industrial entrepreneur
able to command more substantial resources of capital and labour.
Villages where this occurred are widespread in distribution, ranging
from Spinningdale in Sutherland to Penicuik in Midlothian,[71] from
Deanston and Stanley in Perthshire to New Lanark in the Clyde Valley
and Newton Stewart on the Solway. There is, however, a heavy concentration of successful examples within twenty miles of Glasgow.
There is also concentration in the period of their construction; almost
all date from the years 1780–1800. Before this date the cotton industry
and the water-frame factory on which its spinning side was based were
unknown in Scotland. After it, for technical and economic reasons,
the industry became centred far more narrowly in the large towns of
the Clyde valley, although those works that were already in the villages near Glasgow did not cease operation.

The function of the factory village, from the landowner's point of
view, did not differ in essence from that of a fishing village or a place
like Ormiston or Cromarty : it provided a market for his tenants'
agricultural produce, and an extension of employment opportunity
for the local population. If it was successful it was much more likely
to provide him with a good return in rents and feu duties than a place
like Laurencekirk, where he had to be continually giving rebates and
premiums to persuade employers to stay at all. It was rather rare for
the landowner to provide any capital at all to the entrepreneur in the
factory village.

Within a factory village, the actual role of the landowner was generally greatly reduced compared with other villages. It was true there
were some, like Spinningdale, Stanley and Newton Stewart, where
the initiative of the landowner had brought the entrepreneur to the
site. Eaglesham was constructed to the Earl of Eglinton's specifications in the traditional way and sounded very nice:
  'two rows of elegantly built houses, all of freestone, with a large
  space between, laid out in fine green fields, interspersed with trees,
  with a fine gurgling streamlet running down the middle... Towards
  the higher end, and on the rivulet, the cotton mill stands'.[72]

Many of the factory villages, however, were the brain-child of the entrepreneur, not of the landowner on whose territory they found themselves – it was David Dale who decided where New Lanark should be, and the landlord in that settlement, Lord Braxfield, appears to have played no part in its history other than that of a passive spectator and drawer of feu duties.

It was perhaps inevitable that a factory village should fall under the sway of the factory owner.[73] In a community like New Lanark or Catrine more than two breadwinners out of three worked in the mills, or at ancillary jobs for the firm : they lived in houses built by the firm (Eaglesham was again an exception), and went to schools provided by the firm. Where in another planned village the landowner would have insisted on houses built to certain aesthetic and social standards, in the factory village he let the factory owner have his way untrammelled. The result was almost everywhere worse housing. At Penicuik, for example, the two-room hovels the employers put up were much worse than the two and three-storey buildings the Clerks had insisted upon in the 1740s. Owen at New Lanark has been given much credit for the 'exceptional' way he built houses with two storeys, had the dung-hills cleared before the doors and instituted a regular cleansing service. Exceptional he may well have been among his fellow employers, but he was surely doing no more than the minimum which any good landowner would have insisted upon in the conventional planned community.

In the factory village, formal government was likewise made over to the employers in the majority of cases, and those at Balfron, New Kilpatrick, Deanston, Blantyre and New Lanark (for instance) all took special measures and employed special staff to control the 'morals' of their labour force in the village. Even at New Lanark there was apparently no question of permitting self-governing communities as at Laurencekirk and Letham. Only Eaglesham, a village still under the Earl's constitutional guidance, was managed with the assistance of 'a committee or body of directors annually chosen [by the villagers] for the management of the town'. Neither at Deanston nor at Blantyre was any public houe allowed in the community. At New Lanark 'pot and public houses were gradually removed from the immediate vicinity of their dwellings'. No one regarded the problem from the other end and built a decent inn, as the landowners almost invariably did. All in all, it is difficult to believe that the quality of life for the villagers did not deteriorate as a result of social control passing out of the landowners' hands. They were, for all their obvious short-comings, just a little more respectful of humanity than the entrepreneurial middle-class that came to replace them.

4. *Conclusion and Summary*

Superficially the planned village movement must appear as an enormous and inevitable failure. In the Highlands, the villages were made
meaningless in the chaos and decay which marked the middle decades
of the nineteenth century in that region. Fishing all along the west
coast collapsed shortly after the end of the Napoleonic Wars, and the
fishing villages went with it. The linen, woollen and cotton manu-
factories in the Highlands had never even got started on profitable
lines in the communities that housed them. The typical settlement of
the nineteenth-century Highlands was therefore not an integrated
village providing non-agricultural employment and a nucleus of
traders (as everyone had hoped and worked for between 1745 and
1820) but a crude huddle of crofters' huts crouched by the sea between the potato plots and the inshore boats. Such planned villages
as had been created already (like Ullapool) stayed half-finished while
the population that was to have filled them emigrated to America, or
to the scarcely less alien environment of Glasgow.

In the Lowlands the planned village was killed, hardly less firmly,
by the railway, and by the concentration of industrial activity in the
towns: the first enabled the farmer to bring his surplus cheaply to
the markets and dispensed with the need to bring the market to the
farmer; the second made rural industry uncompetitive. As soon as the
textile industries had mastered the art of utilizing the steam engine,
production moved into the factories, and the factories moved into
towns near their fuel supplies: this killed many even of the factory
villages, especially the outlying ones. The rural linen industry which
had been the basis for so many of the communities of the north-east,
of Perthshire, Angus and Kincardineshire, was ebbing away even
before it reached the stage of factory organization, because of the disadvantages of running the trade in remote rural areas. By 1800 it was
already concentrating on a few towns. The result of this drain of
employment was to strand most planned villages high and dry. Some,
like the Forfeited Estates *colonia* at Benniebeg and Borland Bog, just
vanished. Others were like Fife Keith in Banffshire, started with great
hopes, but described before 1850 as 'commercially a complete failure;
for except for a few merchant shops and some three or four tradesmen,
the villagers may be said to depend on their crofts of land'.[74] Many
places were in this plight, and are left today (Laurencekirk in Kincardineshire is an instance) curiously large and meaningless in a modern rural environment. Still others, like Airdrie, Johnstone and Penicuik grew into prominent towns on the edge of the coalfields or the
conurbations and, though by that measure successful, they totally lost
their 'planned', compact and rural character. The factories and the

H

manufacturers ultimately swamped the little settlement of which Sir John Clerk had once been proud, and when Penicuik grew up it was without much regard to either the aesthetic or social ideals of its eighteenth-century planner : it is only now that the community is trying to unravel the Georgian kernel to make it the focus of a twentieth-century development scheme for the town.

Yet by dwelling overmuch on the failure of the villages we may overlook the limited but nevertheless real contribution to the economic and social life of Scotland which they made in the past and are sometimes making today. Such towns as the Highlands possess at the present time date their foundations in most cases from an eighteenth-century landlord – Oban, Inveraray, Tobermory and Ullapool, Callander, Grantown, Tomintoul and Thurso. In the last half-century their populations have tended to grow while that of the country areas around them has tended to decline, and the people in them have increasingly become involved in non-agricultural activities like shop-keeping and administering to tourists in a manner not so very different from what their founders intended. Indeed, the planned architectural appeal of such places as Inveraray and Ullapool has done much to make them tourist centres, and will do more in the future if they succeed in keeping their character. They can indeed be considered one of the major assets of the modern Highlands.

In the Lowlands, where the most important fact of history since 1740 has been the coming of industrialization, the planned villages may perhaps be judged to have done their bit towards achieving this end. The crucial leading sector in the industrial revolution was in the textile trades : it did mean something in the early days that landowners were wholeheartedly enthusiastic to expand the linen and woollen trades on a rural basis : it did mean something that they gladly accepted the overtures of the early cotton pioneers to provide a site for a factory. We might remind ourselves of the consequences in some underdeveloped countries of modern times where landowners have set their teeth against industrialization – in Scotland in the eighteenth century it was surely important that they befriended the process in its early days, and though some became critical of it later, it was then too late to reverse the economic trends they had helped to set in motion.[75]

Finally, it is worth recalling that in the short period in which planned villages had a vigorous life in their own right, a number did at any rate do some of the virtuous things their promoters hoped for them. Some grew very well, and in a balanced and controlled manner. Robertson wrote in 1790 about Perthshire:

'Several people still alive remember Callander particularly, when it consisted of four families only, the minister's, schoolmaster's, the beadle's, who was also the smith, and the innkeeper, amounting in all to about twenty souls. There are now at least 1,000 souls and the number is rapidly increasing. Comrie is nearly in the same predicament, besides Crieff and others.'[76]

Such a town was able to provide local employment in a good environment (for its period) for people who would otherwise have had no choice but to leave the traditional area of their habitation. It was also sometimes able to provide an opportunity for education that might be even more highly regarded than the opportunity for employment : the Commissioners of Forfeited Estates might have reconsidered their low opinion of the Highlanders had they noted their General Inspector's report in 1767 that at Crieff 'the village is dayly encreasing from the number of families settling there for the education of their children'.[77]

A good village also succeeded in providing a market, and therefore higher incomes for the farmers who dwelt in its vicinity. Its trading activities introduced many in the rural classes to consumption habits they would otherwise have taken longer to acquire. In this paper we have quoted many writers who were friends to the village movement. It is fitting to make our last point with one who was not. He was a minister in the Spey valley, and may have had Grantown in mind:

'Villages, it will be argued, afford a ready market even for trivial articles from a farm. But the profits arising therefrom are only seemingly advantageous. The farmer's wife, or daughter, repairs to the village to dispose of her basket of eggs. This is one advantage arising from the neighbourhood of the village. But, what is the consequence? She returns loaded with tea, sugar, a bottle of wine as a cordial or medicine, some yards of fine muslin, silk and satin: articles she would never have dreamt of, had she not been ensnared by the glare and show of a fine shop, and unfortunately forgot the most necessary petition—"into temptation lead me not".'[78]

Clearly he would have regarded any historian as degenerate who could argue that tea, sugar and satin made an amelioration of life, and that such might be among the most obvious and pleasant consequences that a new planned village brought to those who lived near it towards the close of the eighteenth century. It was very fortunate he never lived to see Babylon disporting itself at modern Coylumbridge in the heart of his very own parish.

NOTES

1. But there was still room in England for new ones. J. D. Chambers in 'Enclosure and Labour-supply in the Industrial Revolution',

Economic History Review, 2S, V (1952–3), 322–3, draws attention to the number of new rural settlements in the east midlands that followed agrarian change in the eighteenth and early nineteenth centuries : such diverse English 'model' villages as Milton Abbas and Saltaire to some extent parallel Scottish settlements like Inveraray and Ormiston.

2. The term clachan is probably only strictly applicable to settlements containing a church.
3. A. McKerral, *Kintyre in the Seventeenth Century* (1948), 140.
4. The fullest description is George S. Pryde's introduction to his edition of *The Court Book of the Burgh of Kirkintilloch, 1658–1694* (SHS, 1963).
5. D. McNaught, *Kilmaurs Parish and Burgh* (Paisley 1912), 322–3.
6. The charter for the burgh of barony was obtained seven years before the feus : G.S. Pryde, 'The Burghs of Dumfriesshire and Galloway : their Origin and Status' (*Transactions of the Dumfries-shire and Galloway Natural History and Antiquarian Society*, 3S, XXIX (1952), 114, calls it 'a clear case of town planning'. For an early visit to Langholm (and the hostelry) see C. Lowther, *Our Journall into Scotland*, ed. 'W.D.' (1894), 11–12.
7. G.S. Pryde, 'Burghs of Dumfriesshire and Galloway', 115–16.
8. *Acts of the Parliaments of Scotland*, V, 530.
9. A. McKerral, *Kintyre*, chapter III.
10. *Acts of the Parliaments of Scotland*, V, 556, 615.
11. Sir John Sinclair, *Analysis of the Statistical Account of Scotland* (London 1826), I, 174–5.
12. SRO Seafield Papers, Castle Grant, Box 38, bundle 1. I am obliged to Mr Ian Grant for bringing my attention to the passage. The 'improvements in the hills' referred to were enclosures.
13. *Statistical Account of Scotland*, VI (1793), 129.
14. Ibid. XI (1794), 401.
15. Ibid. XI, 472.
16. James Robertson, *General View of the Agriculture in the Southern Districts of the County of Perth* (London 1794), 14.
17. SRO Forfeited Estates Papers E/729.
18. *Statistical Account*, II (1792), 42.
19. Robert Rennie, 'Plan of an Inland Village', *Prize Essays and Trans-actions of the Highland Society of Scotland*, II (1803), 265.
20. J. Sinclair, *Analysis*, I, 172, 177.
21. J. Robertson, *County of Perth*, 67–8.
22. J. Sinclair, *Analysis*, I, 172, 177.
23. *Scottish Forfeited Estates Papers, 1715 : 1745*, ed A.H. Millar (SHS, 1909), 159.
24. Ibid. 61–2.
25. EUL MS 316 (c. 1757).
26. John Bellers, *Proposals for Raising a College of Industry* (London 1696). Bellers's ideas, however, were not specifically related to a village environment.
27. The possibility that Owen's management owed something to the ideas of Robert Rennie should not be overlooked. It is instructive to compare Rennie's 'Plan of an Inland Village' (see note 19 above) with descriptions of Owen's rule at New Lanark.
28. Robert Owen, *Report to the County of Lanark* (Glasgow 1821).

29. J.Robertson, *County of Perth*, 68.
30. Quoted in W.H.G.Armytage, *Heaven's Below – Utopian Experiments in England 1560–1960* (London 1961), 80.
31. See for instance *The New Statistical Account of Scotland* (1845) VI, 780–3.
32. W.H.G.Armytage, *Heaven's Below*, 306.
33. There is much information on the Earl of Hopetoun's attitude to Leadhills in Hopetoun House Muniments, Lead papers, especially IV, 90/1–3. I am indebted to the Hope Trustees for permission to examine these.
34. Moray McLaren, *The Shell Guide to Scotland* (London 1965). The Gazetteer from which I have worked was compiled by Dr Jean Munro with the assistance of R.W.Munro, A.E.Truckell, Cuthbert Graham and others. This is a formidable galaxy of scholars with local knowledge, and although the book was not intended as a definitive work of historical scholarship, the historians involved in writing it have gone a long way towards turning it into one.
35. J.M.Houston, 'Village Planning in Scotland, 1745–1845', *Advancement of Science*, V (1948), 129–33; J.G.Dunbar, *The Historic Architecture of Scotland* (London 1966), 196–8, 244–50.
36. David Loch, *A Tour through most of the Trading Towns and Villages of Scotland* (1778), 22–6.
37. James Loch, *An Account of the Improvements on the Estates of the Marquess of Stafford* (London 1820), and Rosalind Mitchison, *Agricultural Sir John* (London 1962), give accounts and plans of the operations of both men.
38. See for instance SRO, Forfeited Estates Papers E/729: 'the surprising effect it has had in his lordship's village of new Keith has many others to follow his example'.
39. *Scottish Population Statistics*, ed. J.G.Kyd (SHS, 1952), 86.
40. For a plan of 1739 see SRO, Forfeited Estates Papers, RHP 3414.
41. Tomintoul has inspired the best historical account of the founding of a planned village: Victor Gaffrey, *The Lordship of Strathavon* (Third Spalding Club, Aberdeen, 1960), 34–61.
42. There is an account and critique of Ormiston in R.H.Matthew and P.J.L.Nuttgens, 'Two Scottish Villages: a planning study', *Scottish Studies*, III (1959–60), 113–42.
43. David Loch, *Tour*, 10.
44. *Letters of John Cockburn of Ormiston to his Gardener 1727–1744*, ed. J.Colville (SHS, 1904), 79–80.
45. *Shell Guide*, 219, 290, 455; J.Dunbar, *Historic Architecture*, 196–8, 244–50.
46. See for example J.Robertson, *County of Perth*, 67–8.
47. V.Gaffrey, *Strathavon*, 58.
48. SRO, Seafield Papers, Castle Grant, Box 38, bundle 1. I must again acknowledge Mr Ian Grant's help with this reference.
49. J.Robertson, *County of Perth*, 67–8.
50. David Loch, *Tour*, 19, 29, 54.
51. See Francis Garden, Lord Gardenstone, *Letter to the People of Laurencekirk* (1799).
52. J.M.Houston, *Village Planning*, 130, 132
53. J.Sinclair, *Analysis*, I, 186.
54. SRO, Forfeited Estates Papers E.730/29, 1–5.

55. SRO, Forfeited Estates Papers E.783/70 : also *Forfeited Estate Papers*, 263.
56. SRO, Forfeited Estates Papers E.783/68, 87.
57. For debt, and the dilemma of the Highland landowners in this respect, see Malcolm Gray, *The Highland Economy, 1750–1850* (1957).
58. Dr Jean Munro's Edinburgh PH.D. thesis (1952) is an excellent account of the society : Jean Dunlop, 'The British Fisheries Society, 1786–1893'.
59. John Knox, *A discourse on the expedience of establishing Fishing Stations or Small Towns in the Highlands of Scotland and the Hebride Islands* (London 1786).
60. John Gray, *Some reflections intended to promote the success of the Scotch Fishing Company* (London 1789), 50. Note the early use of the phrase 'working class'.
61. The belief that great cities will arise in the north is still cherished by the Highland Development Board. The M.P. for the Western Isles asked in Parliament whether they would be populated by fairies or professors.
62. This, at least, is the factor's version. There is no good reason to disbelieve him. James Loch, *Account*.
63. Report of the Manuscripts of the Right Honourable Lord Polwarth, V (HMC, London 1961), 146–7,
64. David Loch, *Tour*, 66.
65. John Ramsay of Ochtertyre, *Scotland and Scotsmen in the Eighteenth Century* (ed. Alexander Allardyce, 1888), I, 376–7. The comment was made about 1800.
66. *Statistical Account*, I (1791), 421.
67. Ibid. IX (1793), 529–30.
68. 'Linnen manufacture, Michaelmas 1750', NLS, Saltoun MSS, Box 72.
69. *Statistical Account*, XII (1794), 145.
70. David Loch, *Tour*, 54.
71. The factory settlement at Penicuik, which can still be seen, was contiguous to the older planned village, which the Clerks had been developing since before 1740. See *Memoirs of the Life of Sir John Clerk of Penicuik*, ed. J. M. Gray (SHS, 1892), 254–5.
72. *New Statistical Account* (1845), VII, 402.
73. There is an excellent account in Sidney Pollard, 'The Factory Village in the Industrial Revolution', *English Historical Review*, LXXIX (1964). The administration at New Lanark is concisely described in H. G. Macnab, *The New Views of Mr Owen of Lanark Impartially Examined* (London 1819).
74. Quoted in J. H. Houston, *Village Planning*, 130.
75. For a wider consideration of the landowners' attitudes to industrialization, see my article 'Scottish Landowners and Economic Growth, 1650–1850', *Scottish Journal of Political Economy*, XI (1964), 218–34.
76. J. Robertson, *County of Perth*, 64.
77. SRO, Forfeited Estates Papers E.729.
78. *Statistical Account*, XXI (1799), 88.

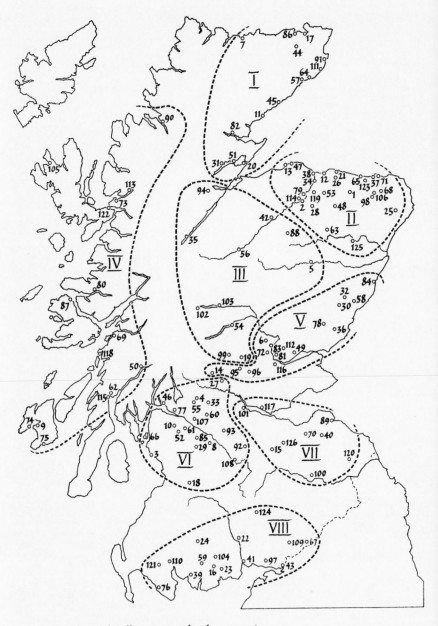

The Planned Village in Scotland, 1730–1830

Appendix

1. Aberchirder, 1764.
2. Aberlour, 1812.
3. Ardrossan, 1805.
4. Balfron (Ballindalloch, 1789).
5. Ballater, 1808.
6. Bankfoot (a group of three planned villages, Bankfoot, Waterloo and Carniehill built about 1815).
7. Bettyhill, before 1815.
8. Blantyre, 1785.
9. Bowmore, 1768.
10. Bridge of Weir, 1790.
11. Brora, 1811.
12. Buckie (Port Gordon, 1797).
13. Burghead, 1805.
14. Callander, 1730.
15. Carlops, 1784.
16. Castle Douglas, 1792.
17. Castletown, 1824.
18. Catrine, 1787.
19. Crieff, 1731.
20. Cromarty, 1772.
21. Cullen, 1820.
22. Dalswinton, c. 1780.
23. Dalbeattie, 1780.
24. Dalry, c. 1780.
25. Deer (a group of five planned villages in a small radius, viz. Stuartfield 1772, Fetterangus 1772, Longside 1801, Mintlaw 1801, and New Deer 1805).
26. Deskford (a group of three planned villages from c. 1760, Deskford, Lintmill, Tochieneal).
27. Doune (Deanston, c. 1790).
28. Dufftown, 1817.
29. Eaglesham, 1796.
30. Edzell, 1839.
31. Evanton, 1810.
32. Fettercairn, c. 1760.

33. Fintry, 1794.
34. Fochabers, c. 1778.
35. Fort Augustus, 1754.
36. Friockheim, 1830.
37. Gardenstown, 1720.
38. Garmouth (Kingston, 1784).
39. Gatehouse of Fleet, c. 1790.
40. Gifford, mid-eighteenth century.
41. Glencaple, 1746.
42. Grantown-on-Spey, 1766.
43. Gretna (Springfield, 1791).
44. Halkirk, c. 1790.
45. Helmsdale, 1814.
46. Helensburgh, 1776.
47. Hopeman, 1805.
48. Huntly, c. 1765.
49. Inchture (Baledgarno, c. 1815).
50. Inveraray, 1743.
51. Invergordon, mid-eighteenth century.
52. Johnstone, 1781.
53. Keith, 1750.
54. Kenmore, 1760.
55. Killearn, c. 1800.
56. Kingussie, c. 1780.
57. Latheron, eighteenth century.
58. Laurencekirk, c. 1770.
59. Laurieston, late eighteenth century.
60. Lennoxtown, 1785–6.
61. Linwood, 1792.
62. Lochgilphead, early nineteenth century.
63. Lumsden, 1825.
64. Lybster, late eighteenth century.
65. Macduff, 1783.
66. Millport, late eighteenth century.
67. Newcastleton, 1793.
68. New Pitsligo, c. 1780.
69. Oban, mid-eighteenth century.
70. Ormiston, c. 1740.
71. Pennan (New Aberdour, 1798).
72. Pitcairngreen, late eighteenth century.
73. Plockton, late eighteenth century.
74. Port Charlotte, 1828.
75. Port Ellen, 1821.

76. Port William, 1770.
77. Renton, 1782.
78. Restenneth (Letham, 1788).
79. Rothes, 1766.
80. Salen, probably late eighteenth century.
81. Scone (New Scone, 1805).
82. Spinningdale, 1790.
83. Stanley, 1785.
84. Stonehaven (New Stonehaven, 1797).
85. Thornliebank, 1778.
86. Thurso, c. 1810.
87. Tobermory, 1788.
88. Tomintoul, 1779.
89. Tynninghame, c. 1770.
90. Ullapool, 1788.
91. Wick (Pultneytown, 1808).
92. Wilsontown, 1779.
93. Airdrie, between 1760 and 1790.
94. Beauly, c. 1760.
95. Benniebeg, 1763.
96. Borland Bog, 1763.
97. Brydekirk, c. 1803.
98. Cuminestown, c. 1740.
99. Comrie, late eighteenth century.
100. Galashiels, between 1770 and 1790.
101. Grangemouth, 1777.
102. Invercomrie, 1763.
103. Kinloch Rannoch, 1763.
104. Kirkpatrick Durham, 1785.
105. Loch Bay, 1788.
106. Newbyth, 1764.
107. New Kilpatrick, early nineteenth century.
108. New Lanark, 1784.
109. New Langholm, 1778.
110. Newton Stewart, eighteenth century.
111. Sarclet, c. 1800.
112. Strelitz, 1763.
113. Jeantown, c. 1800.
114. Archiestown, 1764.
115. Ardrishaig, early nineteenth century.
116. Bridge of Earn, 1769.
117. Charlestown, c. 1765.
118. Easdale, early nineteenth century.

119. Fife Keith, eighteenth century.
120. Gavinton, late eighteenth century.
121. Kirkcowan, about 1800.
122. Kyleakin, 1811.
123. Longmanhill, late eighteenth century.
124. Moffat, late eighteenth century.
125. Monymusk, mid-eighteenth century.
126. Penicuik, mid-eighteenth century.

Numbers 1–92 are from *Shell Guide* : the dates are as indicated by the authors of that work except for a few cases where I have been able to be more precise from other information.

Numbers 93–113 (other eighteenth-century villages mentioned in the text of this paper) are dated as accurately as possible from the *Statistical Account* and other sources.

Numbers 114–126 are additional villages, mostly those mentioned in either of two other works of significance bearing on this topic, but not otherwise mentioned either in *Shell Guide* or elsewhere in this paper. These works are J. M. Houston, 'Village Planning in Scotland, 1745–1845', in *The Advancement of Science*, v (1948), 129–32, and John Dunbar, *The Historic Architecture of Scotland* (1966), 196–8, 244–50.

5. *Some Eighteenth-Century Ideas of Scotland*

JANET ADAM SMITH

What is Scotland? A nation, a province, a lost kingdom; a culture, a history, a body of tradition; a bundle of sentiments, a state of mind; North Britain or Caledonia? Such are the questions which Scots have been asking themselves, implicitly or openly, ever since 1707; and this essay is an attempt to discover what 'Scotland' signified for a number of Scotsmen in the century after the Union of Parliaments. It is not by any means an exhaustive survey, but the result of readings in and about David Hume, Alexander Carlyle of Inveresk, Robert and James Adam, James Boswell, Allan Ramsay, Robert Fergusson and Robert Burns, with this question in mind. In the first section, and again in the third, I have grouped men of similar background. In the first Hume, Carlyle, and their friends the Adams, men whose kinship extended far among the Lowland gentry, who had travelled and resided in other countries than their own. In the third the three poets – wigmaker, clerk and farmer, men with no pretensions to gentle birth – who all their lives were firmly planted in Scotland, whose experience of England and the world beyond came through their reading. In between comes Boswell, *sui generis*.

Hume (1711–76), Carlyle (1722–1805) and the Adam brothers (Robert, 1728–92, James 1732–94) were born into families that accepted the Revolution Settlement of 1688 and the Union of Parliaments of 1707. Carlyle, surveying the Roman wall as he travelled from Newcastle to Carlisle in 1762, felt that

> 'while it demonstrates the art and industry of the Romans, brings full in our view the peace and security we now enjoy under a government that unites the interest and promotes the common prosperity of the whole island.'[1]

In the same year James Adam was basing his designs for the Houses of Parliament on the fact of the Union:

> 'This is what I strongly aim at in my Parliament House – that making the improbable supposition of its being built, ruined and no mention made of it in history or records, that notwithstanding, posterity who have ever read of Great Britain or its constitution

should not be at a loss to say, two thousand years hence, this is the Hall for Coronations; this is the House of Commons and that the House of Peers; here are the Courts of Justice and there the committee rooms &ca. Nor would there be any risk that it be suspected to be raised by any other people but the British, nor at any period before the Union, as I have taken care that North Britain shall bear its own share in all decorations.'[2]

So the fountains at the foot of the great stairs, decorated with oaks and roses, birks and thistles, were to personify Thames and Forth.

Both James Adam and Carlyle imply the fact of Britain, of which Scotland is the northern part; so does Hume when he says that 'London is the Capital of my own Country'; and Robert Adam, on reaching London in 1758 after his years in Rome, signs himself 'my dearest Mother's British boy'. But consciousness of being British is rather for special occasions; in their everyday consciousness, Scots and English are two separate nations. Carlyle, describing the company at Harrogate in 1763, draws a composite picture of 'John Bull'; Hume, referring to Addison's views on Germany, denounces 'John Bull's prejudices'. John Bull stands for England only.

They were specially conscious of being Scots when they were in London. It was partly the limitations of Scotland that brought them south; the city's chief attraction for Hume (who for a while thought of settling there) and for the Adams (who did settle, in 1758) was the chance that it offered of an ampler stage for their talents. 'Scotland is but a narrow place', wrote Robert Adam in 1755, explaining that he needed 'a greater a more extensive and more honourable scene I mean an English Life'.[3] Soon after, he outlined his plan to his sister in Edinburgh:

'I often think what a pity it is that such a genius [as myself] should be thrown away upon Scotland where scarce will ever happen an opportunity of putting one noble thought in execution. It would be a more extensive scheme to settle a family also in England and let the Adams be the sovereign architects of the United Kingdom.'[4]

Four years later Hume was writing to Adam Smith that 'Scotland is too narrow a Place for me'. Yet once in London, citizens of the United Kingdom, the sense of Scottishness was strong. Often it was the straightforward gregariousness and heightened national consciousness of any exiles: as when the London Scots dined regularly in a coffee-house in Savile Row or Sackville Street, or when Carlyle, with Robert and James Adam and John Home, drove out to dine with Garrick at Hampton, taking their golf-clubs, and the party was cheered by the Coldstream Guards at Kensington –

'in honour of a diversion peculiar to Scotland; so much does the remembrance of one's native country dilate the heart, when one has been some time absent. The same sentiment made us open our purses, and give our countrymen wherewithal to drink the "Land o' Cakes".'[5]

The sense of being Scottish was sharpened by English criticism and hostility. Carlyle was in a London coffee-house with Smollett when the news of Culloden came through in 1746 and sent the town into 'a perfect uproar of joy'. As the two Scots walked home

'The mob were so riotous, and the squibs so numerous and incessant that we were glad to go into a narrow entry to put our wigs in our pockets, and to take our swords from our belts and walk with them in our hands, as everybody then wore swords; and, after cautioning me against speaking a word, lest the mob should discover my country and become insolent, "for John Bull", says he, "is as haughty and valiant tonight as he was abject and cowardly on the Black Wednesday when the Highlanders were at Derby".'[6]

Smollett, Carlyle then explains, 'though a Tory, was not a Jacobite, but he had the feelings of a Scotch gentleman on the reported cruelties that were said to be exercised after the battle of Culloden'.

So did 'this Rage against the Scots' – Hume's phrase for the anti-Bute agitation of the 1760s, whipped up by Wilkes and the *North Briton* into a general anti-Scots feeling – sharpen a sense of Scottishness. This feeling – and the cool reception of his *History* ('by the Barbarians who inhabit the Banks of the Thames') – decided Hume not to settle in London. He, who had been ready to integrate with the English, had been rebuffed: 'Some [English] hate me because I am not a Tory', he wrote to Gilbert Elliot in 1764,

'some because I am not a Whig, some because I am not a Christian, and all because I am a Scotsman. Can you seriously talk of my continuing an Englishman? Am I, or are you, an Englishman? Will they allow us to be so?'[7]

Increasingly after 1760, acceptance of the fact of Union was tempered by a sense of the unfairness with which it was working out for Scotland. The Union was conceived as a partnership, Scots like Hume and Carlyle intended to make it a true partnership, the English made it an unfair and uneasy one. One recurring complaint is about the Militia Act of 1757, which applied to England only because, says Carlyle's editor Hill Burton, 'ministers were afraid to arm the people among whom the insurrection of 1745 had occurred'.[8] This stigma on Scottish loyalty provoked the founding of the Poker Club in Edinburgh (so-called because it was to poke up feeling) which had Carlyle, Hume and Adam Ferguson among its members, 'zealous friends to a Scotch militia, and warm in their resentment on its being refused to us, and an invidious line drawn between Scotland and England'.[9] Causes of irritation and complaint abound in Carlyle's autobiography and Hume's letters: Englishmen encroaching on the Scottish political scene (like Charles Townshend, who aspired to represent Edinburgh at Westminster), Parliament's mean provision for the established Church of Scotland as compared with that for the Church of England, English criticisms of Scots backwardness and provincialism. Such criticisms were countered by Scots boasting. When Carlyle noted how well Scotsmen did in the Royal Engineers, and as head gardeners to the English nobility (in both fields because of the good teaching of mathematics and mensuration in Scottish schools), he was making factual observations which redounded to Scotland's credit. When he and others in Edinburgh were in 'an uproar of exultation' over John Home's *Douglas*, the cause was frankly patriotic: 'a Scotchman had written a tragedy of the first rate'. Similarly Hume, praising the verses of Blacklock and William Wilkie, was scoring for Scotland. And, in sentences now famous, Hume showed how necessary to national morale such successes were. In a letter to Gilbert Elliot in 1757, he put Scotland's situation thus:

> 'Is it not strange that, at a time when we have lost our Princes, our Parliaments, our independent Government, even the Presence of our chief Nobility, are unhappy, in our Accent & Pronunciation, speak a very corrupt Dialect of the Tongue which we make use of; is it not strange, I say, that, in these Circumstances, we shou'd really be the People most distinguish'd for Literature in Europe?'[10]

'Are unhappy, in our Accent & Pronunciation, speak a very corrupt Dialect of the Tongue which we make use of.' In one crucial sense these Scots – Hume, Carlyle, the Adams – wished fervently not to be Scots. Carlyle was proud that as a little boy of seven he had learnt 'to read English, with just pronunciation and a very tolerable accent – an accomplishment which in those days was very rare'.[11] When that Londonized Scot, Lord Mansfield, commented on the un-English style of Hume's and Robertson's *Histories*, Carlyle explained that

> 'to every man bred in Scotland the English language was in some respects a foreign tongue, the precise value and force of whose words and phrases he did not understand, and therefore was continually endeavouring to word his expressions by additional epithets or circumlocutions.'[12]

When in England, Carlyle noted how the Scots he met now spoke. The English of one doctor in London was so bad that he could neither understand nor be understood; another, though an Aberdonian, had no accent, for he had gone very young into the Navy as a surgeon's mate and had 'entirely lost his mother-tongue'.

Hume considered the acquisition of English so important that, on being asked for advice about his nephew's schooling, he recommended Eton for this reason:

'There are several Advantages of a Scots Education; but the Question is whether that of the Language does not counterballance them, and determine the Preference to the English. He is now of an Age to learn it perfectly; but if a few Years elapse, he may acquire such an Accent, as he will never be able to cure of.... The only Inconvenience is, that few Scotsmen, that have had an English Education, have ever settled cordially in their own Country, and they have been commonly lost ever after to their Friends.'[13]

The Open Sesame to equal partnership (when that seemed attainable) or to regard – or to making a living in England – was an ability to write and speak English. As the Select Society put it in their statement in 1761:

'As the intercourse between this part of Great Britain and the capital daily increases, both on account of business and amusement, and must still go on increasing, gentlemen educated in Scotland have long been sensible of the disadvantages under which they labour, from their imperfect knowledge of the ENGLISH TONGUE, and the impropriety with which they speak it.'[14]

The Society proposed to import qualified English teachers to give instruction. Some years before Hume (who would ask Wilkes and David Mallet to correct his written English) had drawn up a list of Scotticisms to be avoided with the correct English alternatives: 'a park' should be replaced by 'an enclosure', 'part with child' by 'miscarry', 'a compliment' by 'a present', and so on.[15] In the light of his concern for correct English, we can look again at Hume's boast to Gilbert Elliot, quoted earlier:

'Is it not strange...that we should really be the People most distinguish'd for Literature in Europe?'

What literature? The works most likely to be in his mind as giving distinction to Scotland were his own *Essays* (1748) and the first volume of his *History* (1754), John Home's *Douglas* (produced in 1756), Robertson's forthcoming *History of Scotland* and two volumes which Hume had done much to forward, Thomas Blacklock's *Poems* (1754) and William Wilkie's epic, the *Epigoniad* (1757), which he praised to the skies in this same letter to Elliot – all works written in standard Southern English. A later enthusiasm (whatever his subsequent doubts of its origin) was Macpherson's supposed translation from the Gaelic. In 1759 Hume showed some fragments to Carlyle who reported him as 'highly delighted', and they agreed it was a precious discovery and must as soon as possible be published to the world. For both men it must have had a twofold appeal: it was a Scottish production, and so something to notch up to Scotland's credit, but the words on the page were pure English.

Within Hume's circle there was some sense of the loss involved in this anglicization of tongue and pen. William Robertson, in his *History of Scotland*, allowed himself to speculate on the gain in language had there *not* been a Union:

'If the two nations had continued distinct, each might have retained idioms and forms of speech peculiar to itself; and these, rendered fashionable by the example of a court, and supported by the authority of writers of reputation, might have been considered in the same light with the varieties occasioned by the different dialects in the Greek tongue; might have been considered as beauties; and, in many cases, might have been used promiscuously by the authors of both nations. But, by the accession, the English naturally became the sole judges and lawgivers in Language, and rejected, as solecisms, every form of speech to which their ear was not accustomed.'[16]

But, as there had been a Union, Scotsmen must keep off their mother-tongue if Scotland were to count.

A composite notion of Scotland drawn from Hume, Carlyle and the Adams, might go like this. A nation still, but not independent; firmly united to England in supposedly equal partnership that all too often worked unequally; stripped of much – a court, a centre of government – that fosters a culture and gives scope to men of large ideas; its language now become a dialect to be unlearned, its literary superiority to be demonstrated by out-Englishing the English; its future unquestionably with England, in a United Kingdom. Theirs is a forward-looking, rational North-British patriotism, that of men of the world; the spirit in which the New Town of Edinburgh was planned and built.

II

Like Hume and Carlyle, James Boswell (1740–95) was a travelled man and familiar with London, and shared many of their sentiments about being Scots – though one must always be cautious about pinning down too definitely a man given, as he owned, to 'such changes of sentiment as would hardly be conceived to arise in a mind whose judgement was not totally overthrown'. He, too, was bothered by questions of language and pronunciation: 'Love reconciles me to the

Scots accent', he wrote of a young woman met in Moffat in 1766; but a homely evening with Scots in London was spoiled for him because 'the Fife tongue and the Niddry's Wynd address were quite hideous'. He was gratified when Sir John Pringle told him that 'you have the advantage of possessing the English language and the accent in a greater degree than any of your rivals', but five years later, in 1772, Sir Alexander Macdonald was still 'correcting several Scotch accents in my friend Boswell'. His feelings about the language were more ambivalent than Hume's: from his first travels abroad he had in mind to compile a Scots Dictionary.

Like Hume, Boswell had found Scotland cramping : he was irked by the prevailing 'narrow notions of religion' and by 'the Scots strength of sarcasm which is peculiar to North Britain' and which he considered 'checked all endeavours at excellence'. He too found his patriotism (constantly sharpened on Johnson's teasing) flare up when the English were in anti-Scots mood. One evening in 1762 he went to Covent Garden to see *Love in a Village*:

'Just before the overture began to be played, two Highland officers came in. The mob in the upper gallery roared out, "No Scots! No Scots! Out with them!", hissed and pelted them with apples. My heart warmed to my countrymen, my Scotch blood boiled with indignation. I jumped up on the benches, roared out, "Damn you, you rascals!", hissed and was in the greatest rage. I am very sure at that time I should have been the most distinguished of heroes. I hated the English; I wished from my soul that the Union was broke and that we might give them another battle of Bannockburn. I went close to the officers and asked them of what regiment they were of. They told me Lord John Murray's, and that they were just come from Havana. "And this", said they, "is the thanks that we get – to be hissed when we come home. If it was French, what could they do worse?" "But", said one, "if I had a *grup o yin or twa o the tamd rascals I sud let them ken what they're about*."'[17]

Scots fight Britain's battles and their reward is to be hissed in London. The Union is not working equally.

But this 'brave Scot of antient line' (as Boswell described himself to his Sienese mistress) was unlike Hume and Carlyle in forever looking back at Scotland's past – a selective past, which did not include the Covenanters. At the start of his journey from Edinburgh to London in 1762 he –

'made the chaise stop at the foot of the Canongate...walked to the Abbey of Holyroodhouse, went round the Piazzas, bowed thrice: once to the Palace itself, once to the crown of Scotland above the gate in front, and once to the venerable old Chapel.'[18]

I

Two months later in London he watched the splendid equipage driving to Court on the Queen's birthday and

> 'recollected all the stories of the old Scottish magnificence when our monarchs resided at Holyroodhouse, and I wished to see such days again.'[19]

When he met Scots abroad, the talk would turn to Scotland's past greatness. In Berlin in 1764 he 'talked against the Union' with the Earl Marischal, who took down Barbour's *Brus* from his bookcase and inscribed it 'Scotus Scoto' before giving it to Boswell with the injunction to read it once every year.[20] On his way home he visited two Jacobite exiles in Avignon and 'recalled the ancient days of Scottish glory', particularly the routing of the Danes at the Battle of Luncarty:

> 'My Lord asked me seriously. "Are the greatest part of the people in Scotland reconciled to the Union?" BOSWELL: My Lord, I fear they are; that is to say, they have lost all principle and spirit of patriotism.'[21]

When the Union came up in conversation with Rousseau in 1764, Boswell learnt that the Earl Marischal had asked Rousseau to write the life of Fletcher of Saltoun;

> 'ROUSSEAU: Yes, Sir; I will write it with the greatest care and pleasure. I shall offend the English, I know. But that is no matter. Will you furnish me with some anecdotes on the characters of those who made your Treaty of Union, and details that cannot be found in the historians? BOSWELL: Yes, Sir; but with the warmth of an ancient Scot.'[22]

Boswell's patriotism looked back to heroes – Fletcher of Saltoun, Montrose, Bruce, Wallace – and to the cause they served. In Leipzig in 1764 he was shown round the Magistrates' Library and his eye fell on Anderson's *Diplomata Scotiae*:

> 'My old spirit got up, and I read them some choice passages of the Barons' letter to the Pope [the Declaration of Arbroath]. They were struck with the noble sentiments of liberty of the old Scots, and they expressed their regret at the shameful Union. I felt true patriot sorrow. O infamous rascals, who sold the honour of your country to a nation against which our ancestors supported themselves with so much glory! But I say no more, only Alas, poor Scotland!'[23]

When he published his *Account of Corsica* in 1768, he used a sentence from this Declaration of Arbroath as epigraph:

> 'Non enim propter gloriam, divitias aut honores pugnamus, sed propter libertatem solummodo, quam nemo bonus nisi simul cum vita amittit.'

Boswell is here associating the cause of Scotland's independence with the struggle for independence going on in Corsica. There is nostalgia in his feelings about 'the old Scottish magnificence when our monarchs resided at Holyroodhouse', but Wallace and Bruce and the Declaration of Arbroath are not a matter of nostalgia, but of inspiration. Recalling them, Boswell recalls Scotland's prime virtues; independence and love of liberty, which must be exercised in the eighteenth century as in the fourteenth if Scots are to be truly Scots. In 1775 he was an early sympathizer with the American colonists.

This feeling for Scottish independence was by no means wholly political, and for all his railing against the Union Boswell was not a rebel. He was no political Jacobite, as he made plain to the Earl Marischal and others who were, though Jacobitism served as a channel for some of his Scottish sentiment. He regarded Scottish independence in a moral light: if Scots did not cherish and practise their love of independence the virtue would go out of them and they would be denying a part of their own nature.

So Boswell's Scotland is a more metaphysical concept than Carlyle's or Hume's. It is the past as well as the present, a virtue to be practised, a source of feeling (as he said, weeping over Culloden) with which sober rationality has little to do, an inspiration to liberty.

III

Hume regarded words as 'instituted by men, merely for conveying their ideas to each other',[24] so in his writing, concerned with ideas, there was no loss in using only English. But for those who used words imaginatively, Scots was vital. The word that is coloured by the use of generations, the word that touches a chord of feeling, the word that calls to mind a complex of traditional experience – when Burns calls the devil a 'tousie tyke' he opens up a whole area of Scottish folk-lore that no English equivalent could do – these words, for Ramsay, Fergusson and Burns, would mainly be Scots. There was patriotism in their sticking to their own tongue, but to write in Scots was not primarily a patriotic gesture, it was the only way in which they could write at all of certain areas of their experience. Scotland was their language.

The poets do not talk of North Britain, a prosy geographical or administrative concept, but often of Caledonia – a name which spoke of Scotland's Roman past, and also of that patriotic moment just before the Union when the Darien colonists sailed to plant the flag of Scotland in New Caledonia.[25]

'The end of ane auld sang' was the comment of Scotland's last Lord Chancellor on the Union. Allan Ramsay (1685–1758) was determined that in the most literal sense this should not be so. His answer to the loss of one of Scotland's possessions, her political independence, was to preserve another, her poetry. It was not as an antiquarian that he collected the poems of Dunbar, Henryson, Scott and Montgomerie in his *Ever Green* (1724)[26], but as a patriot who felt that poetry was a living part of a nation's life. A poet could be an active patriot – whether by affecting events, as Lindsay did –

> 'Sir David's satyres help'd our nation
> To carry on the Reformation,
> And gave the scarlet whore a box
> Mair snell than all the pelts of Knox –'[27]

or simply by being a good poet and so increasing his country's renown:

> 'The Chiels of *London*, *Cam*, and *Ox*,
> Hae'e rais'd up great Poetick Stocks
> Of *Rapes*, of *Buckets*, *Sarks* and *Locks*,
> While we neglect
> To shaw their betters. This provokes
> Me to reflect
> On the lear'd Days of *Gawn Dunkell*,
> Our Country then a Tale cou'd tell,
> *Europe* had nane mair snack and snell
> At verse or Prose;
> Our Kings were Poets too themsell,
> Bauld and Jocose.'[28]

So he could claim, in an address to the Duke of Roxburgh, that as a Scots Poet he had deserved well of his country: through his poems in Scots and in traditionally Scots measures, as through his collecting, he was affirming that Scotland, to be herself, must have her own literature.

His concern was not only with the classics of Scottish poetry, the work of the Makars and the court poets of the sixteenth century; he wished also to preserve and give fresh life to the Scots songs which he collected in the *Tea-Table Miscellany* (1724–37). Scotland's heritage was 'The Bonny Earl of Moray' and 'An thou wert my ain thing' as well as 'The Golden Targe' and 'The Cherrie and the Slae'.

'Had he enjoyed life and health to a maturer age', wrote Thomas Ruddiman in his preface to the 1779 edition of the *Poems* of Robert Fergusson (1750–74), 'it is probable he would have revived our ancient Caledonian Poetry, of late so much neglected or despised.' Certainly Fergusson felt it the duty of Scottish poets to make their country famous in song:

> 'The ARNO and the TIBUR lang
> Hae run fell clear in Roman sang;

But, save the reverence of schools!
They're baith but lifeless dowy pools.
Dought they compare wi' bonny Tweed,
As clear as ony lammer-bead?
Or are their shores mair sweet and gay
Than Fortha's haughs or banks o' Tay?
Tho' there the herds can jink the show'rs
'Mang thriving vines an' myrtle bow'rs,
And blaw the reed to kittle strains,
While echo's tongue commends their pains,
Like ours, they canna warm the heart
Wi' simple, saft, bewitching art,
On Leader haughs an' Yarrow braes,
ARCADIAN herds wad tyne their lays,
To hear the mair melodious sounds
That live on our POETIC grounds.'[29]

Fergusson serves other national ends in his poetry. He can voice complaints against the unequal partnership of the Union:

'Black be the day that e'er to England's ground
Scotland was eikit by the UNION's bond:
For mony a menzie of destructive ills
The country now maun brook frae *mortmain bills* –'

says the ghost of George Heriot to the ghost of George Watson in Greyfriars kirkyard of the proposed legislation to compel the trustees of Scottish schools to invest in government stock (so removing the capital from Scotland) and reduce their scholars to

'Starving for England's weel at *three per cent*.'[30]

He can recall lost grandeur and lost independence:

'Or shou'd some canker'd biting show'r
The day and a' her sweets deflow'r,
To Holyrood-house let me stray,
And gie to musing a' the day;
Lamenting what auld *Scotland* knew
Bien days for ever frae her view:
O HAMILTON, for shame! the muse
Would pay to thee her couthy vows,
Gin ye wad tent the humble strain,
And gie's our dignity again:
For O, waes me! the Thistle springs
In *domicile* of ancient kings,
Without a patriot to regret
Our *palace* and our ancient *state*.'[31]

He can expose by mockery the snobberies of the genteel who prefer the English and the foreign to the Scotch – brandy to whisky, snails and roast-beef to haggis and partans, Italian airs to 'The Birks of Invermay'. In 'The Farmer's Ingle' Scottish food – bannocks, porridge and kail – is directly associated with Scottish independence:

> 'On sicken food has mony a doughty deed
> By Caledonia's ancestors been done;
> By this did mony wight fu' weirlike bleed
> In *brulzies* frae the dawn to set o' sun:
> 'Twas this that brac'd their *gardies*, stiff and strang,
> That bent the deidly yew in antient days,
> Laid Denmark's daring sons on yird alang,
> Gar'd Scottish *thristles* bang the Roman *bays*;
> For near our *crest* their heads they doughtna raise.[32]

Fergusson makes Scottish food almost a question of morals – as porridge (unsweetened) still is for some Scots. At times there seems something narrow in his championing of native food, drink and music – as if he were praising them merely because they were Scottish – but his concern is really at a deeper level. He sees them as standing for Scotland's separate identity; nationality is for him not just a matter of institutions, or of 'high' culture, but of all the elements that make up the texture of life. A Scots poet can be active in preserving Scottishness, from a love of freedom to a love of whisky.

'Freedom and whisky gang thegither', wrote Robert Burns (1759–96) at the end of his 'Earnest Cry and Prayer to the Scotch Representatives in the House of Commons'. He too was using poetry to fight Scotland's battles, in this case 'a most partial tax...to favour a few opulent English Distillers, who, it seems, were of vast Electioneering consequence'. The same point – that it is a question of freedom – was made in his letter on the subject to the *Edinburgh Evening Courant* (9 February 1789):

> 'An ancient Nation, that for many ages had gallantly maintained the unequal struggle for independance with her much more powerful neighbour, at last agrees to a Union which should ever after make them one people –'[33]

and is then cheated like this! For Burns, whisky is never just a major item on the Scots bill of fare, but one of the symbols of Scottish freedom, and also (as in 'Scotch Drink' or 'John Barleycorn') of the poet's inspiration; and Scots poets have a patriotic part to play. They must speak for Scotland.

Burns's view of what a poet should be doing for Scotland is defined in 'The Vision'. 'The rustic bard' is visited by his Muse – Coila, who presides over the Kyle of Ayrshire, but whose mantle is emblematic of all Scotland. On it are the heroes of independence:

> 'My heart did glowing transport feel,
> To see a race heroic wheel,
> And brandish round, the deep-dyed steel
>> In sturdy blows;
> While back-recoiling seem'd to reel
>> Their Suthron foes –'

and on it too are Burns's contemporary Dugald Stewart and his father, Matthew Stewart: Scotland is to be proud of her present philosophers and mathematicians, as well as of her ancient warriors. The Muse explains that she and her sisters are charged to inspire Scots to serve their country in their various ways:

> 'Some fire the soldier on to dare;
> Some rouse the patriot up to bare
>> Corruption's heart:
> Some teach the bard, a darling care,
>> The tuneful art.'

Coila then exhorts Burns to do his country honour by his poetry as Wallace did by his battles or as a few politicans still do by standing up for Scotland's rights at Westminster. The poet Beattie is bracketed with Dempster the Member of Parliament as having earned well of Scotland.

It vexed Burns that so many of the poets 'who composed our fine Scottish lyrics' should be unknown; and he looked on the collecting of old Scots songs, or the writing of songs to old Scots tunes – the work to which he devoted his last years – as a patriotic service, for which he would not take payment. And as an emotional service too: 'There is a certain something in the old Scotch songs', he wrote, 'a wild happiness of thought and expression',[34] and in collecting them he was safeguarding something that Scotsmen needed, something (as Fergusson had put it) 'to warm the heart'.

In 'To William Simpson, Ochiltree' Burns develops the idea that poets *make* a country:

> 'Ramsay an' famous Fergusson
> Gied Forth an' Tay a lift aboon –'[35]

and his own duty is to bring renown to *his* part of Scotland, the Kyle – in an almost literal sense, to put it on the map:

> 'Nae poet thought her worth his while,
> To set her name in measur'd style;
> She lay like some unkenn'd-of isle,
>> Beside New Holland,
> Or where wild-meeting oceans boil
>> Besouth Magellan.

For this work, Wallace again is invoked.

Burns is full of Scottish history. When he visited Bannockburn in 1787 –

'I knelt at the tomb of Sir John the Graham, the gallant friend of the immortal Wallace; and two hours ago I said a fervent prayer for old Caledonia over the hole in a blue whinstone, where Robert de Bruce fixed his royal standard on the banks of Bannockburn.'[36]

He read Blind Harry's *Wallace* and John Barbour's *Brus*, Knox's *History of the Reformation*, books on 1715 and 1745; one of his treasures was the dirk of the Jacobite Lord Balmerino. When a minister, supposed to be celebrating the blessing of the Glorious Revolution, gratuitously attacked from the pulpit 'the bloody and tyrannical House of Stuart', Burns spoke up for them in a forceful letter to the *Edinburgh Evening Courant*.

After the first success of his *Poems*, the Earl of Buchan advised Burns 'to fire my Muse at Scottish song and Scottish scenes'. This he was doing without prompting – but to what end?

Burns is not nostalgic; he uses Scottish history as a guide and inspiration to action. Memories of independence must fire the poet to protest against supposed injustice to Scotland (as with the distillery tax) or to Scotsmen (as when, in the 'Address to Beelzebub' he attacks the Highland landowners who wished to prevent their tenants emigrating). But Burns's appeal to history is for a wider end than the liberty of Scotland or Scotsmen. The final charge laid on him by Coila in 'The Vision' is:

> 'To give my counsels all in one,
> Thy tuneful flame still careful fan;
> Preserve the dignity of Man,
>   With Soul erect;
> And trust the Universal Plan
>   Will all protect.'

So when Burns thinks of the Stuarts in 1688 and the Glorious Revolution, he also thinks of the glorious revolution across the Atlantic. He ends his letter to the *Edinburgh Evening Courant* by pointing out that it was all very well to celebrate the rights and liberties won in 1688, but how odd then that –

'a certain people, under our national protection, should complain, not against a Monarch and a few favourite advisers, but against our whole legislative body, of the very same imposition and oppression, the Romish religion not excepted, and almost in the very same terms as our forefathers did against the family of Stuart! I will not, I cannot, enter into the merits of the cause; but I dare say, the American Congress, in 1776, will be allowed to have been as able and as enlightened, and, a whole empire will say, as honest, as the

English Convention in 1688; and that the fourth of July will be as sacred to their posterity as the fifth of November is to us.'[37]

For Burns in 1793 Bannockburn is directly associated with the French Revolution, as for Boswell in 1768 the Declaration of Arbroath is directly associated with the liberation of Corsica. From 1789 Burns was openly enthusiastic about the Revolution: in 1792 he bought at auction four carronades from a captured smuggler and sent them as a gift to the French Convention; by 1793 (the year of the trial in Edinburgh of Muir and Palmer, the Friends of the People), he was a marked man and in danger of losing his government appointment as excise officer. To his patron Robert Graham, to his superior officers, he had – for the sake of his family – to explain, excuse, retract. During these months he was also engaged at his work of collecting Scots airs, and, where necessary, supplying them with words. In August 1793 he wrote to George Thomson, editor of the *Select Collection of Original Scottish Airs*, of the tradition that the old tune of 'Hey tutti taitie' was Bruce's march at Bannockburn:

> 'This thought, in my yesternight's evening walk, warmed me to a pitch of enthusiasm on the theme of Liberty & Independance, which I threw into a kind of Scots Ode, fitted to the Air, that one might suppose to be the gallant ROYAL SCOT's address to his heroic followers on that eventful morning.'[38]

Then comes his first version of 'Scots wha hae', followed by 'So may God ever defend the cause of Truth and Liberty, as he did that day!' In sending copies to Maria Riddell and the Earl of Buchan, he expressly associated the Bannockburn Ode with Liberty; and he was cautious about publication, telling Patrick Miller that the London *Morning Chronicle* was welcome to print it, 'only, let them insert it as a thing they have met with by accident, & unknown to me'.[39] The issues of Bannockburn were all too topical.

Scotland's fight for independence could be the channel of expression, the 'objective correlative', for feelings of independence that were not confined to Scotland. Burns's pride and independence as a man, his pride in his country's struggle for independence, led him to value freedom everywhere. Scots must be inspired by their past to a concern for the freedom of others. The swords and staves of Bruce's army must become the carronades sent by Boswell to the Corsicans, by Burns to the French Convention. The sad irony in Scott's *Redgauntlet* is that Redgauntlet himself (showing his nephew the spot where Edward I died on the Solway shore) associates the cause of Scotland's liberties with the cause of the Stuarts, already hopelessly lost, but for Burns it is associated with the living cause of revolution in America and France.[40]

Burns, 'the lad was born in Kyle', is parochial but not narrow. He moves outward from the affirmation of personal and national independence to the general idea of Liberty. Nor is he narrow or backward-looking in his words: in poems like 'The Vision' and the 'Address to the Unco Guid' he moves from Scots to English as he moves from the area of personal and local experience to that of general ideas.

Burns believes in history as a motivating power. To Mrs Dunlop he writes in 1790:

> 'Nothing can reconcile me to the common terms, "English ambassador, English court" &c....Tell me, my friend, is this weak prejudice? I believe in my conscience such ideas as "my country; her independance; her honor; the illustrious names that mark the history of my native land" &c. – I believe these, among your *men of the world*, men who in fact guide for the most part and govern our world, are looked on as so many modifications of wrongheadedness.[41]

To him such ideas are guiding lights. Scotland is an old song; a declaration of independence; the dignity of man.

All those whom I have discussed were concerned – some steadily, some intermittently – with what Scotland is and what duties or actions being a Scot implies. For Carlyle and Hume the duties were practical, to do with government, with manners, with civic improvement: to defend Scottish institutions, to expose and correct injustice (as by agitating against the Militia Bill), to demonstrate by their speech, their writing and their arts, that in civility the Scot could take his equal place beside the Englishman.

The poets too were concerned with defending institutions and correcting injustice, and were not opposed to improvement. Where they diverged from Hume and Carlyle was in defending ways of living and feeling as well as ways of governing and dispensing justice, and in questioning the direction that improvement should take. It must not, all their work implies, be at the expense of cutting Scots off from their roots, in history, language and sentiment. To define this basic Scottishness which must be cherished, to insist that independence and a love of liberty must be the groundwork of a Scot in the eighteenth century as in the fourteenth, and that those who turned their back on this Scottishness would be not only the less Scotsmen but the less men – this is the theme sounding in all the poets, but most steadily in Burns. So concern for Scottishness becomes a moral concern, not directly associated with any definite strategy of action. Thus isolated and detached, with no structure of programme or party to mesh into, the moral concern could and often did degenerate into a patriotism either bellicose-wha's-like-us or couthy-kailyard, the Burns sentiment skimmed off without the reason and moral fervour that underpinned it originally.

NOTES

1. John Hill Burton (ed.), *The Autobiography of Dr Alexander Carlyle* (1910), 447.
2. John Fleming, *Robert Adam and his Circle* (London 1962), 303.
3. Letter quoted in A. J. Youngson, *The Making of Classical Edinburgh* (1966), 290.
4. J. Fleming, *Robert Adam*, 351.
5. *Autobiography*, 359. Till I read this in Carlyle, I had assumed that George IV's reference to the Land o' Cakes in his toast at the Holyrood banquet in 1822 ('The Chieftains and Clans of Scotland – and prosperity to the Land o' Cakes') came from Burns's 'On the late Captain Grose's Peregrinations through Scotland' which begins 'Hear, Land o' Cakes'. But the O.E.D. gives references going back to 1669 for Land of Cakes as a name 'applied (originally in banter) to Scotland, or the Scottish Lowlands'.
6. *Autobiography*, 199.
7. J. Y. T. Greig (ed.), *The Letters of David Hume* (Oxford 1932), I, 470.
8. *Autobiography*, 418n.
9. *Autiobiography*, 439.
10. Hume, *Letters*, I, 255.
11. *Autobiography*, 4.
12. *Autobiography*, 543.
13. Hume, *Letters*, II, 154.
14. Quoted in E. C. Mossner, *Life of David Hume* (1954), 372.
15. The list appeared in the *Scots Magazine*, XXII (1760), 686–7.
16. William Robertson, *Works* (1819), III, 197 (*History of Scotland*, Book VIII) quoted in the Introduction to John Jamieson's *Etymological Dictionary of the Scottish Language* (1808). Jamieson compiled his Dictionary in a spirit of patriotism, pointing out that, however beneficial the union of crowns and the union of Parliaments had been, they had resulted in the decline of Scots : 'I do not hesitate to call that the Scottish *Language*, which has generally been considered in no other light than as merely on a level with the different provincial dialects of the English. Without entering at present into the origin of the former, I am bold to affirm that it has as just a claim to the designation of a peculiar language as most of the other languages of Europe'.
17. Frederick A. Pottle (ed.), *Boswell's London Journal, 1762–1763* (Yale editions, London 1950), 71.
18. Boswell, *London Journal*, 41.
19. Boswell, *London Journal*, 148.
20. Frederick A. Pottle (ed.), *Boswell on the Grand Tour : Germany and Switzerland, 1764* (Yale editions, London 1953), 83.
21. Frank Brady and Frederick A. Pottle, *Boswell on the Grand Tour: Italy Corsica and France, 1765–1766* (Yale editions, London 1955), 265.

22. Boswell, *Germany and Switzerland*, 218. Professor Pottle suggests that the Earl Marischal proposed this to Rousseau to deflect him from *his* proposal to write the biography of the Earl's brother, Field-Marshal Keith.

23. Boswell, *Germany and Switzerland*, 126.

24. Hume, *Letters*, 11, 298.

25. I reject the temptation to contrast the different areas of Scotland formerly served by the *North British* and *Caledonian* railways on the the lines of their being, e.g., the forward-looking East and the backward-looking West.

26. and often 'improved' them. But I am not concerned here with the quality of his editing, only with the motive of his collecting.

27. Allan Ramsay, *Selected Poems*, ed. H.Harvey Wood (1940), 19, 'Epistle to James Clerk Esq. of Pennycuick'.

28. A. Ramsay, *Poems*, 24, 'Familiar Epistles between Lieutenant William Hamilton and Allan Ramsay'. *Gawn Dunkell* is Gavin Douglas, Bishop of Dunkeld, translator of Virgil ; Ramsay's name in the Easy Club was Gavin Douglas.

29. Robert Fergusson, *Scots Poems*, ed. Bruce Dickins (1925), 85, 'Hame Content'.

30. R.Fergusson, *Poems*, 63, 'The Ghaists : a Kirk-yard Eclogue'.

31. R.Fergusson, *Poems*, 80, 'Auld Reikie'.

32. R.Fergusson, *Poems*, 39.

33. J. De Lancey Ferguson (ed.), *The Letters of Robert Burns* (Oxford 1931), 1, 305.

34. R.Burns, *Letters*, 1, 133.

35. This personification of a country by its rivers – practised as we have seen by James Adam in his proposed decorations for Parliament – has a later echo in the *Life and Letters of James David Forbes* (London 1873), 247. On revealing, at a village in the Ardèche, that he was a Scot, 'a pettifogging *notaire*...immediately quoted 'Le Tay' and 'La Clyde' as classic streams'.

36. R.Burns, *Letters*, 1, 120.

37. R.Burns, *Letters*, 1, 271.

38. R.Burns, *Letters*, 11, 195.

39. R.Burns, *Letters*, 11, 240.

40. George Dempster, the politician whom Burns admired, was another keen Scottish patriot ('Often have we disolved the unequal union of our country to England, converted it into a republic, marshal'd Scotia's warlike sons, cultivated her barren fields, fortified her avenues and strong places, and re-established her long-lost independence') with an imaginative sympathy for the American Revolutionaries and (up to 1791) for the French. James Fergusson (ed.), *Letters of George Dempster to Sir Adam Fergusson* (London 1934), 32, 94, 198.

41. R.Burns, *Letters*, 11, 18.

6. Scottish Public Opinion and the Union in the Age of the Association*

N.T.PHILLIPSON

The whig historians of Scotland used to speak of extra-parliamentary agitation in the age of the American revolution as a symptom of the 'political awakening of Scotland'. What they meant, of course, was that because Scotsmen had sought to reform their electoral system and the government of the royal burghs at the same time as their English brethren and had used the same techniques and the same ideology, it was possible to think of the two countries as forming part of the same political unit for the first time.[1]

This view of the politics of the early 1780s as forming a particular stage in the political assimilation of Scotland to England raises several difficulties. In the first place although it is no doubt true that the electoral reformers received help and advice from Christopher Wyvill on various problems of organization, the extra-parliamentary movement was *sui generis*.[2] In the 1750s and 1760s agitation was in full swing for the introduction of a Scottish militia. In 1779, when such agitation was still only in its infancy in England, the Protestant Association in Scotland had won well-deserved notoriety for showing the faithful in England how public opinion could be mobilized in order to stop the progress of noxious reforms like those designed to grant civil rights to Roman Catholics. As far as the electoral reform movement was concerned, in spite of all Wyvill's efforts to coordinate the efforts of the English and Scottish reformers, the Scots seemed to prefer to follow their own path rather than to follow the lead of Yorkshire. By this time, extra-parliamentary activity had so well taken root, that by 1784, when the English movement was on the wane, it was still continuing to gain ground in Scotland. In that year a campaign was launched to reform the internal government of the royal burghs which was to continue to prosper for the next nine years. As Mr E.C.Black observes, 'when Wyvill withdrew from active leadership of the reform movement in 1786 the Scots were proud to take the lead'.[3]

Nor is it clear that an ideology shared with the English reform

* I am very grateful to Dr T.C.Smout and to Professor J.D.B.Mitchell for their comments on this essay.

movement necessarily indicates a particular stage in the process of assimilation; indeed it could be argued that precisely the reverse is true. No doubt Wyvill and the Scots agreed that the electoral systems of England and Scotland were corrupt because, as the Elginshire gentlemen put it, they placed freeholders in a state of 'servile dependence' upon 'a few overgrown proprietors and lords superior'.[4] But what provided their campaign with inspiration and drive was the example of the recent American and Irish attack on what they believed was a corrupt constitutional structure manned by factious, ambitious, greedy and incompetent aristocrats. The Americans had successfully carried their attack to the point of denying that this corrupt parliament had any right to legislate for America. In 1782 the Irish, fortified by this success and by the activities of the Volunteers, had fought for and won legislation which would render their parliament independent of that of Britain. If the ideology of the reform movement, then, has in it a strong element of what Sir George Savile once called an 'anti-parliament spirit',[5] it is worth noting that one of its seventeen authors was none other than Andrew Fletcher of Saltoun, that arch-opponent of the Anglo-Scottish Union of 1707.[6]

In short it may be asked whether so far from marking a particular stage in Scotland's political assimilation to England the association movement should be seen, along with the American and Irish rebellions, as a symptom of separatism. It is a question which receives added point both from the remarkably widespread sympathy with which Scotsmen viewed the cause of the Americans and from Horace Walpole's remark to Sir Horace Mann in the year of Yorktown and Irish parliamentary independence:

'I shall not be surprised if our whole trinity is dissolved, and if Scotland should demand a dissolution of the Union. Strange if she alone does not profit of our distress.'[7]

Some light can be shed on the general significance of the association movement in Scotland as a symptom of separatism or assimilation by considering a hitherto almost unnoticed agitation in 1785, in which several of the gentry and nobility successfully averted an attempt by the government to reduce the number of judges of the court of session from 15 to 10.[8] In fact the bill was modest and of little importance in itself and the agitation it provoked was something of a mountainous molehill. Nevertheless the confused and remarkable reactions of the bill's opponents do suggest paradoxically that both the assimilationist and the separatist hypotheses are true, and that many of the landed class saw Scotland as standing apart from England and, at the same time, moving into a closer relationship with it.

I

The purpose of the judges' bill was gradually to reduce the size of the bench of the court of session from 15 judges to 10 by leaving places unfilled as they fell vacant by death or resignation. The money thus saved was to be used to increase the salaries of the remaining judges.[9] The problem of the Scottish judges' salaries was a long-standing one. Apparently they had been fixed at the rate of £700 p.a. for an ordinary lord of session in 1759 and had remained there ever since in spite of the fact that those of the English judges had been increased to £2,400 in 1779.[10] On that occasion the lord advocate, Henry Dundas, had sought a comparable increase for the Scottish judges only to be told by Lord North that no public money would be forthcoming for the purpose. 'He thinks', Dundas reported, 'the labours of the Judges of the Court of Session and Justiciary are amply compensated by their sallaries, but that he thinks that the Diminution of their number is the only way by which their Sallaries ought to be augmented.'[11] With that the matter was allowed to drop until 1783 or 1784 when, apparently, the coalition ministry proposed to increase salaries without reducing the size of the bench.[12]

It is common for historians to see Dundas as one of the classic political operators of the later eighteenth century, as a man cheerfully and cynically out to exploit the patronage machine in order to extend his own electoral empire in Scotland. Seen in this light his move to abolish five valuable judicial gowns may be difficult to understand – particularly as there is no evidence to suggest that the judges' bill was simply a capitulation to the economical instincts of the treasury. The standard view of Dundas's political motivation is no doubt correct but there are signs that in the first flush of his career he was something of a reformer. His correspondence for 1782 contains plans (never executed) for overhauling the customs and excise administration in Scotland[13] and it may be suggested that the judges' bill was proposed as a mild but probably genuine piece of legal reform. Good arguments could be adduced for saying that a smaller bench would work more efficiently. For one thing, as the new lord advocate Ilay Campbell tactfully pointed out, so large a bench was 'better calculated for debate than for decision'.[14] What was more important, as Dundas told the Commons on 3 June, the existence of so many gowns could not but attract the politicians who could argue, quite plausibly, that the presence of one or two placemen on so large a bench could not materially impair the efficiency of the whole.[15] Such a misuse of legal patronage had enjoyed a long and dishonourable history in Scotland and it had not been until Lord Hardwicke's time that any real steps had been taken to stamp it out. That he succeeded was not a little due to the help he got from the Dundas family, from Henry's father, who had been lord president of the court from 1748 until 1754 and from his half-brother Robert, who was lord advocate from 1754 until his appointment to the presidency in 1760 and who was still in the chair in 1785. Unfortunately, that had not been an end of the problem. There are signs that the confused and unstable politics of the 1760s had taken their toll and that placemen had once again begun to find their way onto the bench.[16] It was, then, perfectly understandable that the Dundases should want to reopen the offensive on placemen, particularly if it would at the same time solve the salary problem.

The danger was, of course, that the bill would be misunderstood; the more so as Ilay Campbell made a hash of introducing it to the Commons on 27 April. He had just told members that the government proposed to reduce the size of the court of session and to use the money saved to increase the judges' salaries, and, no doubt, was just about to expatiate on the benefits the measure would bring, when he was interrupted by Sir Adam Fergusson, M.P. for Ayrshire, who rose to remind him that the bill touched on the structure of the court of session, that its constitution was guaranteed by Article 19 of the Act of Union and that, constitutionally, the king's prior consent was needed before the matter could be discussed. With that the discussion had to be adjourned.[17]

Given that they had only the bare facts to go on, it was inevitable that many Scots should leap to the obvious conclusion. As James Boswell wrote, the total cost of the proposed increase would only be £6,000 p.a. 'and cannot that miserable sum be spared off some corner of the sinecure establishment?'[18] Lord Fife observed that the sum involved was so small that 'it was degrading the dignity of the nation to raise it in a manner so humiliating'.[19] A writer to the *Caledonian Mercury* saw it as a symptom of something far worse:

'We pay our share of taxes and public burdens in support of the state. Have we not, then, a right to demand that our Judges shall have adequate salaries? Why proceed in so pitiful, cringing, and begging a way! So degrading of the honour of a nation never subjected by conquest, as our neighbouring island was, but independent in its laws and government, and now united, by solemn treaty, upon terms of equality with England, and having equal right that our Judges shall be suitably provided, according to their rank and dignity, as in England?'[20]

The matter came up again on 3 June and it was clear that the government was in trouble. Campbell announced that he did not intend to proceed with the matter further that session, and that he simply sought agreement to the principle that the numbers of the judges ought to be diminished. But, in spite of Dundas' attempt to explain the benefits of a smaller bench, even this motion had to be withdrawn after a short and apparently hostile debate, and another was substituted which moved simply that the salaries of the judges ought to be increased.[21] What had happened was that the Scots MPs, with an uncharacteristic display of independence, had rebelled. Robert Dundas, the Scottish solicitor-general, later recalled

'We did everything in our power to carry it through. But tho' the interest and influence of Administration was at that time most intensive, and tho' every exertion was needed to persuade people of the necessity of some such change, our most steady and zealous Personal friends even deserted us.'[22]

If Dundas and Campbell had openly accepted defeat and simply announced that they proposed to introduce a bill based on the resolution of 3 June, that would have been an end of the matter; by postponing the issue until the next session they simply kept alive fears that they would try to reverse their defeat. Even before June the bill had begun to attract interest in the Edinburgh press and James Boswell had contributed a characteristically vivid and latterly influential pamphlet to the discussion. At Michaelmas the country gentry assembled at their annual county meetings to deal with all the routine business of county government and to voice their opinion on public affairs. Here, events took a new turn and provoked the freeholders to express themselves in language which allows the historian to reflect on the way in which Anglo-Scottish relations were developing in the age of the American revolution, of the Irish independence movement and of the Association movement in England. In the end, when parliament reassembled in December Dundas was forced to rise to announce:

'So great a prejudice has gone forth in Scotland against the proposition, that the design had been necessarily abandoned.'[23]

II

At the heart of the agitation against the bill lay the belief that there was something more fundamental at stake than treasury cheeseparing. The point was first put on 7 May by the anonymous author of a letter, which appeared in the *Caledonian Mercury* addressed to 'The Sheriffs-depute of the Counties, and Magistrates of Royal Boroughs [sic] of Scotland'. It read:

'A question is speedily to be agitated in the British Parliament, which deeply affects the interest of every Scotsman. The articles of Union, which are the *palladium* of our *abridged* national liberties, are

K

no longer secure against the prevailing spirit of innovation. A Scottish member of Parliament proposes to bring in a bill for overturning the constitution of the Supreme Courts of Justice in this country; and the matter is regarded as of such total insignificance, that only *one* member opens his mouth upon the subject, and that solely to put the Honourable Proposer right as to a small matter of form, of which it seems he was ignorant, viz. that it was necessary previously to obtain the King's consent to any bill which touched on the treaty of Union. Did it never occur to these gentlemen, that something like the consent of a nation may be thought requisite to an alteration of its constitution in the most material part, next to its Religion, its Laws and Courts of Justice? That nation would be supine indeed, and aptly fitted for the yoke of servitude, that should tamely suffer her most valuable rights to be canvassed, and a fundamental alteration of her constitution attempted, while, thus neglected and overlooked, she is deemed to have no interest in the question.'

'We should', the author went on, 'rouse ourselves from this state of torpor', '[to] take the sense of the nation upon this important subject' and, in particular, consider whether the bill was not an infringement of Article 19 of the Acts of Union which stated that the court of session was to remain as it was constituted in all time coming except for regulations made 'for the better administration of justice'. At Michaelmas at least nine of the 33 Scottish counties stirred themselves and passed resolutions hostile to the bill. These were Ayr, Elgin, Fife, Haddington, Inverness, Kirkcudbright, Linlithgow, Perth and Stirling.[24] Of these, all but Elgin and Fife believed that the bill raised constitutional issues.[25]

Some said that the Haddington resolutions were drafted by disgruntled lawyers, and others pointed out that Stirling and Linlithgow belonged to the political opposition, but it would be wrong to see the agitation simply as a case of 'outs' versus 'ins'.[26] Just as the parliamentary opposition to the bill had come from friend and foe alike, so too did the opposition from the country. If Stirling and Linlithgow were opposition counties, Haddington, Perth and Elgin were normally sympathetic to government. It is significant, too, that ministers did not try, either publicly or privately, to blame the failure of their bill on the opposition. Indeed, it was not until the whole affair was nearly over that the Scottish whigs began to ask whether political capital might not be made of it. Thus on 30 December, Sir Thomas Dundas wrote to Henry Erskine, 'Pray, will not all these meetings upon the Judges Bill, and distilling, [agitation against revised distillery legislation was also in progress] brew into something?'[27]

What makes it possible to think of the nine counties together is that they all had considerable experience of association politics. Stirling and Elgin had begun the agitation for the reform of the Scottish electoral system; Fife and Haddington had been among their earliest supporters and they had soon been joined by the remaining five counties. As recent scholarship has shown the association movement in England was independent of party politics and even directed against it. For this reason opposition politicians were extremely wary of associating with something that was ultimately directed against themselves as much as against their opponents.

It was this distrust of the omni-competent pretensions of parliament, which Sir George Savile had called 'anti-parliament spirit', that formed the most interesting part of the agitation. The *Caledonian Mercury* of 7 May had spoken of the Union as 'the palladium of our abridged national liberties which are no longer secure against the prevailing spirit of innovation'. This point worried many freeholders. The gentlemen of Linlithgow, using language that owes much to that of the American colonists, feared that if a bill infringing the Union was allowed to pass, it would open the door to other violations, for, as someone put it, 'the infringement of one article...unhinges the whole'. James Boswell saw the whole affair in highly coloured terms. If this attempt were to succeed, horror upon horror would ensue; the land tax which had been kept down by the Union would rise, the kirk itself would be assailed.[28] 'Where', asked one of the *Caledonian Mercury's* more despondent correspondents, 'is it to stop? If [parliament] may take away four [sic] [judges] may they not take away five, or eight, or ten? And may not Scotland be left to sing the loss of her judges as she once did of her Heroes "For the flowers of the forest are all fled away". '[29] Such laments about the wickednesses done to a defenceless nation (and one wonders whether such laments form any part of the ideology of the more pessimistic elements in the American and Irish independence movements) clearly appealed to Scotsmen then as indeed they do now. Thus an anonymous Scottish David lamented in the *Courant* of 5 October:

'It is not improbable that this bill is brought into Parliament, to try if the people of Scotland will submit to have the Articles of the Union broke; and the next thing will be to break through them with regard to the land-tax, etc.

America would not submit to be taxed without its own consent; Ireland will legislate for itself; but Scotland, which, by the Union gave up its honour and independence, it is presumed, will submit to have the Articles of that very Union broke.

Oh Scotland! Oh my country! How do I weep over your fallen

dignity, your forfeited honour, your lost independence! – A bill is
brought into Parliament breaking through the Articles of Union,
without your knowledge; you are insulted, and not consulted; you
are poor, and you are insulted for your poverty; you are poor, and
since the Union, made to bear every tax equal to your more opulent
neighbours:– And the only consolation you have left is, to have
your richest Noblemen and Gentlemen sent four hundred miles
distant from their country and your capital, to tax you, and spend
the rents of their own great estates; and yet, notwithstanding all
your taxes, your Judges cannot have sufficient salaries, without an-
nihilating one third of them, to your prejudice.'[30]

Such gloomy fatalism although significant was not altogether typical. In August a correspondent of the *London Chronicle* had expressed
the hope that 'the successful magnanimity of the Irish [would] probably rouse the latent spirit of the Scotch against any infringement of
their judicial establishment, as secured by the treaty of Union, which
if violated in one article, will no longer be a bulwark.'[31] And it was in
this spirit that the freeholders addressed themselves to the original
problem that had been raised by the original *Caledonian Mercury* letter;
was the bill a violation of the Union and was parliament, therefore,
acting beyond its competence?

Seven of the nine counties (Elgin and Fife were exceptions) and a
great many letter writers to the Edinburgh press agreed that it was. As
the Ayrshire freeholders observed, 'the articles of the Union between
England and Scotland, cannot be infringed by the British Parliament,
without the consent of the people of Scotland; because of the number
of members [of parliament] from Scotland being inconsiderable,
compared with the number of members from England, those articles,
upon the faith of which Scotland resigned her independency would
be nugatory'. The trouble was that this only raised the question of
how the act of Union could be amended because, as is well known, the
act itself made no provision for amendment either of particular clauses
or of the act as a whole. In the past successive governments had not
taken this question very seriously and had simply assumed that the
Union could be amended by statute in the same way as any other piece
of legislation. Thus the extraordinary lords of session had been abolished in 1723 as had the heritable jurisdictions in 1747 even though it
could be argued that each was a violation of the Union. In 1781 Lord
Stormont had been assured by lord chancellor Loughborough (himself a member of the Scottish bar) that there was no constitutional
objection to reducing the size of the court of session.[32] In the autumn
of 1785 Ilay Campbell, once again rather too late in the day, published
a pamphlet to explain the bill, and in it restated this classic whig view

with certain diplomatic reservations. He agreed that it would be a violation of the Union to abolish Scots law and the court of session, but that was only likely to happen 'when the Legislature of Great Britain becomes *non compos*'. Until that time parliament had a clear power to make whatever amendments it pleased 'consistently with the fundamental principles of the law and constitution of Scotland and evidently intended for the utility of the people'.[33]

The strong point in the government's case was the technical one that it was not easy to see how 'the consent of the nation' could be obtained. What did this mean, asked one critic? The English had signed the Union as well as the Scots; were they to be consulted now? And how were the sentiments of the Scottish nation to be obtained?

Will it be enough to call the heritors of counties together, who are few in number, compared to the whole body of the people? Will it be enough that a majority of any meeting, either of heritors or people, consent to the measure; or must the whole concur? In a word, if the Union is to be altered, is it possible that this can be done without a new Parliament of England and another of Scotland, to treat together as before; and how are these Parliaments to be called?[34]

The opponents of the bill were not impressed by such *reductiones ad absurdum* and had no intention of allowing the power of amending the Union to pass by default to parliament. On 19 November, the *Caledonian Mercury* printed the following reply to the previous letter.

'Were a Scottish Parliament now to be called, of whom would they consist? If you do not know, I will tell you. The Parliament would just be a convention of representatives chosen by those very persons who are now convening themselves, and expressing their dissatisfaction with your favourite measures, viz. the freeholders and heritors of counties, and the citizens or communities of burghs, whom you are pleased to consider as factious convocations, because they meet in their own proper persons, and not in the sacred form of a Parliament, by a set of representatives whom you consider as in no shape bound to regard their opinions and wishes. Is not the sense of the people, therefore, by your own showing, better collected by these conventions, as you are pleased to call them, than they would by any Parliament they might elect?

Have not the resolutions of six counties [not all the counties had yet held their meetings] already shown the possibility of getting the sense of those counties?'[35]

For this author, the innovation was quite unnecessary because the necessary machinery already existed for formally obtaining the sentiments of the nation in the form of the county meeting. The country gentlemen agreed. The freeholders of Ayr, after passing resolutions to the effect that neither the act of Union or the constitution of the court could be changed without the consent of the people went on to resolve 'that *we* [my italics] will not consent to a change in the constitution of the Court of Session...etc'. Nor were the Ayrshire gentlemen alone in assuming that they were the watchdogs of the Scottish constitution, for this assumption pervades all the resolutions passed by the nine counties. Inverness insisted that ministers should allow sufficient time for any bill touching the union to be discussed by the country 'in order to be satisfied of its utility to Scotland'. Kirkcudbright resolved that the consent of the people of Scotland should be 'previously obtained in a public manner'. Linlithgow claimed that the bill 'was a surprise upon the country and disrespectful to the people, and particularly to the landed interest, when no means had been used to apprise them of the design, and when there was no complaint of evil'.

This last remark provoked what was, in the age of association politics, the classic response of the parliamentary apologist, in a letter, possibly by a government spokesman, printed in the *Caledonian Mercury* and the *Edinburgh Evening Courant* of 31 October. The author asked,

'whether it is now held to be an established part of the constitution, that the proceedings of Parliament must be authorised and directed by conventions of the people; and what means have been provided, by which papers may be called for, evidence adduced, information obtained, and parties or counsel heard before such conventions?

2. Whether a member of the House of Commons, standing up in his place, and proposing any measure which he thinks of public utility, is liable to be censured as guilty of *disrespect* to the *people*, because he has not *without doors* given previous notice of his design to all and sundry, according to some new form not explained?'[36]

The Americans and the Irish, on challenging the omni-competent pretensions of parliament, had threatened armed force in support of their case. The Scots, too, had means of enforcing their claims. Six of the nine counties sent formal 'instructions' to their MPs (although we do not know what form they took) and General Skene, MP for Fife, no doubt anticipating the inevitable, wrote his constituents asking what action he should take. At Ayr, Perth, Haddington and Stirling committees were set up to correspond with other counties on the progress of the bill. In Fife, where no resolutions were passed, the freeholders resolved to adjourn until the bill should be re-introduced. In the face of such active opposition from one-fifth of the Scottish counties and the undoubted tacit hostility of a great many others

Dundas and Campbell had no option but to accept, as the solicitor-general put it, 'the general and unbiased voice of the country being ascertained against us',[37] the bill had better be abandoned.

By claiming that they, acting through their county meetings, were the judges of what was or was not contrary to the articles of Union, the Scottish freeholders had, of course, directly challenged the power of parliament freely to legislate for Scotland.[38] In so doing they had ventured farther along the anti-parliamentary path than the English freeholders had ever dreamt of going and had ranged themselves alongside the American colonists and the Irish. In England, the closest the Association movement had got to challenging parliament's supremacy was in John Jebb's address to the freeholders of Middlesex on 20 December 1779.[39] There he had argued that if counties sent delegates to meet together to promote some favoured object, M P s when discussing the measure should remember that the delegates were more truly representative of the people than were they who had been returned to parliament by a corrupt electoral system. Jebb believed that any decision of the delegates should be properly authenticated by being called 'the public ACT of the combined counties' and he appears even to have envisaged them entering into a federal relationship with the independent American colonies. In all of this, though, the threat to parliament is implicit rather than anything else for Jebb never made a frontal attack on the doctrine of parliamentary supremacy as did the Americans in the Stamp Act crisis, and as the Irish and the Scots were to do in 1782 and 1785.

III

But this was only one side of the agitation, for not all opinion had reacted as militantly to the bill. Some had regarded it as the sort of threat to national identity which a small and defenceless nation was ill-equipped to withstand. And such a mood was all the more significant for foreshadowing one which was to be of growing importance to future generations of the Scottish bourgeoisie and which is by no means unknown even now. As Lord Swinton remarked in 1789, this sort of talk could be used as a cover for doing nothing; 'Who knows what parliament may do with us; better to bear some inconveniencies, than trust the constitution of our Courts to the handling of Parliament.'[40] But not everyone was agreed that inaction was the best policy and the most remarkable aspect of the agitation is that it produced its own reform proposals which were far more radical and far-reaching than anything contained in the original bill. What was sought was the introduction of civil jury trial into the ordinary practice of the court of session.

Lord Sydney, the home secretary, confessed that he was astonished to learn that 'the Right of Trial by Jury could be connected with [the judges bill]';[41] and well might he be. But in order to understand the implications of demanding civil jury trial and in order to understand why the question should ever have been raised in this context, it is necessary to make a couple of diversions.

As we shall see, agitation in favour of civil jury trial was directed towards the introduction of the system as practised in the common law courts of England. The principles on which the common law courts operated were these. Parties to a dispute first decided out of court what points were at issue between them and then presented them for trial by a jury under the direction of a judge. The jury would normally return a verdict settling the facts of the case, leaving it to the judge to apply the law to them. Such a system assumed that the points at issue were fairly simple. Complex cases, in which the definition of the points at issue was too difficult a task to be left to the parties themselves and in which the points of fact were too complex to be settled according to a single method of proof, were tried in chancery, where the judges in equity used their powers both to define the points on which the case rested and to prescribe appropriate methods of proving each of these facts. It was then up to the bench to decide both the facts and the law of the case. In Scotland, as in all countries administering civilian systems, the court of session was both a court of law and of equity. As such the judge had to reserve the right both to define the points at issue and to prescribe appropriate methods of proving disputed facts. On the face of it, then, it seemed clear that the effect of demanding the introduction of civil jury trial would be to make necessary the transferring of the equitable jurisdiction of the court of session to a separate court. It would mean, in short, the assimilation of the Scottish civil courts to those of England.

That was exactly what the freeholders intended. Scotsmen had long been fascinated with the English jury system and in this they shared in the general admiration of enlightened opinion in the civilized world. By giving to the jury the duty of deciding whether an offence to life or property had been committed and by leaving it to the judge to apply the law to the determined fact, the English seemed, in theory, at any rate, to have developed a system in which the interests of a fixed and stable law so necessary to a civilized society could be combined with the no less necessary interests of individual liberty. Blackstone's classic eulogy of jury trial as 'the glory of the English law…the most transcendent privilege which any subject can enjoy or wish for'[42] was one with which few would have disagreed.

Respect for jury trial as a bulwark of individual liberty had developed steadily in Scotland since 1726. Before then, as Professor Willock has shown, the criminal jury in Scotland had run the risk of extinction because, over a long period of time, the bench gradually undermined their undoubted right to return a general verdict of guilty or not guilty.[43] From 1726 onwards, it would seem that there were a series of spirited encounters between the jury, the bar and the bench in which the protagonists of the rights of juries, fortified by arguments about the liberties of the individual, ultimately won their case. It is interesting that the most recent of these encounters (Spence's case) had taken place as recently as 1784 and was still fresh in the mind of the public because of a pamphlet on the subject by a well-known Edinburgh publisher, William Smellie, and because James Boswell reminded his readers of the subject in a pamphlet which we shall later consider.

While the corresponding virtues of civil jury trial had not been very strongly canvassed before 1785 the subject was probably ripe for discussion. It had been discussed in a tentative way in 1747 and had cropped up periodically in the agenda of one or two debating societies – notably the Select and Belles Lettres Society.[44] It was to reappear in 1789 and, by 1802, when the long debate over the future of the court of session was reopened, it was clear that it had been given a lot of thought.[45] However, none of this explains why the subject should come up in 1785.

That the subject came up in 1785 was due to the efforts of James Boswell. He was deeply involved in the agitation against the bill although exactly how far we cannot be sure. He called the Ayrshire meeting, wrote a pamphlet and persuaded Capel Lofft, one of Christopher Wyvill's most experienced propagandists, to publish a letter on the unconstitutionality of the bill.[46] Indeed, although there is no direct evidence on this point, it is just possible that he saw himself as a Scottish Wyvill. He had known Wyvill since 1768, and had attended and been impressed by the great Yorkshire county meeting in March 1784.[47] Nor is it without significance that he described his own county of Ayr as 'the Yorkshire of Scotland'.[48] Be that as it may, what is important here is the pamphlet, composed and published in May 1785, and entitled *A Letter to the People of Scotland on the Alarming Attempt to Infringe the Articles of Union and Introduce a most Pernicious Measure by Diminishing the Number of Lords of Session*. It makes excellent reading and was widely read both in its original form and in an extracted version published in the *Scots Magazine*. Indeed, such was its effect that Ilay Campbell felt obliged to answer it in his pamphlet to which we have already referred. It is racy, full of good stories and animated by zest, intelligence and good humour. Structurally, it is rambling and incoherent, and wanders from one subject to another as the author's own inimitable train of consciousness directed it. In the section which concerns us it wanders from its author's completely uninhibited exasperation with a bill that threatened to put paid to his delusion that he would someday find his way onto the bench and ends with a demand for civil jury trial.

Having deplored the current rage for innovation of which the bill was a product and the servility of Scotsmen who allowed themselves to be governed 'by some person or other who for the time is brought forward, or who puts himself forward, as a *minister for Scotland*' (p. 8) he turned to his English readers with more evidence of the servility of his fellow countrymen:

> 'It will hardly be believed, in England, that we have no juries in civil causes; still more strange will it seem, that we once had that inestimable privilege, and lost it – nobody can tell how. [Here Boswell refers to a favourite contemporary myth that Scotland had once possessed the same sort of judicial institutions as England, and that she lost them in 1532, when the civilian court of session, borrowed from a despotic France, usurped her free constitutions.] That a country should, in the progress of civilisation in every other respect, become more barbarous in its executive jurisprudence, is a wonderful and a disgraceful phaenomenon. Nay, we have no grand jury in Scotland. There is no such thing as finding a bill by the country...etc.' (pp. 12–13).

Perhaps this turn in the argument from civil to criminal juries was inevitable for criminal juries were very much in Boswell's mind. Indeed, one of the most honourable episodes in his career, too long neglected by Boswellians, is the part he played in fighting for the rights of juries. His most recent encounter had been as counsel for the accused in Spence's case in 1784 – a point to which he refers in the appendix to the *Letter*. Nevertheless, it is clear from this and from what follows that Boswell's strong reason for wanting civil jury trial, like his strong reason for fighting for criminal jury rights, was not because it would help the existing system to work better but because it would change it altogether. Thus he went on to refer to a characteristically tendentious remark that Lord Kames had once made to the effect that the court of session was a standing grand jury of the nation *in civilibus* – a confusing point, because the grand jury as commonly understood has no place in civil litigation. He concluded triumphantly that the only condition on which this standing grand jury could legitimately be reduced in size was if it were accompanied by civil jury trial in all its glory. Only then, Boswell commented, would Scotsmen agree to an amendment of the Act of Union because they would have something better than their 'ancient aristocratical court' (p. 17).

The search for an institution which would transform rather than reform the court of session clearly appealed to the gentlemen at Ayr, Haddington, Kirkcudbright, Perth and Stirling, not to mention the various writers of letters to the press. At the Ayrshire meeting Colonel Crawfurd talked of 'the inestimable privilege of trial by jury in civil causes as in England' and surveyed the development of the legal system since the days of Alfred to show how much more conducive it was to liberty than that of Scotland. In drafting their resolutions, the Ayrshire lairds spent much time debating whether they should insist explicitly on the need for civil jury trial.

'It was argued on the one side, that it was *impossible* to have any mode so good as a trial by jury. On the other side, that, *perhaps*, something as good, or better, might be proposed, and we ought not to preclude ourselves.'

One enthusiast 'looking to Mr. Boswell' remarked that the man who should obtain it for this country 'would deserve a statue of gold'.

The same sort of thinking extended throughout the other four counties. Haddington and Kirkcudbright talked of trial by jury as part of 'the ancient law of Scotland'. In Perth there was a fear that 'the diminution of the number of judges would lessen the security of property in a country which does not enjoy the inestimable privilege of trial by jury in civil cases'. Stirling sought 'the trial by jury in civil causes, as enjoyed by their fellow subjects in England'. Nor was the effect of the agitation confined within these circles, for on 28 November, the farmers of Berwickshire, threatened by the prospect of a strike of local procurators in protest against a proposed tax on attorneys, wondered whether some local jury system might not be set up as a substitute for lawyers' justice.[49] Of this, one enthusiastic observer remarked,

'Consider ourselves, and consider your posterity. Cast your eyes beyond the Tweed. Behold in the vigorous exertion of a free people, in support of every circumstance connected with liberty, the spirit which ought to animate you. Catch their zeal, and, if it is directed by wisdom, success will crown your efforts. You complain of the want of a jury in civil causes. Accustom yourselves, accustom your connections, to consider the sentences of their fellow-citizens as the best criterion of right and wrong in litigation. This opinion will extend from you to the most northern corners of Scotland; it will infallibly procure for your country that bulwark of liberty; and secure to you the applauses and the blessings of posterity. This is the important moment. Your interest, the interest of liberty, and that of the minister, coincide. The intimation you have given to the public shews that you are sensible of it. The resolutions you adopt will I hope confirm the opinion already conceived of your wisdom and of your vigour. Let the spirit which formerly desolated the borders, which has since improved your country, now direct itself to the interests of liberty, and secure to you, *of your own right*, that freedom which you at present possess only by your connection with the English.'[50]

It was left to another writer to make explicit the assumption that underlies all this, that the proper end of government should be the assimilation of Scottish legal institutions to those of England.

'Let [Scotland] consider maturely consider [sic] if she might not with safety and much advantage exchange part of her Judges for that lofty Privilege Tryal by Jury – the Glory of the English Constitution and thus without Danger assimilate herself to the sister kingdom.

Thus might that Grievance arising from our voluminous mode of Procedure, the *Law's Delay* be redressed, then should we restore our ancient rights – And the Liberty of the Subject be enlarged – while it would add lustre to the Crown of George the Third.'[51]

With that the matter was allowed to drop, not again to become a subject of serious discussion until it was taken up by the judges of the court itself in 1802. But the court had to wait until 1815 before Blackstone's 'transcendent privilege' was ultimately conferred upon it.

IV

Let us now try to unravel some of the more perplexing strands in the agitation, in particular the relation between the challenge to parliament's claim to legislate freely for Scotland, the demand for the assimilation of the practice of the court of session to that of the common law courts of England and the gloomy laments of the Jeremiahs. A suggestive clue is to be found in a clause in the resolutions of the Linlithgow freeholders. They had resolved that 'the motion in parliament was a surprise upon the country and disrespectful to the people *and particularly to the landed interest* [my italics] when no means had been used to apprise them of the design and when there was no complaint of evil'. What this amounted to, in effect, was a claim that the responsibility for reforming such national institutions lay with them.

Such a claim was by no means unreasonable in the more general context of Scottish legislation in the eighteenth century. In the early years of the union the attempts of English ministers to interfere with Scotland's institutions had been none too happy. In 1709 the law of treason had been assimilated to that of England only after a prolonged and bitter parliamentary battle. In 1712, Harley had embarked on a far more dangerous exercise when, in an effort to secure the support of the Scottish tories, he had steered legislation through parliament restoring lay patronage to the kirk, to the delight of the gentry and to the intense anger of the general assembly. Thereafter successive ministries had walked more warily; for the rest of the century there was very little legislation impinging on Scottish institutions and what there was was initiated in Scotland. Thus the act of 1727 which set up the Board of Trustees for improving Fisheries and Manufactures was the work of the convention of Royal burghs and the enterprising landlords who belonged to the Society of Improvers in the Knowledge of Agriculture in Scotland. The only three major changes in the law, the Election Act of 1743 (7 Geo. II, c.16) the Entail Act of 1770 (10 Geo. III, c. 51) and the Bankruptcy Act of 1772 (12 Geo. III, c. 72) were all of them Scottish acts in the sense that they were devised by the Scottish law officers, and (with the possible exception of the Election Act) approved by the judges, the law societies and the freeholders before being forwarded to parliament. In only one case was this procedure not followed. In 1747–8 the judges refused Lord Chancellor Hardwicke's request that they draft legislation to abolish the heritable jurisdictions. Yet even here, there was no real divergence from the rule. No one in Scotland seriously disagreed with the intention of the measure; the only quarrel was about the amount of compensation that ought to be given. If the court refused to do the drafting, it was only because it did not want to get embroiled in bitter quarrels on this account.[52]

There are signs – one can put it no more strongly than this – that by the latter part of the century, much of the initiative in bringing about reform of Scotland's institutions was passing to the landed classes. Perhaps the turning point was the agitation for a Scottish militia which flourished in the late 1750s and early 1760s and which was still active in 1782 – a movement which deserves to be studied in detail. The agitation, which drew its strength from a contemporary distrust of standing armies and from a corresponding belief that in a free state the citizen-freeholder was the best guardian of his and his country's liberties, provoked widespread excitement and expressed itself in a flood of pamphlets, petitions and public meetings. It was even underwritten by the intelligentsia who belonged to the Poker Club whose object was, in the words of Henry Mackenzie, 'to stir up the spirit of the country'. Although the agitation was unsuccessful it did not discourage future activity. The Entail Act of 1770 was the product of prolonged agitation on the part of the landed class, and, having sponsored campaigns for a militia and for the reform of the

land law, it was not surprising that in 1782 and '3 they should have
taken up the case of the reform of the county electoral system to
which we have already referred; however much that campaign owed
in terms of technique to the association movement in England (and
this, again, is a subject for research) it clearly had a lineage of its
own.

Ministerial initiative in matters of reform of national institutions
then, could not but seem an unwelcome new departure to the country
gentry. It threatened to usurp their guardianship of Scottish liberties
and also by implication challenged their position as Scotland's
governing class. Under these circumstances their irritation was perfectly understandable.

But it was irritation and little more. That at least is clear from the
ideology which underlay their attack on parliament. For although it
was justified by the part which the landed class and the lawyers had
played in the past decades, it was terribly immature by comparison
with those which united the freeholders of England and the colonists
of America (the Irish case is more or less unstudied). Narrowly based,
on a single trivial incident, itself the product of governmental bung-
ling, the ideology the movement produced neither extended to all the
various parts of the Scottish constitution, nor did it come to grips
with the problem of defining the precise stranding or constitutional
powers of the county meeting. The fact that the Act of Union had
been consistently ignored by the government since 1707 – often with
the active support of the gentry – was conveniently forgotten. Nothing was worked out; this ideology was a product of a vaguely felt
sympathy with the roughly analogous situation of the Americans and
the Irish, fired with the enthusiasm of the moment and given colour by
a certain quality of self-dramatization.

And under all this lies the hard fact that the gentry and lawyers had
sold out to deeply rooted assimilationist ideology which was represented in 1785 by the demand for civil jury trial. I have already suggested that there was nothing particularly Scottish about an admiration for the civic virtues of English legal institutions. Nevertheless
the history of so many other areas of Scottish life can be told in terms
of the pressures operating for assimilation that it is hard not to feel
that this participation in a general admiration for English legal institutions was something of a noble lie to justify the assimilation of the
legal establishment. Mrs Mitchison, Mr Clive and Miss Adam Smith
have, elsewhere in this book, considered some of the ways in which
these assimilationist pressures made themselves felt. For my purposes
the important thing is that for much of the eighteenth century assimilation was regarded not so much as a threat to Scottish life as a

stimulus to it. English civilization seemed to provide new and exciting categories in which to think about the problems of progress and the Union provided Scotsmen with a series of opportunities to be exploited. The spirit was well caught by Alexander Wedderburn, the future lord chancellor Loughborough, in the preface to the *Edinburgh Review* of 1755–6:

'The memory of our ancient state is not so much obliterated, but that, by comparing the past with the present, we may clearly see the superior advantages we now enjoy, and readily discern from what source they flow.'

And Scotland's relations with England are summed up thus:

'If countries have their ages with respect to improvement North Britain may be considered as in a state of early youth, guided and supported by the more mature strength of her kindred country.'

Wedderburn's view of Anglo-Scottish relations is to be seen along with that of the secretary to the Society of Improvers in the Knowledge of Agriculture which perfectly captures the sense of the sort of stimulus that many Scotsmen felt that England provided.

'If our Agriculture and Manufactures were improved and carried on to the Height they could bear, we might be near as easy and convenient in our circumstances, as even the People of our Sister Kingdom of England; seeing neither our soil nor our climate is unfriendly, and since we enjoy the same Privileges of Trade with them ...if we are far behind, we ought to follow further.'[53]

It was within a framework of categories built up of sentiments like these that the Scottish landed classes sought to improve the economy the institutions and the manners of their country and to draw it, where necessary, into a closer relationship with England.

The landed classes, then, believed that Scotland was progressing rapidly from rudeness to refinement under their leadership and the feeling that a new age required new, or at least rethought, institutions was natural enough. It was this that led Boswell to remark that civil jury trial would provide a system that was better than 'our ancient aristocratical court'. It was this that led a judge, Lord Swinton, to argue in 1789 for the introduction of jury trial into a court like the court of session which had been founded on a French model.

'Considering the great difference between the political systems of France and those of this kingdom, it may be thought, that our courts of judicature will never be completely sound till every drop of French blood shall be purged away, and discharged from their constitution. And this is an observation which the French themselves, in their present humour, would not take much amiss.'[54]

One of the most yawning gulfs which divided eighteenth-century

Scotland from nineteenth lay in attitudes to assimilation. If the process had been seen in the eighteenth century as controllable from within, in the nineteenth it appeared as a pressure operating from without, as something which was controlling the development of much of Scottish life but which Scotsmen could not themselves control.[55] Scott, in his remarkable *Letters of Malachai Malagrowther* (1826) was to speak with a passionate anger of the complete disregard shown in England for national peculiarities and of the rage for uniformity; in English eyes, Scott believed, Scotland was little more than 'a subordinate species of Northumberland'.[56] Such a belief in the impending extermination of Scottish national characteristics finds an early expression in the melancholy laments that the judges bill provoked. Indeed, in terms of the history of assimilation and of its impact upon the consciousness of the Scottish ruling class, perhaps the agitation may be regarded to be as a watershed between the eighteenth and nineteenth centuries. For it contains possibly the last and certainly the most extreme and self-conscious statement of the gentry's right to direct Scotland's future and to control the process of assimilation and one of the earliest expressions of the melancholy with which a later generation was to regard the process of uncontrolled assimilation. 1785 perhaps marks the end of what Henry Cockburn once called 'the last purely Scotch age'.[57]

NOTES

1. Vide W. L. Mathieson, *The Awakening of Scotland, 1747–1797* (Glasgow 1910), ch. III; H. W. Meikle, *Scotland and the French Revolution* (Glasgow 1912), ch. I. See also J. D. Mackie, *A History of Scotland*, (Penguin Books, 1964), 283–5.
2. For the association movement in Scotland, see E. C. Black, *The Association : British Extra-Parliamentary Organistaion, 1769–1793* (Cambridge Mass. 1963), ch. 3–4; H. W. Meikle, *Scotland and the French Revolution*, 5–12; I. R. Christie, *Wilkes, Wyvill and Reform* (London 1962), 160–74.
3. E. C. Black, *The Association*, 122.
4. J. Brooke and L. B. Namier, *The History of Parliament : the House of Commons* (London 1964), i, 480.
5. Quoted E. C. Black, *The Association*, 51.
6. For the ideological history of this period and for Andrew Fletcher's place in it, see J. G. A. Pocock, '"The Onely Politician" : Machiavelli, Harrington and Felix Raab', *Historical Studies Australia and New Zealand*, 12, no. 46, 196; J. G. A. Pocock, 'Machiavelli, Harrington, and English Political Ideologies in the Eighteenth Century'. *William and Mary Quarterly*, 3rd Ser., xxii, no. 4, 1965. I owe a great deal to discussion of this subject with Professor Pocock.

7. *The Letters of Horace Walpole, fourth earl of Orford*, ed. Mrs Paget Toynbee (Oxford 1913–15), xii, 252.
8. The movement is treated in passing in Sir H. Craik's neglected *A Century of Scottish History* (Edinburgh and London 1891), ii, 130 and, although in a different context, by I.D. Willock, *The Jury in Scotland* (Stair Society, 1966), 247–8.
9. For the text of the bill see *S[cots] M[agazine]*, vol. 47, 475–6.
10. *Memorial on the Scotch Judges Bill of 1785* H[ome] O[ffice] MSS, Public Records Office, 102/3/383–6. See also *Memo on the Salaries of the Scotch Judges, May 1828*, Melville MSS, N[ational] L[ibrary of] S[cotland], 13/173–8. G. Brunton and D. Haig, *An Historical Account of the Senators of the College of Justice from its institution in 1532* (1832), xlvii.
11. H. Dundas – Sir J. Dalrymple, 24 July 1781, Melville MSS, S[cottish] R[ecord] O[ffice] 5/396.
12. C[aledonian] M[ercury], 8 June 1785.
13. Melville MSS, NLS, acc, 2761.
14. [I. Campbell], *An Explanation of the bill proposed in the House of Commons, 1785* (1807 edition edited by H. Erskine), 6.
15. *S.M.* 47, 332–3. cf. H. Dundas – J. Boswell, ND [9/10 Nov. 1786] '[I] cannot admit that Political merit of any kind is the Proper Road to Judicial Promotion. That opinion was one of the foundations for thinking that the Judges in Scotland were too numerous. If they were less so, such kind of merit would be urged for such a purpose'. Melville MSS/SRO/5/400/2. See also H. Dundas – I. Campbell, 9 April [1792], Succoth MSS.
16. N. T. Phillipson, *The Scottish Whigs and the Reform of the Court of Session, 1785–1830* (Cambridge, PH.D. 1967), 12–14.
17. *S.M.* 47, 279–9.
18. J. Boswell, *A Letter to the People of Scotland on the Alarming Attempt to infringe the Articles of the Union and introduce a most pernicious innovation by diminishing the number of the Lords of Session* (London 1785), 39.
19. *C.M.* 9 Nov. 1785.
20. *C.M.* 24 Sept. 1785; cf. [*Edinburgh Evening*] *Courant*, 5 Oct. 1785.
21. *S.M.* 47, 332–3; *C.M.* 8 June 1785.
22. R. Dundas – W. Dundas, 11 Oct. 1805, Succoth MSS.
23. *Parlt. Hist.* xxv, 1369.
24. The *Scots Magazine* published resolutions, or summaries of resolutions, of all the counties concerned in *S.M.* 47, 516–8, 569–70. More information on the Ayrshire meeting is to be found in *C.M.* 29 Oct. 1785 and in *Ayr County Records, Minute Book of Commissioners of Supply, 1775–88* (Scottish Record Office), 215–6, 220–2, 225–6. For Elgin see *C.M.* 9 Nov. 1785, *London Chronicle*, 1–3 Nov. 1785; Inverness, *C.M.* 16 Nov. 1785; Perth, *C.M.* 26 Nov. 1785; Stirling 5 Nov. 1785.
25. The Elgin meeting was very firmly controlled by Lord Fife, the county M.P. who disliked the bill but was clearly determined not to allow the constitutional issue to raise its head. At Fife, the earl of Balcarras carried a motion by 20 to 8 adjourning the meeting till it should be clear whether or not the bill was to be reintroduced.
26. *London Chronicle*, 19–21 Jan. 1786.
27. A. Fergusson, *The hon Henry Erskine, lord advocate for Scotland* (1882), 265.
28. J. Boswell, *Letter to the People of Scotland*, 25–7.

L

29. *C.M.* 23 Nov. 1785.
30. There is an amusing parody of this sort of thing in *C. M.* 7 Nov. 1785. The author of the letter quoted above is referred to as 'the reverie writer of Ayrshire'. One wonders if, by any chance, it was Boswell.
31. *London Chronicle,* 23–5 Aug. 1785.
32. H. Dundas – Ld North, 18 Nov. 1781, Melville MSS/NLS/16/40–1.
33. I. Campbell, *Explanation,* 67, 51 ; cf. the angry and exasperated expostulation of ABC in *C.M.* 16 Nov. 1785.
34. *C.M.* 31 Oct. 1785 and *Courant,* 31 Oct. 1785.
35. cf. *Memorial of the Scotch Judges Bill of 1785,* 22 Oct. 1785, HO/102/2/383–6.
36. Cf., for example, the whole tone of the debate in the House of Commons on 8 May 1781 on Sir G. Savile's motion respecting the Petition of the Delegated Counties for a Redress of Grievances. (*Parlt. Hist.,* xxii, 138–200) – and in particular, the speech of the solicitor-general for Scotland, A. Murray (161–4). The *Scots Magazine* republished letters from English writers on the constitutionality of county meetings and on the question, was the M P a delegate or representative?
37. R. Dundas – W. Dundas, 11 Oct. 1805. Succoth MSS.
38. I have not used the word sovereignty here because it is a matter for scholarly doubt how far a fully fledged, formal, doctrine of parliamentary sovereignty existed, or was seen to exist, in 1785. There is, however, no doubt that the Americans, both in the events which led up to the Declaration of Independence and the War, did much to help the emergence of the modern conception of sovereignty.
39. *The Works, Theological, Medical, Political and Miscellaneous of John Jebb, etc.,* ed. J. Disney (London 1787), ii, 453–90.
40. J. Swinton, *Considerations concerning a proposal for dividing the Court of Session into classes or chambers,* etc., (1789), 118.
41. Ld Sydney – Ld Hopetoun, 13 Dec. 1785, HO/102/59/ Unnumbered and unfoliated.
42. W. Blackstone, *Commentaries on the Laws of England* (London 1749), ii, 378.
43. I. D. Willock, *The Origins and Development of the Jury in Scotland* 220–1. See also a review of the same by A. Harding and N. T. Phillipson, *Scottish Historical Review,* xlvi (1967), 153–6. For particular cases, see *The Trial of James Carnegie of Findhaven* (1729), H. Arnot, *Celebrated Criminal Trials* (1785). See also Deacon Brodie's case (1788). A. Morison, *The Trial of William Brodie...and of George Smith* (1788), 192–3,249–52. See also Macdonald's case, *C.M.* 22 July 1782, and W. Smellie's *An Address to the People of Scotland on the Nature, Powers, and Privileges of Juries* (1784). The role of ideology in the rescuing of the powers of criminal juries would well repay study.
44. The subject had been periodically debated both by the Select Society and the Belles Lettres society. D. D. McElroy, *The Literary Clubs and Societies of 18th Century Scotland* (Edinburgh, PH.D 1952), 600, 616, 634.
45. N. T. Phillipson, *The Scottish Whigs and the Reform of the Court of Session,* ch. III–VIII, passim.
46. *C.M.* 3 Sept. He even sent a deputation of his tenants to petition the king against the bill – something for which he was rightly taken

to task by his neighbour Col. Hamilton of Grange.[*Private Papers of James Boswell from Malahide Castle*, ed. G. Scott and F. A. Pottle (Privately printed, 1930), xvi, 109.] Grange told him that his behaviour 'was now like Lord G. Gordon'.

47. *Private papers of James Boswell*, vii, 187 ; xvi, 45. Boswell's own political career was one of activity and constant disappointment. He had been closely connected with the county reform movement in 1782 and in the following year he had organized a petition against Fox's India Bill and had written an effective pamphlet on the subject. In 1784 he had launched into electioneering. All of this was, of course, directed towards squeezing a place out of government and in this he was dismally unsuccessful, outmanoeuvred at every point by an exasperated and occasionally amused Henry Dundas. What prompted him to interfere in the judges bill agitation was very largely irritation at the thought of yet another object of preferment being denied him. [F. Brady, *Boswell's Political Career* (New Haven 1965), passim, esp. chs. 3–4.] I am very grateful to Professors Brady and Pottle for help on this point.

48. J. Boswell, *Letter to the People of Scotland*, 56.

49. *Courant*, 28 Nov. 1785.

50. *Courant*, 5 Dec. 1785.

51. *Memorial on the Scotch Judges Bill*, 22 Oct. 1785, HO/102/2/383–6.

52. N. T. Phillipson, *The Scottish Whigs and the Reform of the Court of Session*, 4–6.

53. Quoted, D. D. McElroy, *The Literary Clubs and Societies of 18th Century Scotland*, 20.

54. J. Swinton, *Considerations*, 15–16 ; cf. 119.

55. I have explored the development of nationalist ideology more fully in my essay 'Nationalism and Ideology' in *Government and Nationalism in Scotland*, ed. J. N. Wolfe (1969), 167–88.

56. [W. Scott], *Thoughts on the Proposed Change of Currency and other late alterations as they affect or are intended to affect the Kingdom of Scotland* (1826), 17. It is interesting to notice that the tone of Scott's letter bears a quite remarkable resemblance to that of Boswell's *Letter to the People of Scotland* and to the laments of the Jeremiahs.

57. H. Cockburn, *Life of Lord Jeffrey with a selection from his correspondence* (1852), i, 157.

7. Law and Society in Eighteenth-Century Scottish Thought

PETER STEIN

The second half of the eighteenth century was the classical period of Scots law, the period when it came of age as a mature system of law.[1] It had received its first comprehensive statement from Lord Stair at the end of the seventeenth century. He laid out the foundations on which the lawyers of the next hundred years gradually built up a structure of rules having the distinctive features which can be recognized in the Scots law of today. By the end of the eighteenth century, the field of private law was largely covered by the court decisions which formed the basis of the great synthesizing works of George Joseph Bell in the early nineteenth century.

Thought about law and its relation to society in the first half of the eighteenth century still reflected the ideas of the rationalist natural law philosophy of which Stair was an exponent.

Stair's *Institutions of the Law of Scotland* (1681) was intended both to provide a compendium of the established rules of Scots law of his time and also to show how those rules formed a coherent and logical whole. His aim was partly publicist: to show that Scots law conformed to the common dictates of reason and that therefore it could be approached not as a mere collection of authorities but as a rational discipline, having certain basic principles from which particular conclusions could be deduced. As we might expect from one who had been a teacher of philosophy, his work shows that he was familiar with the doctrines of the leading writers of the contemporary Protestant revival of natural law on the continent – in particular Grotius and Pufendorf. His definition of law echoes that of Grotius, 'Law is the dictate of reason, determining every rational being to that which is congruous and convenient for the nature and condition thereof.'[2]

But Stair differs from these continental natural lawyers in two significant respects. First, they held, though they were for the most part devoutly religious, that a rational theory of law could be independent of theological assumptions. Although the obligation to obey natural law might come from God, yet the whole contents of natural law could be ascertained by logical deduction from man's nature as a rational being. Stair did not go along with them in this view. He was attached to the Presbyterian form of Protestantism, and the sincerity of his attachment was demonstrated by his refusal to take the Test. In the Westminster Confession of Faith, accepted by the Church of Scotland, the freedom of the human will and the doctrine of divine predestination are asserted side by side, free will in Chapter IX and effectual calling in Chapter X. So the natural lawyer had to walk warily. He might incur the displeasure of the Church authorities if, by giving undue prominence to the role of reason, he denied that the principles of human action come directly from God. Or he might antagonize them, as did later Lord Kames, by asserting a strict necessitarianism – by holding that the freedom of the human will is illusion and that man is bound by a necessity in the nature and constitution of things. For in either case he would be denying that God is the principle of order in the universe. He would be elevating the law above God and putting man out of immediate relation with the Highest. Stair adopted a middle line. We can assume that God will act according to reason, that His law is rational. But law is founded primarily on the will of God. Reason is rather a subsidiary instrument. 'Divine law is that mainly, which is written in man's heart....Such are the common practical principles, that God is to be obeyed, parents honoured, ourselves defended, violence repulsed, children to be loved, educated, and provided for.'[3] Reason was given to man that from these principles he might deduce God's law in more particular cases. As Professor Campbell[4] puts it, 'Stair was still prepared to rely on God at an indefinite number of points as the author of an indefinite number of principles of human action, which are directly known without reasoning or experience, which therefore do not require logical proof of their validity.'

Stair also seems to deviate from the continental natural lawyers in a second respect. They not only tended towards a secular set of natural law principles ; they held further that from these principles a complete and self-sufficient system could be deduced by logic. The most detailed solutions could be derived from the smallest number of postulates. Their view is illustrated by the attraction they felt for mathematical analogy. Grotius[5] had averred that 'just as the mathematicians treat their figures as abstracted from bodies, so in treating law I have withdrawn my mind from every particular fact'. This Stair did not do. Despite his predilection for reason, he did not admit that reason alone, working on the principles implanted by God, could provide a satisfactory legal system. His attitude corresponded rather with that of the Philosopher in Hobbes's *Dialogue between a Philosopher and a student of the Common Laws of England*;[6] the

Lawyer asks, 'What makes you say that the study of the law is less rational than the study of mathematics?' The Philosopher replies, 'I say not that; for all study is rational or nothing worth; but I say, that the great masters of mathematics do not so often err as the greatest professors of law.' Stair did not agree with much of Hobbes's ideas. But I think he would have recognized the truth of the Philosopher's observation. Although he apologised for it, Stair admitted that some of his statements were asserted on mere authority – for no other reason than *quia majoribus placuerunt*.[7] For no legal system can dispense with authority completely. Take his attitude to customary law.[8] The happiest nations are those whose laws have been wrung out over a long period from debates upon particular cases until they reach the consistence of a fixed and known custom. For in this way the inconveniences of a rule are seen experimentally and can be easily avoided before the rule attains the maturity of a law. When the law is not hardened into a statute, greater discretion is left to the judge. At first the people run some hazard of their judges' arbitrement, 'yet when that law is come to a full consistence, they have by much the advantage in this, that what custom hath changed is thrown away and obliterate without memory or mention of it: but in statutory written law, the vestiges of all the alterations remain, and ordinarily increase to such a mass, that they cease to be...securities to the people, and become labyrinths, wherein they are fair to lose their rights, if not themselves.' Clearly Stair favoured a system in which the bulk of the law is stated in judicial decisions and would not have advocated codification.

There is a tendency to express the problem of the nature of law as a dichotomy, the formula being, law is not x but y. The history of legal thought is littered with aphorisms like: law is not *jussum* but *justum*: law is not made but found: law is not logic but experience. Stair was aware that these are false dichotomies: that law is neither entirely logic nor entirely experience but a mysterious mixture of the two.

When he came to describe the system of Scots law, Stair used as his framework of organization three principles of equity, whose validity he regarded as self-evident, supplemented by three principles of positive law, whose aim was 'the profit and utility of man'.[9]

The three principles of equity are: 1. That God is to be obeyed by man; 2. That man is a free creature, having power to dispose of himself and of all things, in so far as by his obedience to God he is not restrained; 3. That this freedom of man is in his own power and may be restrained by his voluntary engagements which he is bound to fulfil.'

These are the 'efficient causes' of men's rights; the 'final causes' are the three principles of positive law, namely, 1. that *societies* should be formed for mutual defence, and protection of rights; 2. that limits be set to each man's *property*; 3. that free *commerce* be maintained. But the whole system of law can be rationally treated around the three equitable principles of *obedience, freedom* and *engagement*. Freedom is the central condition. For where man's obedience to God ends, freedom begins. Man by his nature is free in all things, unless he voluntarily obliges himself – so that engagement begins where freedom ends.

As obligations were for the most part 'anterior to and inductive of' property, Stair treats first of obligations, and distinguishes between *obediential obligations*, which are imposed on us by the will of God and so are for the most part 'natural', and *conventional obligations*, which bind us through our own will or engagement. Obediential obligations include obligations between husband and wife and between parents and children, the obligations of restitution and of recompense, and the obligation of reparation of damage by delinquence. Conventional obligations are those voluntarily assumed by promise or contract, by which we give away part of the freedom God has left us. These are also binding by natural law; for 'there is nothing more natural than to stand by the faith of our pactions.'

Thus, although Stair's introductory discussion speaks of rights, his actual treatment is based on the idea of law as a series of obligations of various kinds, limiting a general freedom which is itself part of the law of nature. Contract and property are both derived from that general freedom. Treating them from the point of view of obligations meant that just as Stair stressed that the contractual obligation, being an obligation to keep faith, was sacred, so he also made it clear that property carried with it certain obligations. God granted the dominion of the creatures of the earth to man. This dominion was originally held in common, but the fruits of the creatures and the products of art and industry were proper to individuals. Normally they could be disposed of at will; but there was an implied obligation of commerce or exchange in cases of necessity and even, where there was nothing to receive in exchange, an obligation to give.[10] (Stair adds that it must be a real and not a pretended and feigned necessity.) Thus property, in Stair's eyes, was subject to definite restrictions in the public interest.

Stair's conception of law governed legal thought in Scotland for the first half of the eighteenth century. Even John Erskine, whose *Institute of the Law of Scotland* was published posthumously in 1773, still follows the general line laid down by Stair, when he treats of

Laws in general. He does, however, adopt the Grotian view when he says that the law of nature is not made known by any formal notification of God's will but is impressed on men's minds by the internal suggestion of reason.[11] Erskine distinguishes between the primary and the secondary law of nature, the first applying to men in the state of nature and the second to men in independent states. 'The essential reason of things teacheth us...to adhere strictly to our obligations and engagements'[12] and that duty therefore formed part of the primary law of nature, like the duty to honour and obey our parents.

On the other hand, the right of property derives from the nature of society and so forms part of the secondary law of nature. 'By the first, or original law, all things were common....But as men multiplied, experience soon taught, that society could not long subsist if this common use of things continued: A right of property was therefore established.'[13] Erskine stresses the restraints on the use of property. 'The law interposes so far for the public interest, that it suffers no person to use his property wantonly to his neighbour's prejudice.'[14] He recognizes what Grotius called *dominium eminens*, 'the universal right in the public over property...in virtue of which the supreme power may compel any proprietor to part with what is his own', although this right may only be exercised when there is evident utility to the public and full compensation is paid.

The institutional writers, then, followed the natural law line, which considered legal principles to be dictated by man's natural reason, regarded strict adherence to agreements as dictated by nature and the contractual obligation as therefore sacred, and, on the other hand, considered the holder of property to be subject to such restrictions imposed by nature in the public interest that he was theoretically almost a trustee of his property on behalf of the community.

However, professional lawyers, such as Stair and Erskine, were not the only writers to speculate about the nature of law and society. The eighteenth century was notable for the tremendous growth of interest in moral philosophy and the enormous scope which the subject was considered to have. The moral philosophers focused attention on the function of law in ordering men's relations with their fellows in society, and the challenge which they offered to the traditional explanations of the origin and nature of law made lawyers less confident of the absolute character of some well-established legal notions and more critical of some legal institutions which had served their purpose.

Francis Hutcheson, who became Professor of Moral Philosophy in the University of Glasgow in 1729, divided his course into two parts, 'ethicks', and 'the knowledge of the law of nature'. The latter was subdivided into '(1) the doctrine of private rights, or the laws obtaining in natural liberty; (2) Oeconomics, or the laws and rights of the several members of a family; and (3) Politics, showing the various plans of civil government and the rights of states with respect to each others.'[15]

At first sight Hutcheson seems to follow the standard natural law attitudes of Grotius and Pufendorf. His predecessor in the Chair of Moral Philosophy at Glasgow, Gershom Carmichael, had produced for his students' use an edition of Pufendorf's *De officio hominis et civis* and was described by Hutcheson as 'by far the best commentator on that book'. No doubt when he succeeded to the chair, Hutcheson did not make any abrupt changes in the content of the course. But there are definite changes of emphasis discernible in his treatment. Hutcheson was an intuitionist who was strongly influenced by Stoic ideas of the 'citizenship of the world' and 'universal good'.[16] In 1738 he was charged before the Presbytery of Glasgow with holding that the standard of moral goodness was the promotion of the happiness of others and that we could have a knowledge of good and evil without a prior knowledge of God. Holding that 'virtue is in a compound ratio of the quantity of good and number of enjoyers', he was led to enunciate for the first time in English the utilitarian formula: 'That Action is best, which procures the greatest Happiness for the greatest Numbers.'[17]

Although Hutcheson did not work out this principle to any great degree, its influence can be seen in his practical approach to property, 'compleat unlimited property', as he calls it.[18] Hutcheson followed Locke in stressing that it is not the spontaneous fruits of uncultivated earth which maintain mankind but general diligence and labour. Unless labour leads to property, neither our self-love nor our affection for others will make us work. 'The common interest of all requires that all should be obliged by their own necessities to some sort of industry; now no man would employ his labours unless he were assured of having the fruits of them at his own disposal.' Thus Hutcheson holds security of private property to be essential in the interest of all, but he says little about restrictions on user.

Similarly Hutcheson recognizes that the keeping of contracts is 'of absolute necessity in life'. But what he calls 'the sacred obligation of faith in contracts' is demonstrated not only 'from our immediate sense of its beauty', but also 'from the mischiefs which must ensue upon violating it'.[19] By justifying the enforcement of contracts on grounds of public utility, Hutcheson leaves it open to others to maintain that contracts need not be enforced when the public interest would not be served by enforcement.

Hutcheson still explained the origin of society in terms of a social contract whereby men in their natural state made mutual promises to live together as a community, This doctrine was subjected to severe criticism by David Hume in Book III, Part 2, of his *Treatise of Human Nature*, published in 1740.[20]

According to Hume, the state of nature was historically a fiction. It is true that society has obvious advantages for men over the solitary life, but society was not formed by the conscious, rational method of contract. Rather self interest gradually led to the recognition of the benefits flowing from life in society. For man in society can both achieve more and be more secure that he could by himself. 'By the conjunction of forces, our power is augmented: By the partition of employments, our ability encreases: And by mutual succour we are less expos'd to fortune and accidents.' As a result, man is 'in every respect more satisfied and happy, than 'tis possible for him, in his savage and solitary condition, ever to become.'[21]

The individual is mainly concerned with his own immediate needs but there is an insufficiency of goods to supply everyone's desires. Man is confronted by 'the concurrence of certain *qualities* of the human mind with the *situation* of external objects. The qualities of the mind are *selfishness* and *limited generosity*: And the situation of external objects is their *easy change*, join'd to their *scarcity* in comparison of the wants and desires of men.' But for this situation, laws would have been unnecessary. 'If men were supplied with everything in the same abundance, or if *every one* had the same affection and tender regard for *every one* as for himself; justice and injustice would be equally unknown among mankind.' Consequently it is 'only from the selfishness and confin'd generosity of men, along with the scanty provision nature has made for his wants, that justice derives its origin'.[22]

People are not expressly conscious of the advantages of living according to rules of justice, but 'custom and habit operating on the tender minds of the children'[23] make them sensible of them, and gradually they reach a convention that everyone shall have peaceable enjoyment of whatever he may acquire by his fortune and industry. 'This convention is not of the nature of a *promise*', for promises themselves arise from conventions. Rather it is 'a general sense of common interest' which induces men to regulate their conduct according to rules. 'Two men, who pull the oars of a boat, do it by an agreement or convention, tho' they have never given promises to each other.' Similarly the rule concerning stability of possession 'arises gradually, and acquires force by a slow progression, and by our repeated experience of the inconveniences of transgressing it'.[24]

'After this convention, concerning abstinence from the possessions of others, is entr'd into, and every one has acquir'd a stability in his possessions, there immediately arise the ideas of justice and injustice.' It is in like manner 'that languages [are] gradually establish'd by human conventions without any promise. In like manner do gold and silver become the common measures of exchange.'[25] Thus law and justice, like language and money, are seen as developing social institutions, and it is not nature but the artifice of man which establishes the rules of justice.

Only in the light of this characteristic of justice can the ideas of property, right and obligation be understood. For 'the origin of justice explains that of property. The same artifice gives rise to both.... The convention for the distinction of property and for the stability of possession, is of all circumstances the most necessary to the establishment of human society.'[26] Although Hume discusses in considerable detail the circumstances which give rise to property – Occupation, Prescription, Accession and Succession – and then its transference by consent, he nowhere mentions any of the restrictions imposed by the natural lawyers on the owner. Indeed he lays down categorically, that 'possession and property shou'd always be stable, except when the proprietor consents to bestow them on some other person',[27] and actually applies the phrase 'sacred and inviolable'[28] to private property. Hume concludes that 'this system, therefore, comprehending the interest of each individual, is of course advantageous to the public; tho' it be not intended for that purpose by the inventors.'[29] Private interest is thus made to coincide with public interest.

The stability of possession and its transference by consent are both described by Hume as 'fundamental laws of nature'.[30] This usage is at first sight inconsistent with his assertion that the rules in question are not natural but 'artificial'. But earlier Hume explained, 'Tho' the rules of justice be artificial, they are not *arbitrary*. Nor is the expression improper to call them *Laws of Nature*; if by natural we understand what is common to any species, or even if we confine it to mean what is inseparable from the species.'[31] The third law of nature is that compelling the performance of promises. Hume argues that promises have no natural obligation and are merely artificial contrivances for the convenience and advantage of society. Thus force, for example, invalidates all contracts and frees us from their obligation. Yet force is not essentially different from other motives for making promises and laying ourselves under obligations.

'A man, dangerously wounded, who promises a competent sum to a surgeon to cure him, wou'd certainly be bound to performance; tho' the case be not so much different from that of one, who promises a sum to a robber, as to produce so great a difference in our sentiments of morality, if these sentiments were not built entirely on public interest and convenience.'[32]

The conclusion of Hume's argument is succinctly stated in the *Enquiry concerning the Principles of Morals*: 'The good of mankind is the only object of all these laws and regulations.'[33]

Despite (or perhaps because of) the startling contrast between Hume's views and the prevailing opinions on law and society, they made little immediate impact either on other philosophers or on the legal profession. It was rather the publication of Montesquieu's great work on *The Spirit of Laws*, which appeared eight years after Hume's *Treatise*, that marks the watershed which divides the conception of the law as reason from the idea of law as originating in the circumstances of society. While recognizing that reason is an attribute common to all men, Montesquieu pointed out that when reason was applied to find solutions for the special requirements of different nations, it had to take account of many things – the climate, the soil, the main occupations of the inhabitants, their religion, inclinations, manners, customs. So universal solutions were impossible.[34]

This way of looking at law is commonplace today. But before Montesquieu, such a view of law was unusual. There is barely a hint of it in Stair. *The Spirit of Laws* had an immediate impact in Scotland.[35] Its ideas were taken up by a group of philosophical thinkers, of whom the most prominent at the time was probably Lord Kames.[36] Their influence took longer to permeate the outlook of the practitioners of Scots law, but by the end of the century the profession was more conscious than it had been of the need to keep the law in touch with the changing social and economic state of the country, and more conscious too of its particular attributes as Scots law, a system peculiar to the Scots.

Kames was a typical eighteenth-century figure; vigorous mentally and physically, curious about all manner of topics, optimistic about his ability to improve the world. It is characteristic of him that in his eightieth year he turned away from discussion of the elements of criticism and the principles of morality and published *The Gentleman Farmer, being an attempt to improve agriculture by subjecting it to the test of rational principles*. But he was by profession a lawyer and a Lord of Session for thirty years, so that his views on law carry especial authority.

Opening a Kames tract, the reader is immediately struck by the contrast between Kames's manner and the cool, reasoned, smoothly running periods of Stair. Kames addresses the reader as if he were a public meeting. In his *Elucidations respecting the Law of Scotland*[37] he is deprecating the way legal studies are conducted. 'No science', he declares, 'affords more opportunity for exerting the reasoning faculty than that of the law; and yet in no other science is authority so prevalent.' 'What are our law-books,' he cries, 'but a mass of naked propositions drawn chiefly from the decisions of our supreme courts, rarely connected either with premise or consequences?' Even Stair's *Institutions* are not without fault in Kames's eyes. 'Stair tends to cite decisions as all of equal authority, though they are not always concordant.' As a result, law students, trained to rely on authority, seldom think of questioning what they read: 'they husband their reasoning faculty as if it would rust by exercise'. Professors of law, of course, get short shrift. 'They load the weak mind with a heap of uninteresting facts, without giving any exercise to the judgement.' Kames, as a practical lawyer, does not wish to exclude authority altogether. 'The authority of men of eminence has deservedly great weight; for nature gives its weight. But authority ought to be subservient to reason; which the God of nature has bestowed on man as his chief guide in thinking as well as in acting.' Authority then there must be: what Kames condemned was too rigid an adherence to authority and precedent by those who failed to see the principle behind the decision.

It is important to see the exact nature of Kames's championship of the cause of reason in the law. He was not in fact appealing primarily for a greater application of logic. His meaning becomes clear in his remark that law 'becomes then only a rational study, when it is traced historically, from its first rudiments among savages, through successive changes, to its highest improvements in a civilised society'.[38] When Kames pleaded for reason, he was in fact pleading for a more historical approach. Kames had learned from Montesquieu to look for the connection between the law and the social and economic circumstances of society. But he recognized the limitations of Montesquieu's own application of this conception. 'That celebrated writer abounds with observations no less pleasing than solid. But a sprightly genius, prone to novelty and refinement, has betrayed him into manifold errors.'[39] In particular, though he does not expressly say so, Kames recognized the essentially fragmentary character of *The Spirit of Laws*. It lacked an organizing principle around which its author's acute observations could be marshalled.[40] This lack Kames attempted to supply in the principle of the progress of society – through successive stages from barbarism to civilization. He visualised the law as the River Nile. 'When we enter upon the municipal law of any country in its present state, we resemble a traveller, who crossing the Delta, loses his way among the numberless branches of the Egyptian river. But when we begin at the source and follow the current of law...all its relations and dependencies are traced with no greater difficulty, than are the many streams into which that magnificent river is divided before it is lost in the sea.'[41]

Kames hoped that by comparative study of different legal systems, some general principles of legal development would emerge, so that one could explain the growth of one system by reference to that of another.

'We must be satisfied with collecting the facts and circumstances as they may be gathered from the Laws of different countries: and if these put together make a regular system of causes and effects, we may rationally conclude, that the progress has been the same among all nations, in the capital circumstances at least; for accidents, or the singular nature of a people, or of a government, will always produce some peculiarities.'[42]

The difficulty about such a drawing of general conclusions from a comparative study of the institutions of different legal systems was that it tended to become too philosophic for the lawyer and too technical for the student of civil society. In a letter to Adam Smith in 1759, Hume wrote of the work from which the last quotation was taken: 'I am afraid of Kames' *Law Tracts*. The man might as well think of making a fine sauce by a mixture of wormwood and aloes as an agreeable combination by joining metaphysics and Scottish law.'[43]

Although Kames accepted the principle of the progress of society, he did not apply it with much success himself. Perhaps the reformer in him prevented him. For most of his essays on the history of law were tracts supporting some particular improvement favoured by their author. His underlying purpose was to develop the law more rapidly in accordance with the needs of the times. It seems at first sight paradoxical that a judge, who was among the first to interest himself seriously in the history of the law, should be so anxious to change it. But in fact only one who has a sure grasp of the historical origins of a rule of law, and of the connection of that rule with a particular set of social or economic conditions, can see that the time has come to abandon it when the changed circumstances no longer require it. An historically minded judge, in other words, can see the direction in which the law is moving and this insight gives him a certain freedom in handling his authorities.

In the matter of property and contract, Kames was led to conclusions not very different from those of Hume. In one of the *Historical Law Tracts*[44] he traces the progress of the idea of property from barbarian times, when it is inseparable from possession and therefore liable to be dissolved by the slightest accident, until, as society advances, the relation between the subject appropriated and its owner becomes indissoluble except by consent of the owner. Men have a moral sense, he argues, which dictates to them that goods stored up by individuals are their property and that property ought to be inviolable.

In the case of contracts, Kames stresses not so much the binding character of the obligation as the circumstances in which the promisor is relieved from his obligation. 'The moral sense, bending to circumstances, is accommodated to the fallible nature of man; it relieves him from deceit, from imposition, from ignorance, and from error; and binds him to no engagement but what fairly answers the end proposed by it.'[45]

Kames acted to some extent as a bridge between the lawyers and the moral philosophers. He was thoroughly familiar with the practice of the law, and wrote works for the practitioner as well as for the philosopher, while his position as a judge ensured that his fellow-lawyers paid attention to his views, even if they did not accept them. His general influence on the thought of his time has perhaps been underestimated because it was exercised not so much through his writing as by personal contact with the coterie of scholars whom he gathered about him. Pre-eminent among these was Adam Smith. When Smith was congratulated on the number of able writers Scotland had produced, he observed, 'We must everyone of us acknowledge Kames for our master.'[46] Smith's achievement from the point of view of legal thought was to combine the sociology of Montesquieu with the historicism of Kames. The progress of society became for him a principle of historical investigation. In Dugald Stewart's words, 'he attempted to account for the changes in the condition of mankind, which take place in the different stages of their progress, for the corresponding alteration which their institutions undergo.'[47] Actually Stewart was applying these words to Montesquieu, but as Mr Duncan Forbes has observed, this is just what Montesquieu does not do. Stewart was reading back into *The Spirit of Laws* the contribution of Montesquieu's Scottish disciples. John Millar, Professor of Law at Glasgow, who was a pupil of Adam Smith and a member of Kames's circle, put the matter more accurately when he said, 'The great Montesquieu pointed out the road. He was the Lord Bacon in this branch of philosophy. Dr. Smith is the Newton.'[48]

Adam Smith never seems to have made a formal study of law, but it was a subject which deeply interested him[49] and he originally projected 'an account of the general principles of law and government, and of the different revolutions they have undergone in the different ages and periods of society'. He never fulfilled the project, but an adumbration of his ideas can be found towards the end of *The Theory of Moral Sentiments*, and in the *Lectures on Justice*, preserved in students' notes.[50]

Law for Smith was but one aspect of the historical world of human experience which was waiting to be studied 'scientifically', that is without any *a priori* assumptions dictated by reason. Smith distrusted the reason of fashionable philosophers. For example he says, 'That kings are servants of the people, to be obeyed, resisted, deposed, or punished, as the public conveniency may require, is the doctrine of reason and philosophy; but it is not the doctrine of nature.'[51] By nature, he meant not a mythical state of nature, but man's conduct in society. Again, since man is a free agent, explanations of human institutions in terms of systems are to be suspected.

'The man of system...seems to imagine that he can arrange the different members of a great society with as much ease as the hand arranges the different pieces upon a chess-board. He does not consider that the pieces upon the chess-board have no other principle of motion besides that which the hand impresses upon them; but that, in the great chess-board of human society, every single piece has a principle of motion of its own, altogether different from that which the legislature might chuse to impress upon it. If these two principles coincide and act in the same direction, the game of human society will go on easily and harmoniously, and is very likely to be happy and successful. If they are opposite or different, the game will go on miserably.'[52]

Although Smith and his followers reacted against the deductive law of reason of their contemporaries, they would not have admitted to rejecting natural law. Their object, said Francis Jeffrey,[53] was 'to trace back the history of society to its most simple and universal elements – to resolve almost all that has been ascribed to positive institution into the spontaneous and irresistible development of certain obvious principles'. They had considered previous attempts to establish systems of the natural rules of justice, independent of positive institution, and they regarded that of Grotius as the best. But they rejected them on two main grounds.

First, these writers, though proposing to give rules abstracted from any particular system, in fact adhered closely to one, namely the Roman law. Smith and his followers were conversant with the rules of Roman law and respected it, but for them it was no longer 'reason in writing'. Indeed the extreme Millar could even describe it as 'in many of its doctrines erroneous, and in some of its principles narrow and illiberal'.[54]

A second and more important criticism of previous writers on jurisprudence was that they did not sufficiently mark the boundary which separates strict law from mere morality. They were concerned with what the good man, the man with the most delicate scruples of conscience, should think himself bound to perform, and their systems are sets of rules for the conduct of such a man. This, says Smith,[55] is casuistry, not jurisprudence. Jurisprudence is concerned not with what the good man should be disposed to do, but with what a judge should compel him to do. Smith thus saw the necessity to distinguish law and morals and adopted as a working distinction the different ways in which each is enforced. A legal obligation is one which the party entitled can exact by force – which a judge will oblige the other party to suffer or perform. In Smith's view the fault of the natural lawyers, from Cicero to Pufendorf and Barbeyrac, was that they tried to do too much. They attempted 'to direct by precise rules what it belongs to feeling and sentiment only to judge of' and what it requires a complete view of their whole circumstances to determine: the so-called laws of chastity and modesty, the rules of veracity, etc. As a result 'books of casuistry, therefore, are generally as useless as they are commonly tiresome'. They did not achieve the desired aim of establishing a system of natural jurisprudence – 'a theory of the general principles which ought to run through and be the foundation of the laws of all nations'.

When he concerned himself with the institutions of law, Smith developed further the ideas, suggested by Hume, that private property was sacred and that contractual obligations should be measured against the standard of public utility.

In the *Wealth of Nations*, he says, 'the property which every man has in his own labour, as it is the original foundation of all other property, so it is the most sacred and inviolable'.[56] Indeed the prime, almost the only, function of the administration of justice is to protect property. 'It is only under the shelter of the civil magistrate that the owner of that valuable property, which is acquired by the labour of many years,...can sleep a single night in security....The acquisition of valuable and extensive property...necessarily requires the establishment of civil government. Where there is no property, or at least none that exceeds the value of two or three days' labour, civil government is not so necessary.'[57]

In a significant footnote, Smith brings out that the characteristic

M

of contract is not so much the sanctity of the promises but the mutuality of benefit. 'In all voluntary contracts, both parties gain. For a long time, however, people were possessed of the idea, that one man's gain is another's loss. Unfortunately, legislation proceeded on this fallacy, and consequently busied itself with restrictions, prohibitions, compensations and the like.'[58]

Smith's pupil Millar went even further. The view that the foundation of government was the good of society was a Whig view, so that utility was the Whig principle in contrast to the Tory principle of authority. 'The obligation of a contract', wrote Millar, 'is liable in all cases to be controlled and modified by considerations of general utility; and a promise inconsistent with any great interest of society is not productive of moral obligation.'[59]

The legal thought of the school of Kames, Smith and Millar – the Scientific Whigs – had two main aspects: realism and historicism. First, they had what may be called a realist attitude to law. They saw clearly the limitations of the law. 'Mere justice,' said Smith, 'is upon most occasions, but a negative virtue, and only hinders us from hurting our neighbour. The man who barely abstains from violating either the person, or the estate, or the reputation of his neighbours,... fulfils, however, all the rules of what is peculiarly called justice, and does every thing which his equals can...punish him for not doing. We may often fulfil all the rules of justice by sitting still and doing nothing.'[60] Side by side with this view of the compulsive aspect of law they saw the intrinsic imperfection which is inherent in the generality of legal rules. They stressed that where many cases are brought within the same general rule, the smaller circumstances in which they happen to differ are overlooked; and so decisions according to the general rule may actually produce injustice in some instances.

Concentration on the method of enforcement in delimiting law and morals led Smith and his friends to look at law from the point of view of the judge, and led them to an awareness of a further aspect of law – its agonistic or competitive character.[61] We often tend to consider the administration of justice in terms of abstract righteousness. We look at a lawsuit as primarily a dispute between right and wrong. But underlying the preoccupation with moral values is the element of winning and losing. The question at issue must be fought out according to the rules of procedure laid down. As Huizinga says, 'Justice is made subservient to the rules of the game.'[62] One side or other must win. Adam Smith in his moral theory was continually appealing to the judgement of an over-worked impartial spectator. He naturally saw the judge in his role as an umpire, whose main function was to see that the parties in presenting their claims and defences observed the rules of the game.

Hume had seen this aspect of law very clearly. In law, he said, right and obligation admit of no degrees – that the law does not recognize half-rights and half-obligations. An object must either be in the possession of one person or another. An action must either be performed or not. Justice may direct a compromise solution to the dispute, but in a lawsuit one side must be chosen to the exclusion of the other. As a result, Hume pointed out, civil judges who 'are oblig'd to give a decisive sentence on some one side, are often at a loss how to determine, and are necessitated to proceed on the most frivolous reasons in the world. Half rights and obligations, which seem so natural in common life, are perfect absurdities in their tribunal; for which reason they are often oblig'd to take half-arguments for whole ones, in order to terminate the affair one way or other.'[63]

This realism in regard to law and its function in society is reflected also in the work of Adam Ferguson.[64] Although Ferguson, who was Professor of Moral Philosophy in the University of Edinburgh, shared many of the attitudes of the school of Kames and Smith, his background was different from theirs and his views differed from theirs in certain significant respects. He was a Highlander and a Gaelic speaker, he was an ordained minister and he had been a chaplain in the Black Watch for several years.

Ferguson could not accept the optimistic assumption that the material and commercial progress of society went hand in hand with an improvement of law and justice. In his main work *An Essay on the History of Civil Society*,[65] published in 1767, he describes the progress of society from a 'rude' to a 'polished' state, but civilization for him belongs less to the accumulation of wealth than to the organization of political life, and the individual might have more freedom in a less polished society than in one commercially more advanced. Ferguson could not share Smith's assumption that the protection of private wealth would inevitably redound to the benefit of society as a whole. For riches carried with them the danger of corruption and abuse of the power which they conferred on their possessors. Ferguson accepted that wealth made possible a certain degree of security and the establishment of the rule of law. But we are apt, he suggests, to exaggerate the beneficial effects of this development.

'Liberty results, we say, from the government of laws.' But what is law? It is a treaty to which different classes in society have agreed. 'Every class propounds an objection, suggests an addition or an amendment of its own. They proceed to adjust, by statute, every subject of controversy: and while they continue to enjoy their freedom, they continue to multiply laws, and to accumulate volumes, as if they could remove every possible ground of dispute, and were secure of their rights, merely by having put them in writing.'[66]

Then, however, we tend to regard laws not merely as the written records of a people's rights but as 'a power erected to guard them, and as a barrier which the caprice of man cannot transgress....If forms of proceeding, written statutes, or other constituents of law, cease to be enforced by the very spirit from which they arose; they serve only to cover, not to restrain, the iniquities of power....And the influence of laws, where they have any real effect in the preservation of liberty, is not any magic power descending from shelves that are loaded with books, but is, in reality, the influence of men resolved to be free; of men, who, having adjusted in writing the terms on which they are to live with their state, and with their fellow-subjects, are determined, by their vigilance and spirit, to make these terms be observed.'[67]

Laws do not enforce themselves; they must be enforced by men who believe in them, and who, moreover have at their disposal the means to enforce them. 'Law without force is no more than a dead letter; and force, if improperly lodged, will frustrate all the precautions of the legal establishment.'[68]

Finally Ferguson reinforced the objections of Hume and Smith to the moralism of the natural lawyers. 'We are not to expect, that the laws of any country are to be framed as so many lessons of morality, to instruct the citizen how he may act the part of a virtuous man. Laws, whether civil or political, are expedients of policy to adjust the pretensions of parties, and to secure the peace of society. The expedient is accommodated to special circumstances, and calculated to repress the specific disorders peculiarly incident to particular situations.'[69]

The other main aspect of the legal thought of these philosophers was its historical bias. Their emphasis was especially on social and economic causes. William Robertson, for example, who was Principal of Edinburgh University, shows how the barbarian invaders of the Roman empire discarded the Roman laws because these laws were repugnant to their own manners and ideas; they were adapted to a state of society with which the invaders were entirely unacquainted. But by the twelfth century, when a manuscript of the Digest was accidentally discovered at Amalfi, the state of society had advanced and ideas had improved, and men were 'struck with admiration of a system which their ancestors could not comprehend', and so the study of Roman law began anew.[70] Millar, who was the extremist of the group, allowed practically no effect to arbitrary or accidental causes. He insisted that 'the greater part of the political system of any country [is] derived from the continued influence of the whole people',[71] and poured scorn on the suggestion that the revival of Roman law was due to the discovery of a manuscript. 'We may be allowed to entertain some doubt, whether an event of that magnitude could have proceeded from a circumstance so frivolous.'[72]

This historical approach to law was shared, though in a rather different form, by others who were not members of the school and who held opposing political views, such as Baron Hume, the nephew of the philosopher, and Professor of Scots Law at Edinburgh. Kames, it will be remembered, saw law as a great river, ever rolling on and dividing into different courses. Hume had a less fluid but no less vivid image of the law. It is described by Sir Walter Scott,[73] who attended Hume's lectures and copied them out twice in his own hand. Hume, he said, presented 'the fabric of the law, formed originally under the strictest influence of feudal principles, and innovated, altered, and broken in upon by the change of times, of habits, and of manners, until it resembles some ancient castle, partly entire, partly ruinous, partly dilapidated, patched and altered during the succession of ages by a thousand additions and combinations, yet still exhibiting, with the marks of its antiquity, symptoms of the skill and wisdom of its founders, and capable of being analysed and made the subject of a methodical plan by an architect who can understand the various styles of the different ages in which it was subjected to alteration. Such an architect has Mr. Hume been to the law of Scotland.' This image is more static and perhaps more romantic than that of Kames – it certainly ascribes more weight to the human element in the formation of law – but it shows the same realisation of the basic connection between the law and the circumstances of society.[74]

The philosophers of the Scottish enlightenment were the first group of thinkers about law to challenge both the natural law ideas which were dominant on the continent of Europe and the Hobbesian positivism that attributed all law to the sovereign's will. They looked on law as a social science and developed a dynamic conception of law, which was the antithesis of 'legalism' and which anticipated several of the dominant ideas of nineteenth- and twentieth-century legal thought. In treating law as a means of social control which could only be understood when it was studied as a developing social institution, they were the precursors of Savigny, of Maine and of Ehrlich, and they would probably have applauded Roscoe Pound's delineation of law as 'social engineering'.

NOTES

1. Much of the substance of this essay is taken from my articles 'Legal thought in eighteenth century Scotland', *Juridical Review* (1957), 1–20, and 'The general notions of contract and property in eighteenth century Scottish thought', *Juridical Review* (1963), 1–13.

2. James, Viscount Stair, *The Institutions of the Law of Scotland*, 4th edn, ed. G. Brodie (1826), i, 1.

3. Stair, *Institutions*, i, 2–3.

4. A. H. Campbell, *The Structure of Stair's Institutions* (Murray Lecture, Glasgow 1954), 28.

5. H. Grotius, *De Iure Belli ac Pacis*, ed. W. Whewell (Cambridge 1853), i, prolegomena, lxxviii.

6. *Works*, 1840, vi, 3.

7. Stair, *Institutions*, i, vii.

8. Stair, *Institutions*, i, 9.

9. Stair, *Institutions*, i, 13 ff.

10. Stair, *Institutions*, i, 190.

11. J. Erskine of Carnock, *An Institute of the Law of Scotland*, (1773), i, 3.

12. Erskine, *Institute*, i, 3.

13. Erskine, *Institute*, i, 4.

14. Erskine, *Institute*, i, 152.

15. F. Hutcheson, *A Short Introduction to Moral Philosophy*, 2nd edn (Glasgow 1753), v.

16. W. R. Scott, *Francis Hutcheson* (Cambridge 1900), 274 ff.

17. F. Hutcheson, *An Inquiry into the original of our ideas of Beauty and Virtue*, 2nd edn (London 1726), 177; W. R. Scott, *Francis Hutcheson*, 254.

18. F. Hutcheson, *Introduction to Moral Philosophy*, 140.

19. F. Hutcheson, *Introduction to Moral Philosophy*, 168.

20. For Hume's legal thought, F. V. L. Kruse, *Hume's philosophy in his principal work* (London 1939), 52 ff.; L. Bagolini, *Esperienza giuridica e politica nel pensiero di David Hume* (Siena 1947); H. Cairns, *Legal philosophy from Plato to Hegel* (Baltimore 1949), 362–89; S. Castignone, 'La dottrina della giustizia in D. Hume', *Riv. int. filosofia del diritto*, 37 (1960) 457–95, and *Giustizia e bene comune in David Hume* (1964); J. B. Stewart, *The moral and political philosophy of David Hume* (New York 1963); F. A. Hayek, 'The legal and political philosophy of David Hume', *Studies in Philosophy, Politics and Economics* (London 1967), 106–21.

21. *A Treatise of Human Nature by David Hume*, ed. L. A. Selby-Bigge (Oxford 1888), 485.

22. *Treatise*, 494, 495.

23. *Treatise*, 486.

24. *Treatise*, 490.

25. Loc. cit.

26. *Treatise*, 491.

27. *Treatise*, 514.

28. *Treatise*, 533.

29. *Treatise*, 529.

30. *Treatise*, 526.

31. *Treatise*, 484.

32. *Treatise*, 525.
33. *Enquiries concerning the Understanding and concerning the Principles of Morals* (Oxford 1902), 192.
34. I. Berlin, 'Montesquieu', *Proc. British Acad.* 41 (1955) 267–96; For Hume's comments on Montesquieu, see *Enquiry*, 197.
35. An English translation was published in Aberdeen in 1756.
36. W. F. Tytler (Lord Woodhouselee), *Memoirs of the Life and Writings of Lord Kames*, 2nd edn, 3 vols. (1814).
37. H. Home, Lord Kames, *Elucidations respecting the Law of Scotland* (1777), vii–x.
38. H. Home, Lord Kames, *Historical Law Tracts* (1758), v.
39. Kames, *Elucidations*, xii.
40. D. Forbes, 'Scientific Whiggism: Adam Smith and John Millar', *Cambridge Journal*, 7 (1954) 646 ff.
41. Kames, *Historical Law Tracts*, ix–x.
42. Kames, *Historical Law Tracts*, 37.
43. Quoted by W. F. Tytler, *Kames*, i, 318.
44. Kames, *Historical Law Tracts*, 123–219.
45. H. Home, Lord Kames, *Principles of Equity*, 2nd edn (1767), 16.
46. W. F. Tytler, *Kames*, i, 218.
47. 'Account of the Life and Writings of Adam Smith', in *Essays on Philosophical subjects by the late Adam Smith*, 1795, xliii, cited by Forbes, op. cit. 646.
48. J. Millar, *An Historical View of English Government* (London 1812), ii, 429–30 n, cited by Forbes, loc. cit.
49. A. Giuliani, 'Adamo Smith, filosofo del diritto', *Riv. int. filosofia del diritto*, 31 (1954), 505–38; P. Stein, 'Osservazioni intorno ad Adamo Smith, filosofo del diritto', *Riv. int. fil. dir.*, 32 (1955), 97–100.
50. A. Smith, *Lectures on Justice, Police, Revenue and Arms*, ed. E. Cannan (Oxford 1896).
51. A. Smith, *Theory of Moral Sentiments*, 11th edn (London 1812), 86.
52. A. Smith, *Theory of Moral Sentiments*, 410–11.
53. *Edinburgh Review*, ix, 84.
54. 'The progress of science relative to Law and Government', in *Historical View*, iv, 283. For Millar, see W. C. Lehmann, *John Millar of Glasgow* (Cambridge 1960) and *Juridical Review* (1961), 218–33.
55. A. Smith, *Theory of Moral Sentiments*, 585, 605–6, 609.
56. A. Smith, *An Inquiry into the Nature and Causes of the Wealth of Nations*, ed. J. T. Rogers (Oxford 1869), i, 128.
57. A. Smith, *Wealth of Nations*, ii, 293.
58. A. Smith, *Wealth of Nations*, i, 15n.
59. J. Millar, *Historical View*, iv, 301.
60. A. Smith, *Theory of Moral Sentiments*, 137–8; cf. J. Millar, *Historical* iv, 267 ff.
61. A. Giuliani, 'Adamo Smith, filosofo del diritto', 534 ff.
62. J. Huizinga, *Homo ludens; A study of the play element in culture*, tr. R. F. C. Hull (London 1949), 79.
63. D. Hume, *Treatise*, 531.
64. W. C. Lehmann, *Adam Ferguson and the beginnings of modern sociology* (New York 1930); D. Kettler, *The social and political thought of Adam Ferguson* (Columbus, Ohio, 1965).
65. Edited with introduction by D. Forbes (1966).

66. A. Ferguson, *Essay*, 263, 165–6.
67. A. Ferguson, *Essay*, 263–4.
68. A. Ferguson, *Principles of Moral and Political Science* (London 1792), ii, 492.
69. A. Ferguson, *Principles*, ii, 144.
70. W. Robertson, 'View of the progress of society in Europe', in *History of the Reign of the Emperor Charles V* (The Works of Wm Robertson DD (Oxford 1825), iii, 59–60).
71. J. Millar, *The Origin of the Distinction of Ranks*, 4th edn (1806), 5.
72. J. Millar, *Historical View*, ii, 321. For comments on these works, see R. Meek, 'The Scottish contribution to Marxist Sociology', in *Democracy and the Labour Movement*, ed. J. Saville (London 1954), 84–102.
73. Autobiographical fragment in J. G. Lockhart, *Life of Sir Walter Scott* (1837), i, 58–9.
74. For a useful survey of these ideas in a wider context, see Bryson, *Man and Society : the Scottish Inquiry of the Eighteenth century* (Princeton 1945) and for selected extracts from their work, L. Schneider, *The Scottish Moralists on Human Nature and Society* (Chicago 1967).

8. *Education and Society in the Eighteenth Century*

DONALD J. WITHRINGTON

The passing of the Act of Union of 1707 is not itself directly significant for Scottish education. However, this is not to deny the influences which England had on Scottish educational thinking and practice both before and after 1707 : for instance, the impact of Lockeian ideas is easily discernible before the Union[1] and it has been shown that English publications were widely used as models for Scottish school textbooks throughout the 18th century.[2] There was undoubtedly a good deal of traffic in educational ideas (in both directions) across the border and there were many instances of English and Scots taking up work in teaching in the country other than the one of their birth and education.[3]

Then as now, schools and universities were always sensitive to the demands made on them by the society they were intended to serve. Scottish society was not changed suddenly in 1707; but even before the Union it was under strain from a developing commercialism which was, at length, to be quickened and enhanced through closer association with England. The resultant, increasingly more marked pressures within society were bound, therefore, to influence its educational establishments.[4] It is these pressures and influences, the forms they took and the effects they had on education, which this essay will endeavour to trace : and the main point of discussion will be the changes which took place in the curricula of schools and universities, especially in the first sixty years of the century.

The few large burghs in Scotland were well supplied with schooling at the beginning of the century. Each had its town's grammar school, supplemented by 'feeder' English (or Scots) schools which taught reading, writing and some arithmetic. Post-elementary subjects which lay outside the traditional grammar school curriculum were frequently available too in these larger burghs, taught separately from the other subjects and usually privately, but under the aegis and with the financial support of the burgh councils. Thus the earliest years of the century found French masters at work in both Edinburgh and Glasgow with the approval and assistance not only of the councils but of the local universities too.[5] No doubt commercial as well as cultural interest lay behind these appointments. The commercial stimulus to the teaching of navigation and book-keeping is even more certain. Robert Whytingdale was employed in Glasgow as 'fitt for teaching the airt of navigation, book-keeping, arithmetic and wryting' from 7 December 1695 until at least 1 April 1704[6]: then on 15 August 1710 a teacher of the same subjects was brought to Glasgow from London and was given an increase of salary on 21 May 1717 because it would be 'hard to get another as expert as he is to serve in that station'.[7] Meanwhile Edinburgh had appointed its accountant, once a merchant, as 'Professor of Book-keeping to the city' in 1705.[8]

In the cases of Edinburgh and Glasgow these extra-curricular subjects were quite certainly taught outside the public grammar and English schools, but the same situation did not obtain in the smaller burghs. Ayr and Dunbar in 1721 also provided teaching of navigation and book-keeping, while book-keeping was introduced in others of these smaller burghs such as Stirling (in 1728) and Perth (in 1729). In these towns, however, the new subjects were offered within the public grammar schools, either by the principal masters or by their assistants. Mathematics and geography were likewise added to the curricula of the smaller burgh schools at about the same time,[9] and the need for instruction in them was explained by the school doctor in Ayr in 1729 : he told the town council there that maps and globes were 'highly necessary for forming the man of business' and that 'as the world now goes, the mathematical part of learning is a principal part of a gentleman's education'.[10]

As commerce grew in strength in 18th-century Scotland so did the numbers wishing to study these directly useful subjects, especially among the merchants, burgesses and craftsmen of both large and small burghs but probably too among landowners and tenantry (not least those with an interest in improving their properties). This wide area of demand formed a positive and compelling inducement to curricular change and development in the burghs. There is evidence, however, that this movement towards adopting the newer subjects began – perhaps quite generally in the Lowlands – before the parliamentary Union.

In 1700 the synod of Glasgow decided to obtain opinions from its constituent presbyteries on the state of education in its area and to gather suggestions for improvements. There is no indication in the returns which have survived[11] of what stimulated the enquiry but the reasons for it may be fairly surmised. As is well known, the middle and later 1690s were years of widespread economic and social distress. In 1696 an act of parliament had reminded the heritors and tenants of their duty to secure a living to the parochial schoolmasters, for it seemed that in times of pinching scarcity it was an easy way of saving money not to pay the schoolmaster his stipend or fees.[12] And there is good reason to think that the situation of schools in parts of the west of Scotland within the synod's responsibilities had become precarious by the later 1690s.[13]

Yet the returns from the presbyteries of Dumbarton, Glasgow and Hamilton show very little concern indeed about the provision of schools in their bounds within the terms of the 1696 act.[14] Their replies are almost wholly taken up with the standard of the available schooling, with the calibre of the masters and with their methods of teaching. Thus, after a lengthy exposé of mostly minor and middling faults in English and grammar schools, the writer of the Dumbarton account ends his comments on the grammar schools in these words:

'And lastly, as the spring of all these faults, we may reckon the general insufficiency of masters. I desire to be charitable but I believe upon tryall it would be found that three parts of 4 of all the masters in the Kindgom are perfectly unfitt for the charge...And how can it be otherwise?...Ordinarily they that are preferred to this office are youths newly come from the university who, having been but ill taught in the Latine themselves, and not allowed time to repair their losses, can make but very indifferent masters themselves. Now the greatest reason of all this is the small provision that's made for that profession. What can a man do upon 3 or 4 hundred merkis?...Hence it comes about that young men, being preferred to this office and not finding it a competent livelyhood, make use of it only as a retirement for the qualifying themselves for the ministry where the emoluments are better.

Now untill this be mended, that is untill sufficient provision be made for scholemasters, it's utterly in vain to overture any thing upon the head, for money is the great instrument of all action; neither can anything be done successfully without it, for at this day there is not one school in the Kingdom sufficiently provided for, no not even in the great touns such as Edinburgh, Glasgow, Aberdeen, for though the principall masters have a considerable competency, yet the undermasters, who doe the greatest part of the work, have not sufficient for bread much less for books, and thence it is that the profession is fallen under the greatest contempt, so that a man of spirit, if he can possibly doe otherwise, will by no means engage in it. Now if either the state can be prevailed with to setle a more comfortable subsistence upon them, or the inhabitants of severall places of their own accord to make a fund for their more liberall maintenance, there may be some hopes that learning may flourish, but without this all things must remain as they are.'[15]

An interesting, and in many respects similar, view is expressed in a pamphlet entitled *Proposals for the Reformation of Schools and Universities, in Order to the Better Education of Youth, Humbly Offer'd to the Serious Consideration of the High Court of Parliament*, published in 1704 and attributed to Andrew Fletcher of Saltoun. The author is also vehement in his strictures on bad grammar-school teaching: 'There are in the Kingdom near to 1000 Parishes and in most of them Latine is pretended to be taught, though not one of 50 of the School-masters is capable to teach it : And no wonder, for not one of 50 of them was tolerably taught it.' But there is also in this pamphlet a great sense of grievance that higher education in the universities is so open and available to 'the Mechanicks and poorer sort of People': the complaint is made that 'One can make his Son what now with us passes for a Scholar, at a much cheaper Rate than he can breed him Shoe-maker or Weaver.' Fletcher sees that the poverty of these scholars keeps down, and for him keeps much too low, the cost of a university education: it restricts the length of the session, and because it holds down the rate of fees ensures that the regents' incomes are too small to attract good scholars to teach in the Scottish colleges. He wishes to see on offer an education which is much more nearly suited to some kind of Renaissance Christian gentleman. As it is, learning in Scotland is 'under disgrace and contempt' : it tends to 'unfitt a Scholar for a Gentleman and to render a Gentleman asham'd of being a Scholar....And till we Reconcile the Gentleman with the Scholar, 'tis impossible Learning should ever flourish. But were this once done, were Learning taken out of the hands of the Vulgar and brought to be as Honourable and Fashionable among the Gentry, as 'tis now contemptible, I think it would be indeed in a fair way of prospering.'[16]

Such complaints about the poor standard of instruction, with their analyses of causes, effects and social implications, form only one element in the assault which was being made on the schools and universities at this time. The return from the presbytery of Glasgow in 1700 also censured the current grammar schooling because it lacked reference to the real educational needs of the community at large, a point of attack far removed from that of Andrew Fletcher. In the words of the Glasgow reply, let

'non be admitted [to grammar schools] who are designed for trades and occupations in the world, wherein they cannot keep it nor yet have use of it, because it is a meer loosing of so much time and that of their best time for learning of things that may be more usefull for them....If it be objected that the learning of Latine is helpfull and usefull to them for their understanding of their own language etc., it may be Answered there are other things to be learned which are more needfull for them, that will be neglected by learning Latine. For caution here add...that it is fitt to make a difference here between those that follow their studies with a designe to gett a livelyhood in the Church or Commonwealth thereby and have no prospect of provision otherwise, and those who have no such designe but have provision to maintain themselves otherwise.'[17]

What then would those not aiming at preferment in the church or at a post in education or law or medicine be taught in their schools? It is not surprising that all the synod returns emphasize the inculcation of piety, virtue and good manners, the reading of the Bible and other worthy books. Beyond this, the Glasgow reply proposes that pupils in English schools or English classes in grammar schools should be taught 'to write weel and to read write [i.e. handwriting as well as print]; and to count also; some of the plainest and usefulest parts of Geometry and Geography; and musick, at least the common tunes [i.e. psalm tunes]; and History, especially of our own church and state.'[18] Those who went on to grammar schools were to go through this course beforehand.

The more predominantly rural presbytery of Hamilton made similar suggestions. It recommended that every parish should not attempt to employ its own Latin master and have a grammar school, because many could afford only inadequate classical masters and would have their children's education bedevilled by poor teaching : the main teaching in rural areas would be better carried on in English schools, well-secured financially because of having good numbers of pupils attracted by a broadened curriculum. In addition to the usual reading and spelling, the children should be taught 'the Fundamental Rules of Arithmetic, and the common Church Tunes; and if their Master could teach them the use of the Quadrant, compass and rule of proportion with some easie and pleasant problems in practical Geometry, it were so much the better.' Also, among the books which ought to be used would be 'some good compend of History.' Able children would be admitted from these schools to a 4 or 5 year public Latin school in the area, and would be instructed throughout the course there in English while Greek and Hebrew would be included in the 5th year. In the course of their grammar schooling the pupils would also study

'Roman and Greek Antiquities, a compend of all Trades and Sciences, Comenii Janua and Atrium, and particularly some knowledge of Geography, both by the globe and plain chart, especially the Geographia Veterum [which] were very profitable for schools and helpful to the understanding of history and reading it with pleasure; also some elements of chronology, all which may be rendered easie and delightful by Tables, draughts and pictures.'[19]

These sharply critical observations on the standard grammar school curriculum are very remarkable. It has been widely maintained that a change in attitude to the centrality of Latin in Scottish public 'secondary' schooling and to the introduction of newer subjects in the curriculum at all levels comes only towards the middle of the 18th century with the delayed post-Union commercial expansion and rising prosperity. Yet here we see, even before the Union, a readiness to doubt the value of a higher schooling given over entirely to the ancient languages. While classical learning was still accepted, of course, as a professional training for those going to be ministers, doctors, lawyers and schoolmasters, its teaching was denounced for repellant dullness. And just as Latin and Greek and Hebrew were practically useful and important for some employments, it was argued, so geography, history, navigation, mensuration and the like ought to be highly valued in the schooling of the merchant's or trader's or landowner's or tenant farmer's sons, destined to follow their fathers' occupations; moreover, since the newer subjects were generally useful and liberalizing they should be taught to the classical scholars as well.

We have seen that in the earlier 18th century changes which reflected at least some of these ideas were being implemented in the smaller burghs : there the range of subjects which was offered in the public schools was being extended. In contrast, however, the public grammar schools of the largest towns still retained their strict curriculum. Yet we need not assume that when a merchant put his son to such a grammar school the boy was restricted entirely to the Latin authors. Writing and accounts might be available within the school, taught privately by one of the masters;[20] and there is plenty of evidence that grammar school boys in the larger burghs could spend periods in the day, during or after the usual school hours, at a conveniently near French or dancing class or in a local mathematical school. It is thus somewhat misleading to contrast, as H. M. Knox does, the large burgh school where 'Latin was practically the only subject taught' with 'some of the smaller burgh schools which by their remoteness escaped the cramping influence of the university [and] offered a wider curriculum.'[21] Nor is the distinction between the organization of schools in larger and smaller burghs to be related only to the presence or absence of a university: it is much more closely related to the size of population on which the school could draw for its pupils. In a large burgh where there were sufficient pupils each year to form one reasonably-sized class which was beginning a full 4 or 5 year classical training (and which would provide good returns for one master throughout that course), it was both possible and sensible to maintain the unexpanded curriculum: in such a situation the erection of a separate school of, say, mathematics would be an economically sound proposition. Additional schools of this kind would be allowed or even provided by the town council, knowing that they were not likely to affect the livelihoods of the classical masters in the main school. In smaller burghs, on the other hand, it was frequently possible to contain the entire school population of the bounds within one building and usually within two classes – one given over to mainly English studies and the other to classics. Here there were not sufficient numbers in most cases to permit the setting up of separate schools of mathematics or other newer subjects without them drawing off pupils from the town's school: and it was unlikely that a private teacher could have made a living without spreading himself into the teaching of reading or writing and so directly threatening the incomes of the public schoolmasters. Most masters in these public schools were not overburdened with numbers in their classes in the earlier 18th century, and were more than ready themselves to offer additional subjects (at appropriately fat fees) for which there seemed to be a demand. And energetic parochial schoolmasters, in the more populous and wealthier parishes especially, could similarly extend the range of their teaching and their incomes.

The livings which public teachers in burgh and parochial schools could derive from the older curriculum are a vital factor, and one generally overlooked, in assessing the rise of the teaching of modern subjects in the earlier 18th century. We have seen that the smallness of the stipends allowed to public teachers was being complained of as early as 1700. The kirk sessions of rural parishes and the sessions and councils of the less affluent burghs, throughout the century, kept low and often maintained almost unchanged the scales of fees which they permitted their teachers to charge for the subjects they taught : this was especially true of the more 'mainstream' English and classical school subjects, and was done in a deliberate attempt to promote universal instruction in reading and writing in the burgh or parish and also to allow the able poor the greatest opportunities for improving their station through an extended education. In these circumstances, therefore, unless a teacher were able to keep the number of his pupils steady, his total income was likely to fall; and unless he could attract more and more scholars, his income was largely fixed. The inflation which hit Scotland hard in the 40 years or so after 1700 was thus crucial for the country's public schoolmasters.

Town council and kirk session records of the period contain very frequent pleas from their teachers for increases in stipend and, less often, in fees. It is in the later 1740s that we find the first instance of concerted action to obtain higher salaries, when meetings of parochial schoolmasters were held in Edinburgh in order to discuss and frame petitions to parliament for augmentation of the legal stipend laid down in the 1696 act.[22] The petitioning failed and the minimum and maximum levels of stipend fixed then remained in force throughout the 18th century. The schoolmasters' circumstances could only worsen in the face of a continuing inflation; and as they worsened so did the general standards of recruitment to and instruction in the public schools of Scotland.[23]

There was therefore an obvious stimulus throughout the century for schoolmasters, in parish as well as in burgh, to adopt new subjects which would produce additional income in fees. In general, these new subjects seem to have been introduced in the earlier years of the century according to a master's interests and expertise and according to his calculation of the likely response from his pupils' parents. On being applied to, councils and sessions would agree to them and to the level of fee to be charged. But to see such developments in the earlier part of the century as a sign of some concerted movement towards a new and principled curriculum is very probably to impose the thinking and practice of a later period. The emergence of a public 'writing or commercial school' in Dumfries in 1723 is unlikely to be more than a very marginal advance, if that, on older and generally haphazard developments.[24]

The casual and incidental introduction of the newer subjects in the public schools, in the separate classes of Latin and English in the smaller burghs or in landward parishes which could support more than one teacher, offered wide opportunities for acrimonious demarcation disputes over who should be permitted to teach what. We find councils and kirk sessions being applied to as arbitrators during the century, and their taking the chance to regulate the various masters' responsibilities. The 'authorities' could take a somewhat larger view of the situation than the disputants : they could try to assess community needs and to formulate a more deliberate curricular planning than had been previously attempted. Something of this kind seems to have occurred in Ayr in 1746, although there is no indication that it arose as the result of a dispute between the masters in the burgh school : indeed it is possible that it was prompted by the masters for educational rather than for personal reasons.

We are told that in 1746 the Ayr councillors 'after much deliberation adopted a method that appeared to them most proper for promoting the purposes of education, that is, the training up of youths in the knowledge of literature and preparing them for business in the most expeditious way possible.' They decided, therefore, to divide the burgh school into three distinct departments : one for classical training, one for teaching English subjects, the third offering instruction in arithmetic, book-keeping, geometry, navigation, surveying, algebra, other parts of mathematical sciences and parts of natural philosophy.[25] The appearance of so exceptionally comprehensive and settled an educational plan within one school appears to be new, not least as an example of local authority enterprise. In contrast, in Edinburgh (and probably also in Glasgow and Aberdeen) the setting up of commercial and mathematical schools had quickly become a matter for private and not public action : the town council protected its grammar school against the rivalry of private Latin masters but otherwise did not interfere.[26] The Ayr burgh school was remarkable after 1746 for being a single, publicly-run institution which comprehended all post-elementary schooling available in the area, classical and English and 'scientific'.

The relationship between the three departments of the Ayr school is not spelled out in the 1746 plan : it is likely that a parent could choose which department (even which subjects in more than one department?) he would send his son to, for we have no evidence of there being a settled and recommended course of study. By 1794, however, the relationship was clearer : in that year the Ayr town council passed a new set of regulations and invited subscriptions for a reorganized school which was to be given the formal and important title of 'academy'. The council now saw the school as 'one seminary' in which all pupils were expected – that is, if they took the full course – to complete their English and classical studies before going on to the scientific classes : 'the Grammar school instructions being over, it is proposed that by employing ten months of the year in teaching, and a proper arrangement of Classes, a complete course of the other parts of this Academical Education may be gone through in two years and a half, or at the most in three years.'[27]

In 1746, therefore, a scientific education might be had in place of a classical training in the local school; but in 1794 instruction in science subjects was to come after the school's classical course, and was to provide a substitute for attendance at a university. In 1746 the Ayr scheme had included this statement : 'The school will thus be converted into a kind of academy where almost every sort of the more useful kinds of literature will be taught and the want of college education in a great measure supplied.'[28] By 1794 this somewhat ambiguous reference to a 'want' of university education had been replaced by a very direct and unequivocal attack on the curriculum

N

and teaching of the Scottish universities. Since these universities mainly prepared their students for the learned professions, the education at them 'must from its nature be tedious and expensive, and ill-suited to the circumstances of the great bulk of people in a commercial country' : furthermore, university studies promoted 'speculative and indolent habits' in the young people who were sent to them. Thus the arguments against grammar schooling which we found in the Glasgow synod returns of 1700 were extended a century later to the next stage in the educational structure. In the 1790s, both in the Ayr regulations and in similar proposals for other academies set up at about the same time, university education is also characteristically complained of for the too-great expense of boarding out students in the university towns and for the assured moral dangers which faced the young lads who were sent there – 'they should have their Education more under the observation of their parents and friends than when sent to distant Colleges.'[29] The fact that these new academies were expected to provide a homely alternative to some parts of a university education is indicated clearly in a letter from the minister of Avoch in Ross-shire, written in 1791 at the erection of the academy at Fortrose : he had contacted Professor Robert Hamilton in Marischal College in Aberdeen about his recommending someone for a mathematical mastership in the school, and felt the need to add a word of reassurance for Hamilton:

'Our Academy at Fortrose will not probably interfere in the least with Alma Mater's interest, being chiefly intended for the benefit of those who cannot afford the time or expense of a compleat course of University Education. Besides this, almost all the University students from Ross and our neighbouring Counties are picked up by Mr Macleod of King's College and his connections, for all the clergy here except myself, having received their Education at Old Aberdeen, are perhaps too partial to that College.'[30]

These later-18th-century academies thus provided the customary English and classical schooling to be found elsewhere; but they added to it a course, lasting two or perhaps three years, comprising mainly scientific or 'practical' subjects, which gave the burgesses and other inhabitants in the neighbourhood a choice of sending their sons to a university or putting them to this cheaper (and pedagogically better?) alternative at home. It was therefore not the student interested in gaining qualifications for one of the professions who would attend the later years of the academy, unless his parents particularly wished him to do so before attending the college classes. The extra years at the academy were aimed rather at the sons of the burgesses and tenant farmers who were usually sent off to the university to attend a few of the classes there as 'occasional' and non-graduating students; that is, to take a selected mixed bag of, say, mathematics, natural philosophy, *belles lettres*, ethics, etc., chosen from the professors' public and private classes, probably with the addition of some extra-mural courses in such subjects as surveying or book-keeping. The academies at the turn of the 19th century provided a somewhat restricted but nonetheless very real threat to the incomes of university teachers : they might not draw off from the colleges many or any of those who wanted and could afford 'a compleat course of University Education', but it is doubtful if, at the end of the 18th century, the numbers of such students formed a large section of those who attended university classes. The resultant competition between universities and academies for the substantial numbers of 'occasional' students at the colleges was, however, no new thing. The academies set up at the close of the century were not the first in the field and the rivalry they provoked had already a lengthy history in Scotland.

There can be little doubt that the later academies owed a great deal to the example of Perth in 1760 when the town council there founded its academy, the first public establishment to bear the title in Scotland. But in terms of later developments such as we have seen, the Perth foundation has one striking difference : in 1760 the town's grammar school was left undisturbed at the erection of the new and quite separate two-year school 'for Arts and Sciences'.[31] Indeed Perth did not combine the local classical school and the academy in one set of buildings or under one plan until 1807, until it in turn had been influenced by the newer style of foundation of that later period.[32] Why then was Perth so early in setting up its academy, and why did that academy take the form that it did?

The narrative of its establishment in 1759–60 states that gentlemen of the town and neighbourhood had 'for a long time expressed a desire of having some of the most essential parts of Science' taught in the place.[33] They had doubtless been pressed hard to do so by Mr John Bonar, minister of the West Church in Perth. As long before as 1752, Bonar had published a sermon he gave to the annual meeting of the SSPCK : in that sermon he concluded that national progress depended on the attention paid to science. 'By the flourishing of art and science, one nation becomes really superior to another…in proportion as the scale of science rises or falls, that of the kingdom rises or falls with it.' Bonar then goes on:

'Was I now to discourse on education in general, this would be the proper place to mention the study of science : but as many have undertaken that part of the subject, I shall confine myself entirely to a religious education; only observing, with regard to the other part, that the study of science is not only an ornament to the mind, but of real advantage in life : of advantage to private persons, and of advantage to society. Thereby a habit of labour is acquired, application becomes less troublesome, and the several powers of the soul are expanded and enlarged. It draws off the youth from idleness, play and debauchery. It usefully fills up those vacant hours which otherwise would hang heavy upon their hands, and gives to the mind an exact and regular way of thinking.'[34]

The implicit criticism here of the effects of a non-scientific (i.e. standard classical?) education is to be noted.

The memorial prepared by Bonar for the Perth council, proposing the erection of its academy eight years later, rests on analogous ideas. He saw it as important that the teaching of science should be expanded and brought into the education of merchants, mechanics and farmers. Some science training was available to the lawyer, physician and divine in the universities, but few of the other groups were able to afford the time or great expense of attending a university 'according to the present Plann of Education' there. Perth, being 'at a considerable distance from any of the Universitys' and a place where the youth would be in much less moral danger than when away from home 'in any of our great Towns', was therefore a good site for an academy for the teaching of science : the new institution could even 'cooperate with the National Plan of Improving and Civilising the Highlands'. A further advantage, Bonar maintained, was the flourishing state of the grammar school : academy students could attend classes there in order to perfect their Latin, Greek and French while 'the Ushers in the Grammar School might be of great use to the Gentlemen in the Accademy in the way of private Tutors, either for the Languages or any Branch of Science.'[35] The prospect of some advanced language scholars for the rector of the grammar school and of tutoring fees for his assistants was intended, no doubt, to turn aside their predictable fears that the new academy might reduce the number of their pupils. Bonar also went out of his way to convince the councillors and citizenry of Perth that his scheme would bring them personal as well as mere educational advantages : the academy, he claimed, would 'keep a good sale of money in the place which otherwise must be spent at a distance in the Education of those who are now sent to Universitys' and also 'not only bring young people from a distance but considerable Familys to settle in the place, the Benefite of which must be immediately perceived by all employed in any Trade or Bussines.'[36]

Perth Academy was, therefore, to be the new local college for the growing middle classes of a town experiencing the benefits of rapid commercial expansion.³⁷ It would serve as a commercial school of the highest standing and would offer a highly concentrated practical scientific education at a much cheaper rate (2 guineas per scholar) than an overlong, under-taught course at a university. The universities, indeed, would be left for those who could endure the style of teaching, to those who might benefit rather than suffer from the freedom and unfilled spare time associated with university study, to those who could and wished to afford it, and to those – typically the lads o' pairts, few as they might be – who needed a full university training in order to enter one of the professions. The others would find all that they required in education in Perth itself. Bonar's views were accepted by the town council and the academy's two masters began teaching in August 1761.³⁸

Bonar's memorial was on the whole only gently disparaging – in 18th-century terms, that is – to the Scottish universities. Another minister, William Thom of Govan, soon afterwards published anonymously a bitter assault on them, directed particularly at his local university in Glasgow. The first of a series of pamphlets which he published for this purpose in 1762 was entitled : *Letter to J——— M——, Esq., on the Defects of an University Education and its Unsuitableness to a Commercial People : with the Expediency and Necessity of erecting at Glasgow an Academy for the Instruction of Youth.*

Thom launches out with a tirade against the waste of over a session spent in Glasgow on logic and metaphysics : he adds that if the college regulations had allowed students to go straight from Latin and Greek to ethics then many more parents would have sent their sons to the university; but as it was the professors insisted that students passed through the needless subtleties of the logic class in their second year. He repeats an old complaint in saying that there was little value to 'a commercial people' in what the university invited their children to study in its standard curriculum. The education which ought to have been available should have included practical mathematics, history in general and the history of Britain and her commercial neighbours in particular, natural history, geography, the history of commerce, and a course in 'practical morality'. His and others' hopes that Glasgow would follow Marischal College's lead of 8 or 10 years before, when its faculty had 'accommodated their course to modern times', had been disappointed, and one reason for Glasgow's unwillingness to change was the lack of competition in the area – 'be the Professors ever so slothful there is no College near to receive the Students from them'.³⁹

Thom also complains that the professors recommend students to attend too many classes in one session, not only those in the basic curriculum but their own private classes besides; and comments sharply that 'we, who ourselves contrive schemes of profit, can easily see for whose benefit the multiplicity of private classes was first set on foot and continues still to be pursued'.[40] There were social pressures at work too in prompting attendance at these extra classes – 'It was esteemed honourable to attend many classes, it was thought shameful and a mark of poverty to be at few' – and the resultant spread of attention and effort left 'an inclination to ramble in pursuit of knowledge [which] stuck fast with us after we left university'.[41] The Glasgow professors, even more than the curriculum, are Thom's main point of attack. Having noted their rapacity in setting up private classes, he condemns the lack of proper professorial concern for their teaching : they had much too little contact with their students, hardly ever directing a student's reading and merely appearing for an hour or so each day to deliver their lectures – as Thom recalled it, 'our professors loved rank and kept themselves at greater distance from their scholars than common schoolmasters do'[42] and they continued to teach their students 'an hour or two and then send them adrift...so little looked after, and having so much time to play, that the lesson, so harshly read over to them, is neglected and immediately forgot'.[43]

Thom believed that the erection of an academy in Glasgow would remedy all these ills. It would be possible to recruit abler teachers than did the university, which mostly appointed professors through 'connection' and not because of their abilities.[44] Longer hours of well-supervised teaching would be offered in the academy, and each year of its course would comprise subjects properly related to each other and chosen so as not to confuse or distract. Thom then sums up : 'If gentlemen's sons made a competent progress in classical learning [i.e. at grammar schools] and were besides instructed in the several things proposed to be taught at the Academy, we aver that they would have a far more complete and genteel school-education than has ever been publicly given in this country.'[45]

It is difficult to decide just how serious Thom was in proposing the establishment of an academy in Glasgow. He mentions the new curriculum at Marischal College and the new academy at Perth and appears to assume that there was already general discussion of educational reform at the time. But it is more than possible that he merely judged it an appropriate moment to draw particular attention to the sorry state of university education in Glasgow, as he saw it and perhaps knowingly exaggerated it, in the hope that by threatening the professors with the direct rivalry of a well-supported alternative college, which would take away both students and fees, he would convince them of their need for reform as well as shame them into it. There seems, at any rate, to have been no move by the town council of Glasgow to act on Thom's suggestion or to follow the Perth example. As was the case in Edinburgh, the range of private teaching available in Glasgow would have provided the facilities which its merchants and traders wanted without the need to dip into the city's funds : those who wished to use these facilities could pay for them. There was no pressure on the town councils of the two largest cities, as there was on those in smaller burghs, to enter into schemes of comprehensive educational planning on their own accounts.[46]

Having reviewed some at least of the motives for the promotion of academies in 18th-century Scotland, can we now judge what constituted the so-called 'academy movement'? In both mid and later 18th-century developments a few common elements stand out. Firstly, academies were publicly organized institutions, not to be confused with private establishments; they were usually supported by subscription funds, but either their management was immediately in the hands of the local burgh councils or the local councillors had a very considerable influence in the controlling bodies; the academies were establishments mainly intended in their higher studies for the middle and upper ranks of the local society, with the addition usually of a few bursaries for poor but able boys. Secondly, the academies offered alternative courses to those in the universities to the extent that they were intended to reduce or remove the need for certain groups of post-grammar schoolboys being sent away from home for a general and perhaps rather inchoate scientific training to those universities. Within these common factors, there are to be found distinctions between the formative attitudes of the 1760s and those of the 1790s and 1800s. In 1760 the academy at Perth (and the one mooted for Glasgow) were meant to be separate local colleges for higher instruction; they were to be 'end-on' (in modern parlance) to the grammar schools, would-be equivalents to the universities in level but not in kind or manner of instruction. (Is this the distinction which caused the Ayr burgh councillors in 1746 to hold back from calling *their* reorganized school an academy?) By the 1790s science courses in the newer academies had become part of a composite school unit, and were being recommended as continuations of a general education available in the English and grammar departments; the courses formed a worthwhile practical training in themselves at a middling sort of level and were also valuable as a preliminary to higher instruction in a similar range of studies at the university.

By the 1790s, therefore, a form of arrangement had become the model which was closer to the Ayr scheme of 1746 than to that of

Perth in the 1760s. It seems, indeed, that the Perth – Glasgow idealism of the 1760s had failed to catch on, and that the reasons for this failure are to be found in the universities rather than in the schools. No less than the schools, the universities were responding – in the long run and in their own ways – to the new educational demands of a changing society.

The universities found that they could not disregard the growing demands for new subjects or for different emphases within the teaching of the traditional curriculum : they had to be ready to change if they were to thrive or, perhaps in one or two cases, even to survive. Edinburgh, in the course of the century, showed the others clearly what could be achieved in attracting greater numbers of students. As early as 1741 the professors there had multiplied the numbers of 'colleges' or classes which they taught – Colin Maclaurin offered as many as four mathematics classes, John Stevenson provided two logic classes and even Charles Mackie, professor of the new subject of history, had two classes (both of which, oddly enough, he taught in Latin).[47] While good and proper pedagogical reasons might be brought forward for these developments, early in Edinburgh and rather later elsewhere, it is hardly to be doubted that it was their financial attractiveness to the teachers which was of the first importance.

It is worth noting that Edinburgh and Glasgow – universities which served increasingly populous areas and could thus draw in large numbers of students in any case – tended to tamper little with the stated curriculum but greatly extended the teaching of private classes and of extra subjects : these same universities also soon drew off the ablest (and most worldy conscious?) teachers from the others. The reputation of Edinburgh, and later in the century that of Glasgow, were important factors here, but so was the lure of large classes and of a steady and worthwhile income.[48] By the time that the University Commission of 1826–30 was taking evidence, there were growingly insistent complaints that the teaching of private classes was distracting the professors from their first duties to the public classes within the degree curriculum : Thom's caustic comments in 1762 were repeated. The income which could be derived from a popular private class might, indeed, be very considerable. An excellent instance of what could be earned in this way in Edinburgh (and above all other university towns in *Edinburgh*) is given in a letter from Henry Cockburn to T. F. Kennedy in 1826 : although taken from a later period than the one presently under scrutiny, this example shows well how financially attractive a private class could be. In fact the class referred to was not only extra-curricular but it was taught to a group of very occasional, non-matriculated students –

'The fashionable place here now is the College; where Dr Thomas Charles Hope lectures to ladies on Chemistry. He receives 300 of them by a back window, which he has converted into a door. Each of them brings a beau, and the ladies declare that there never was anything so delightful as these chemical flirtations. The Doctor is in absolute extacy with his audience of veils and feathers, and can't leave the Affinities, The only thing that inwardly corrodes him, is that in an evil moment, when he did not expect to draw £200, he published that he was to give the fees to found a Chemical prize, and that he can't now retract, though the said fees amount to about £700. Horrible ——. I wish some of his experiments would blow him up. Each female student would get a bit of him.'[49]

The problems which faced the larger universities at Edinburgh and Glasgow in securing adequate incomes for their teachers were simple by comparison with those which faced smaller universities in less populous and less prosperous regions. In St Andrews and in Old and New Aberdeen these problems were aggravated by the existence in each area of more than one college. There, separate institutions vied with each other in attracting the relatively fewer students which their hinterlands provided : and the bad inflationary years of the 1730s and 1740s hit particularly hard at the masters' incomes. As a result two of the three St Andrews colleges began negotiations for their union in 1738, apparently the only means open to the regents to save the colleges and themselves from ruin. These negotiations may well have prompted the faculties in Old and New Aberdeen to consider seriously a similar union. In the later 1730s Marischal College was in a very poor way, its buildings being very badly dilapidated. So great indeed was the regents' anxiety for their future that they took the unprecedented step of renouncing part of their incomes from general college funds to start a subscription for new buildings : the town council of New Aberdeen then granted a year's revenue from the bursary monies and recommended the project to private benefactors.[50] Although it appeared to have nothing to worry about in respect of buildings at the time, from the little we do know about King's College it was also clearly hard pressed financially. These two small universities, Marischal and King's, barely one mile apart, seem to have been well forward with their discussions for a union in early 1747, significantly the year in which the union of St Leonard's and St Salvator's Colleges in St Andrews was later to be completed : developments in the north-east in the following decade merit our particular attention.

It is not to be doubted that there were important and honest educational reasons for Marischal and King's to push forward with a scheme of union : but a memorial from the inhabitants of New Aberdeen in 1747 contended that the college regents wished for union 'of purpose to augment their own salaries'.[51] This memorial also reflected a growing apprehension in New Aberdeen that, with the buildings at King's still in much better condition than those at Marischal, a united university would be sited in Old Aberdeen. The threat of the removal of their college from the seaport-burgh to its decayed neighbour was enough to turn the New Aberdeen town council entirely against union – unless, of course, it was decided to locate the united university within *its* bounds.[52] In the face of the ensuing impasse, the idea of union was dropped for a time; and the prospects of both groups of regents and professors remained dim.

The years which immediately followed 1747 gave little if any relief from the financial difficulties which beset each of the Aberdeen colleges. It is important to note how much attention was given by both faculties to their 'oeconomy', including much-needed investigation of their landholdings and other investments. It is no coincidence that in 1753 both produced new regulations for their regular courses of study : both needed desperately to increase the number of students in attendance, and neither dared let the other steal a march in this matter. It is very likely indeed, that the distatisfactions with the older university curriculum which we have noted in the south were also to be heard in the north and north-east : perhaps the regents had become uncomfortably aware of the appearance of modern subjects in schools in New Aberdeen and elsewhere in their area, and believed that this was causing the numbers of students to decline.[53]

Marischal College made its move first. On 11 January 1753 the faculty concluded that 'the present order of teaching Philosophy, introduced by the scholastics, is, since the reformation in Philosophy, very improper' because it forced students to deal with abstractions about evidence and reasoning before they had much knowledge of particular facts on which they could learn to reason.[54] Moreover, so much time had to be spent on logic and metaphysics that none was left for 'some very useful parts of knowledge'. The faculty therefore suggested a new arrangement of the classes which would follow a first year still given over to Latin and Greek : the remainder of the course would begin with particular facts (a second year comprising mathematics, natural history, geography and civil history), would then proceed to general reasonings on familiar, material objects (a third year which included scientific parts of natural philosophy, mechanics, hydrostatics, pneumatics, optics, astronomy and newer topics such

as magnetism and electricity), and would reach in the last year
abstruser enquiries about the mind, the Deity, and moral and natural
philosophies founded on them (the philosophy of the spirits, pneuma-
tology, ethics and logic). The old regenting system was to end and
professors were to be fixed to a particular branch of philosophy, i.e.
to a stated year and part of the course. In framing the new curriculum
they hoped 'that the following this natural order will tend to render
the study of the Sciences [i.e. all learning] more advantageous in life
than it is generally thought to be, and will remove the prejudices some
have entertained against University Education as useless'.[55] By 1755
when Alexander Gerard, one of the philosophy professors, wrote
and published an official apologia for the new *Plan of Education in the
Marischal College and University of Aberdeen, with the Reasons of It*, he
was able to state that the professors 'have already begun to experience
the public approbation, by the increase of the number of their
students'.[56]

On 17 August 1753 a committee laid before a meeting of the faculty
in King's College a very extensive set of new regulations, dealing with
the length of the session, bursaries, students' lodgings within college
and the college meals, and a revised curriculum. The teaching session
was proposed to be extended by a month, beginning in early October
and not early November; the uniting of small bursaries would, it was
thought, make a more adequate provision for their holders over the
lengthened session; and it was suggested that all students should be
obliged to lodge in College rooms, under the direct educational and
moral care of their masters, unless given a contrary permission by the
principal or sub-principal. In these matters the committee went
beyond the Marischal proposals : but the revised curriculum which
was produced was all but identical to that agreed on by the Marischal
regents several months earlier. After a first year devoted to Greek,
students were to attend classes in mathematics (speculative and
practical), in some more Greek and in an introduction to all the
branches of natural history; the third year was to be given over to
mathematics, and natural and experimental philosophy; and finally
came a year 'to be employed in the Philosophy of the Human Mind,
and the Sciences that depend upon it'. The committee noted that it
had discussed the advantages and disadvantages of changing from a
regenting to a fixed class system, and had finally decided against any
alteration. Another proposal from the committee stated : in order

'that the Students may have the benefit of those parts of Education
which are not commonly reckoned Academical, such as dancing,
writing, book-keeping, French, etc., without losing time in attending Masters at a distance from the College, the Sub-principal and

Regents shall appoint proper rooms in the College, and proper hours when these things may be taught, and shall bespeak Masters of the best characters and qualifications for instructing those who choose to attend them'.[57]

The King's College teachers seem, therefore, to have tried to match those at Marischal College in their revision of the standard curriculum and to remove any advantage that the latter had in the easy availability in New Aberdeen of a range of extra-curricular classes. The rest of the committee's proposed changes were probably intended to impress the northern clergy and schoolmasters on whom King's had always depended for their students: in order to have these supposedly conservative groups swallow the much-altered curriculum, they offered more teaching time for the same fees and the attraction of larger bursaries for competition by their scholars; and it was presumably also thought that King's would gain approval and more students by going against the increasing non-residence which was permitted in other colleges, including Marischal, by affirming that all students not exempted would be always 'under the eye and authority of the Masters'.

A few additions and slight alterations were made to the committee's scheme in April 1754 after correspondence on the subject with 'alumni and other well-wishers of the College'. The necessity to lodge in College was no longer to apply to gentlemen's sons who boarded with the regents and professors – a fairly obvious attempt to attract boarders and so increase the teachers' incomes; as a result of representations from the correspondents it was agreed that the importance of classical learning be emphasized, and thus Latin and Greek were to be taught two hours per week to each of the three philosophy years as well as in the first year; the proposal that the professor of Humanity should teach gratis all classes in addition to his stated, first year class was withdrawn – 'gratis teaching is a thing that will probably turn to no account'.[58]

Despite Gerard's remark that the Marischal changes had resulted in a rise in student numbers by 1755, it appears that both colleges revived their earlier union negotiations in that same year: it is unlikely that matters had improved very noticeably. Once again the attempt at union failed because of disagreements over the siting of the united university, even though the Earl of Findlater was asked to arbitrate on this occasion. Once more the likelihood that Old Aberdeen would be accepted as the better location brought vigorous opposition from the council of the seaport-burgh: and among the points which the council brought to Findlater's notice was the following: 'The inhabitants of Aberdeen are so anxious about having the seat in the town of Aberdeen, that if it were to be otherwise, they would be provoked to set up private Academies for the conveniency of their children's education; and there is too great reason to fear such would be greatly disaffected to our happy establishments both in church and state, and so debauch the minds and morals of the youth, and mislead them in their principles of religion and government',[59] a reminder to the noble earl about the still recent Jacobite troubles in the north and about the well-known private academies set up in that area by renowned Jacobites like William Meston.[60] In the end no settlement was reached and the two small colleges continued to scratch out a somewhat meagre and cheerless existence.

The road was apparently rougher for King's than it was for Marischal. By 1759 the sub-principal and two of the three regents in King's College had decided that the plan of education and discipline passed six years before was 'encumbered with such difficulties and attended with such bad consequences, that they have determined to make some changes in it'.

The first alteration they hoped to see was a return to a shorter session, beginning in early November : 'since the late Alterations made in the length and expense of the session, the Number of Students at this College has greatly diminished'. Uniting the bursaries since 1745 had badly affected attendance too : 'our bursars are reduced from fifty-three to thirty-four; by this means the benefit of a good education is confined to a smaller number; we have no Alumni to teach in Schools or Gentleman's families, those of Marischal College are employed, and they naturally do all they can to support their Alma Mater and to hurt ours.' It was hinted, too, that the patrons of bursaries not in the College's hands were finding it difficult to get applicants for them, since they were thought too small in value to pay for the extended session : these patrons were now considering uniting *their* bursaries, which would result in still fewer students in attendance – 'the consequence of this will be, that the teaching Masters must starve unless they exact a double or triple fee from such Bursars, and then their Numbers will decrease so fast as not to leave the Appearance of a College'. The contrast which King's seemed to be making with Marischal was particularly galling :

'For the Number of Students in the neighbouring College, where they have kept the old session of five or six months, has increased every year for some years past. And ever since the Alteration of our Session, the Number of Students there has been more than double of ours, a thing never known before, and the disproportion is daily increasing insomuch that they had last winter twenty in their first class and we had but thirteen or fourteen, whereof two

or three only were Libertines [i.e. students not holding bursaries].
It appears from this how little encouragement we have had from
the Gentlemen and Clergy of this Country. Tho our Plan be good
in Theory, the Taste and Circumstances of the Country render it
unfit and impracticable in the Execution.'[61]

But the meeting of faculty on 31 October 1759 resolved narrowly to
stand by the 1754 regulations.

Not until January 1760 was there any further discussion on the
topic, when the professor of Humanity pointed out that the attendance of second, third and fourth year philosophy students on his
special classes for them was very poor, and yet it had been made
compulsory in 1754. Principal John Chalmers retorted with a quite
brutal attack on the humanist for not being able to drum up students
for his first year class, never mind attract them to him later on : Chalmers maintained that 'now that he has no scholars of his own, he
makes an attempt to frighten away the students from the other
Professors.' Having remarked that if the humanist had his way, the
result would be to drive students out of the College and give the
country the opportunity to decry the faculty as tyrants and oppressors,
Chalmers then gives his general views of a university education in
1760 in these words :

'It is well known that Students do attend the Universities with many
Views. And now that Education is put upon a more rational and
useful footing, there are many Students who know nothing either
of Latin or Greek. Their plans and schemes for Life do not depend
upon the knowledge of these Languages, and yet by attending the
other classes they may learn a great deal of useful Knowledge. And
therefore the Principal apprehends that it is highly inexpedient, as
well as unreasonable, to think of fixing down one uniform and
determined scheme of education, so as to oblige every individual
Student to learn the same things. The Genius and Capacity of the
Student, his situation and connexions in Life, and the Views and
inclinations of his Parents and his friends must be regarded and a
great deal of Latitude must be allowed on these Accounts. And
therefore much must be left to the discretion of the Master under
whose particular tuition the Student is, and to whose care he is
principally committed. The Professor who pays a just regard to
these things, and keeps them steadily in his View, will always be
respected and regarded. His authority will encrease, and his reputation as a teacher will rise in proportion to his Practice. But if
things are carried so far, as to say, that no Student shall be allowed
to learn Mathematics or Philosophy unless he learns Hebrew and
Greek and French and Latin etc., we expose our Authority to

contempt, and instead of establishing an useful plan, we do all that
we can to defeat the purposes of a free and of a Liberal education.'[62]
This statement, made in the same year as the creation of Perth
Academy and preceding Thom's published attack on the Glasgow
insistence on a fixed progress through its stated curriculum, is notable
indeed. It shows well that, within the universities, there were those
prepared to argue for the greatest amount of flexibility as a means of
gaining students – no doubt because of the welcome income which
would be brought by the occasional and non-graduating students to
whom Chalmers refers (and who were certainly much needed at
King's College); but also and importantly because the task of the
universities in the community was seen as having outgrown an earlier
strong emphasis on training for the learned professions. The service
which universities were to give society was now to go much beyond
this. True, the old curriculum could be retained for bursars and for
others who wished to enter the professions and, generally speaking,
it was – although, as we have seen, both King's and Marischal Colleges were prepared to liberalize the traditional curriculum even for
these students. But it was vital to expand the teaching and to relax
older restrictions on attendance at classes if the universities were to
grow or even to hold their own against a new-style competition from
the schools.

Thus the universities of Scotland showed themselves to be in the 18th
century differently but nicely sensitive to the educational demands
which a changing society was making on them. Their general readiness to allow or promote change, more marked in some universities
than in others and slow as it was in the earlier period, ensured that
they survived their antagonists' sallies and the reduced student numbers of the first sixty years of the century. The public academy movement, which in the 1760s had seriously attempted to draw off some of
those students who still went to the universities, seems not to have
gained the strength its protagonists had hoped for. Perhaps the Scottish middle classes, in contrast to those in England, having been long
used to sending their sons to a university, still had an attachment to
them (born of an honoured tradition) even in their darkest days.[63]
At any rate the universities met the new challenge, survived through
adapting themselves still further to public demands and grew in
esteem. By the last years of the century the older academy movement
had itself altered, probably in response to the revived or reviving
fortunes of most of the universities : a new (or perhaps revised) form
of academy appeared, providing an extended but greatly liberalised
higher schooling, still including grammar as an important feature of

its course, probably instituted in order to obtain and pay for better teaching at school level as much as to offer a restricted alternative training to that available in the universities. Awareness of the changing nature of 18th-century society itself promoted among the professors and schoolmasters some serious reflection about the purposes which Scottish education – at all levels – was intended to fulfil. But in both schools and universities, throughout the century, the elemental challenge of their teachers' declining incomes was the greatest stimulus of all to a rethinking of their educational aims and practice.

NOTES

1. E.g. in the return of the presbytery of Dumbarton to an overture anent schools before the synod of Glasgow in 1700: 'The minds of children are empty and rude: if therefore their empty minds be not furnished with usefull knowledge, and their rude minds formed with suitable manners, their native ignorance will be confirmed into a stupidity and their originall roughness into a savage brutishness' (NLS Wodrow MSS, F. xxxv, 6).

2. A. Law, *Education in Edinburgh in the Eighteenth Century* (London 1965), 193–215.

3. The influence of Scots in the English academy movement, for instance, has not yet been carefully enough looked into. N. Hans, *New Trends in Education in the 18th Century* (London 1951) and J. W. Ashley Smith, *The Birth of Modern Education: the Contribution of the Dissenting Academies* (London 1954) do little more than mention it in passing. Smith particularly refers to tutors who received some part of their education in Scotland, usually a university training, but does not attempt to distinguish expatriate Scots from English dissenters. Hans (p. 22) does note 'an important minority of Scotsmen who migrated to England and settled there to practise their professional knowledge acquired in Scotland' and adds that 'their contribution to English intellectual life was considerable': but he does not work out this point in respect of Scots who took up teaching appointments in the south.

4. This is not at all to imply that the educational developments we are to trace should, in any direct way, be seen as the result of some potent but undefined anglicisation: the evidence for such a view is very meagre. Many other factors were at work in changing Scottish society.

5. *Charters and other Documents relating to the City of Glasgow*, ed. J. D. Marwick and R. Renwick (Glasgow 1906), ii (1649–1707): 2 June 1691, 19 February 1698 and 1 April 1714 when 'the provost represented that some tyme ago the principal of the university had proposed to him and others of the magistrates that for the good of the place a French school might be sett up.' See also A. Law, *Education in Edinburgh*, 165–7.

6. *Charters relating to Glasgow*, ii. This reference to the teaching of book-keeping is apparently a very early one (A. Law, *Education in Edinburgh*, 169–70).

7. *Charters relating to Glasgow*, ii.
8. A. Law, *Education in Edinburgh*, 168. By 1768 it was being said that Edinburgh was overstocked with teachers of book-keeping (*ibid.*, 171).
9. W. Boyd, *Education in Ayrshire through Seven Centuries* (London 1961), 75 ; J. Grant, *History of the Burgh Schools of Scotland* (London 1876), 402.
10. W. Boyd, *Education in Ayrshire*, 75–6. References to the purchase of maps for grammar schools need to be treated with care : the maps were frequently used only to help in the teaching of Roman and Greek antiquities and as a supplement to language teaching, rather than for instruction in general geography (A. Law, *Education in Edinburgh*, 75–6).
11. I.e. the ones which the writer has found so far and which are in the Wodrow MSS in the NLS.
12. See 'Schools in the presbytery of Haddington in the 17th century' in *Transactions of the East Lothian Antiquarian and Field Naturalists' Society* (Haddington 1963), ix, 90–111.
13. E.g. in Ayrshire : *Munimenta Universitatis Glasguensis* (Glasgow 1854), ii, 547–8.
14. This seems to confirm the claim that in the Lowlands at least the 1696 act was not required in order to plant schools : see 'Lists of Schoolmasters teaching Latin, 1690' in *Miscellany of the Scottisl History Society* (1965), x, 121–42.
15. NLS Wodrow MSS, F. xxxv, 6.
16. op. cit., 3–5. The probability that Fletcher wrote this pamphlet is argued by R. A. Scott Macfie in his 'A Bibliography of Andrew Fletcher of Saltoun' in *Papers of the Edinburgh Bibliographical Society*, (1901), iv (1899–1901), 117–48. Similar views to Fletcher's about the too widely-spread opportunities for grammar schooling are found in England at the time of the Restoration, while complaints about the narrowness of the grammar curriculum are also prominent there – corresponding to the criticisms of the returns to the Glasgow synod – in the later 17th century : see two good studies by W. A. L. Vincent, *The State and School Education 1640– 1660 in England and Wales* (London 1950) and *The GrammarSchools, their Continuing Tradition 1660–1714* (London 1969).
17. NLS Wodrow MSS, F. xxxv, 8.
18. Ibid., 8.
19. Ibid., 11.
20. A. Law, *Education in Edinburgh*, 75.
21. H. M. Knox, *Two Hundred and Fifty Years of Scottish Education, 1696–1946* (1952), 12.
22. N. Morren, *Annals of the General Assembly of the Church of Scotland 1739–52* (1838), 376–83 ; *Scots Magazine* (1750), xii, 487–92. The minimum stipend had been fixed in 1696 at 100 merks Scots and the maximum at 200 merks.
23. See J. M. Beale, *A History of the Burgh and Parochial Schools of Fife from the Reformation to 1872* (unpublished Ph.D. thesis, University of Edinburgh, 1953), 234–350 and especially 341–6. The *Old Statistical Account* contains good comment about the poverty of teachers, particularly parochial schoolmasters in the landward areas, towards the end of the century. The minister of Kemback in Fife

O

states that 'at present, the salaries and perquisites of established schoolmasters in the country are, in general, so exceedingly small, that they do not exceed, and often hardly equal, the wages of an ordinary mechanick' (vol. xiv (1795), 308). The minister of St Andrews Lhanbryde, near Elgin, is more expansive : 'Since by the alteration of the times, the salaries of schoolmasters can in no ways support a family, that office has fallen altogether into the hands of mere school-boys, which they abandon as soon as their own education is supposed to be completed, or into that of bankrupt tenants, still less qualified for the duties of it. So that a thicker cloud of ignorance must be settling over the lower ranks of the people, than that which covered their fathers. And while the reputation for learning which Scotland has so long supported among the nations must in a short time be lost, those numbers who, by means of the mediocrity of literature acquired in the parish schools, rose from the lowest stations of life to merit, wealth and rank, must hence-forth be chained down, hopeless and inglorious, to the miserable sphere of their humble birth.' (vol. ix, (1793), 178–9).

24. H. M. Knox, *Scottish Education 1696–1946*, 13, oversimplifies the situation, which is altogether more soundly treated in A. Bain, *Education in Stirlingshire from the Reformation to the Act of 1872*, (London 1965) 132–3.

25. W. Boyd, *Education in Ayrshire*, 76–7. In 1776 and in 1779 the Elgin town council minuted disputes between its Latin and English masters 'on account of their interfering with one another's province' ; but no move was made to unite the schools until 1790. Disputes did not always lead immediately to the formation of a composite school. (*Records of Elgin*, ed. W. Cramond (Aberdeen 1908), ii, 425–8).

26. A. Law, *Education in Edinburgh*, 146–7.

27. W. Boyd, *Education in Ayrshire*, 77.

28. *Air Academy and Burgh Schule, 1233–1895*, (Ayr 1895), 52–3. In the report of the managers in 1804 it is stated that whereas some of the principal schools in Scotland prepared students for the universities by a good classical education and others were 'more particularly subservient to the mercantile profession and the cultivation of the useful arts', the academy at Ayr had aimed to 'unite the advantages of both these plans'. In 1804 the full course there comprised 3 years at the English school (from age 5 to 8), 5 years at the grammar school (8 to 13), and at least 2 years at the mainly science school (14 to 15) where pupils studied geography, natural philosophy, chemistry and more of the French, arithmetic, writing and drawing they had begun in the grammar school (*ibid.*, 140–1).

29. Ibid., 51–2. There was clearly a busy traffic in ideas and plans for academies at this time. Thus on 26 June 1790 the Elgin town council approved a petition from townsmen and people in the neighbourhood for the union of the various town's schools and on 23 October invited subscriptions for a school with three separate departments – English, French and church music; writing, arithmetic and the elements of mathematics; Latin and Greek. But by 28 March 1791 the councillors had been persuaded to adopt an arrangement 'on the lines of Inverness Academy' with four

masters – English, French and church music; Latin, Greek, ancient and modern geography; arithmetic and book-keeping; the elements of mathematics, including geometry, trigonometry, algebra, navigation, surveying, perspective and drawing. Yet on 12 May 1800 it is minuted that 'the magistrates submit a plan of three new schools, similar to those at Montrose.' (*Records of Elgin*, ii, 428–30).

30. Aberdeen University MSS, 456 : James Smith to Robert Hamilton, 1 November 1791. The mathematical master was to have two classes : in the first year he was to teach arithmetic, algebra, book-keeping and a complete course of geography; in the second year the course included geometry, plain and spherical trigonometry, land surveying, gauging, the elements of fortification, navigation and some easy sessions of astronomy.

31. Register of the Proceedings of the Managers appointed by the Magistrates and Town Council of the Burgh of Perth for superintending the Affairs of the Academy there : 27 November 1761. (SRO B59/22/34).

32. The 1807 buildings contained six schools in all : the grammar school with a rector and two doctors, the academy with a rector and a doctor, and the English school, French school, drawing and painting school and writing school, each with one master. (E. Smart, *History of Perth Academy* (Perth 1932), 94).

33. Register of the Proceedings... : 27 November 1761.

34. J. Bonar, *The Nature and Necessity of a Religious Education* (1752), 8–9. Bonar was minister at Cockpen in Midlothian when he gave this sermon : he moved to Perth in 1756 and died there in December 1761.

35. Register of the Proceedings... : 27 November 1761. The curriculum proposed in Bonar's memorial was : 1st year – natural history, arithmetic of integers and fractions, geometry, plain and spherical trigonometry, practical geometry including mensuration, surveying, dialling, fortification, navigation, conic sections, astronomy and some English and writing : 2nd year – history of philosophy and the rise and progress of arts and sciences, natural philosophy, practical geography as an introduction to civil history, history of commerce (particularly in Britain), a short and practical system of logic, the principles of religion and duty, and English composition, accounting and book-keeping. There was therefore a very considerable overlap in the studies to be pursued in Perth and those followed at the universities, but Bonar rather played this down in his concluding statement about the curriculum : 'From this Plan, it will appear how much such an Education would differ from that which is generally pursued in our Universitys and how well it is calculated both for the service of those who, being designed for an Active Life, cannot afford to employ more time in the Study of Science, and as an Introduction to others who may intend to follow any of the Learned Professions and in that view to prosecute their Studys to a greater Length.'

36. Ibid., 27 November 1761.

37. *Old Statistical Account*, (1796), xviii, 513–21. When the rector of the grammar school resigned in 1772, the town council was very dilatory in replacing him despite insistent pressure from the presbytery of Perth – *see* minutes of the presbytery of Perth,

especially from 7 June 1775 to 28 April 1779 when it was at last reported that the council had promoted one of the grammar school doctors to the vacant rectorship (SRO CH2/299/20–1). It seems that there had been a distinct falling-off in the numbers attending the grammar school after the opening of the academy, and there is a clear possibility that the town council were hoping that the grammar school might be incorporated into the new academy. It is important to remember that Perth was strongly seceder at that time, and many burgesses would have been well aware that a private subscription establishment was not so open to interference from the Established Church as was the older type of burgh school; indeed, seceding antipathies to the Established Church may have gained support in the town from those inhabitants who were disaffected to all religion (*Old Statistical Account*, xviii, 531 and a minute of the presbytery of Perth of 27 March 1776). One must wonder whether there was at least an element of anti-Church feeling in the erection of academies elsewhere later in the century. The Peterhead minister who wrote his parish's report in the *New Statistical Account* (xii, 383) in 1840 was aware of it in that year: he noted that the Peterhead voluntaries wished to 'supersede the parish school by the establishment of an academy on a large scale, to be conducted, as has been held out by some of the projectors, independently of the clergy of the Established Church.'

38. Register of the Proceedings... : 27 November 1761. The regulations of the academy included a requirement that the managers and masters should elect annually a rector who was to 'make proper Rules for Conducting the Affairs of the Accademy, and for Securing the attendance and good behaviour of the Students' – a fairly obvious parallelling of rectorial appointments in the universities of the day. The desire of the magistrates of Perth to gain for the town an educational institution of university status was not new in 1760: in 1697–8 Perth had been very ready to offer a home to the masters of the university of St Andrews who were in intense dispute with the townsmen there, and for a time it seemed likely that the entire university would remove to Perth (R. G. Cant, *The University of St Andrews : a Short History* (1946), 79–80).

39. William Thom *Works* (Glasgow 1799), 281.

40. Ibid., 272. Professorial venality is the target of another pamphlet by Thom published in 1764: *Letter from Pr–f——r —————— to H—— M———, Esq., Airshire, explaining the Motives which have determined the University of Glasgow to desert the Blackfriar Church and betake themselves to a Chapel*, printed in the *Works* at pp. 231–62. According to the author, the professors were not only getting money from the manufacturing of private classes for additional honoraria but also by boarding rich lads whose parents paid out large fees in the incorrect belief that their sons would receive extra and private instruction out of college, by taking every opportunity to increase the rents of the university lands, by not paying promptly the stipends of ministers of parishes on those lands and then dividing among them the interest gained from investing the unpaid stipends, by meddling in the bursary funds, and by removing themselves from the local parish church to a large newly-built chapel so that they might gather in seat rents from 'the richer and

politer sort' who would attend worship there rather than in their own parish churches.

41. Thom, *Works*, 271–2.
42. Ibid., 270.
43. Ibid., 287.
44. Ibid., 284 – 'A place in an university is considered as easy, honourable and lucrative. It is almost looked upon as a sinecure : it is not ordinarily the most ingenious and able for teaching that is pitched upon, but he who is connected or whose friends are connected with and can serve the men in power ; and this appears to be growing more and more in fashion. When a vacancy happens we hear everyone saying 'Who will get this place ? Who has most interest with such a duke or such a lord ?' A man's sufficiency is seldom or never mentioned ; his ability is no recommendation of him ; his total ignorance of the things he is to teach is no obstacle to his being preferred to the office.'
45. Ibid., 291. Thom argues against the introduction of an academy, in a rather heavy-handed satirical way in a pamphlet of 1762 entitled *The Scheme for Erecting an Academy at Glasgow set forth in its own proper Colours : in a letter from a Society of the Inhabitants of that City who are not yet tainted with a taste for Literature, to their brethren of the same Principles at Paisley*. He points out that university training as it then existed had the great benefit of teaching students little or nothing else than their professors' 'very laudable attachment to money' and that an academy education, 'being delivered from its present obscurity' and becoming enjoyably comprehensible, would draw attention away from business and be an enemy to both trade and religion.
46. A. Law, *Education in Edinburgh*, 146. In Edinburgh a separate public academy would only have harmed the 'Toun's College', to which increased numbers of students were already being attracted by the introduction of new subjects and additional private classes.

In Glasgow, at the very time when Thom was writing his pamphlets, there had been set up a new private academy which offered an astonishing range of studies. An advertisement in the *Glasgow Journal* (no. 1073, 18–25 February 1762) gives a full description : 'Attentive to the importance and utility of a judicious Plan of Education, and convinced by experience of the impropriety of many different schools for the purposes thereof, William Gordon and James Scruton have been at pains to render their Academy as complete as possible, by procuring the assistance of masters properly qualified for teaching the modern languages, which our commerce hath rendered necessary for the man of business to be acquainted with, and such of the sciences as they themselves could not (without neglecting others as essential) overtake : by which means the youth committed to their care will be instructed in every branch of literature, proper for the merchant, the mechanic, the marine and the farmer, under their own eye, the proper master being always at hand to resolve the difficulties that may occur, without the disagreeable necessity of strolling from school to school at the expiration of almost every hour.' The plan of classes in this private academy was very extensive – writing and flourishing; arithmetic and book-keeping, with private classes also available in both; practical geometry, plain and spherical trigonometry with their application in land surveying, longimetry, altimetry, navigation, geography, astronomy, fortification, gunnery and dialling; a separate class in geography; algebra; Euclid's *Elements* either in Latin or in English; the French language, and Italian and Spanish if required. The advertisement ends by stating that if there was good support for their academy then Gordon and Scruton intended to 'have more masters properly qualified : by whose assistance they may be able to teach Rhetoric; Composition in the Latin, English, French, Spanish and Italian languages; History ; Natural Philosophy ; and the Reading of the English Language with taste and propriety : which addition, it is supposed, would render their academy as complete and extensive as would be requisite in this city.' With private enterprise of this kind at work, there was hardly need for the town council in Glasgow to consider erecting a public subscription academy like the one in Perth.

47. *Scots Magazine* (1741), iii, 371–4.
48. In the 1760s, 1770s and 1780s in Aberdeen frequent and unflattering comparisons were made between the two local universities and those at Edinburgh and Glasgow.
49. *Letters chiefly connected with the Affairs of Scotland from Henry Cockburn...to Thomas Francis Kennedy*, M P..., (1874), 137–8.
50. R. S. Rait, *The Universities of Aberdeen : A History* (Aberdeen 1895), 297–8. The union of the colleges of St Leonard and St Salvator in St Andrews is described in R. G. Cant, *University of St Andrews*, 87–8.
51. R. S. Rait, *Universities of Aberdeen*, 343.
52. *Extracts from the Council Register of the Burgh of Aberdeen 1643–1747*, ed. J. Stuart (1872), 385–7. One objection registered against the removal of their college from New Aberdeen was : 'The town of Aberdeen looks upon it as a considerable addition to its lustre and dignity to have an university situate in the heart of the town where the provost, baillies and councill had such a great interest and concern, and where the inhabitants' children can be taught under the inspection of their parents at a very small expence.'
53. The grammar schoolmaster of Elgin advertised in the *Aberdeen Journal* of 31 May 1748 that, besides English, Latin and writing, 'he directs the studies of such young Lads as incline to Trades, Merchandize, etc.,...to such Branches of Education as are most adapted to the way of life they choose.' The parochial master at Old Deer offered 'Arithmetick, Book-Keeping after the Italian method, Geography, Geometry and Algebra, all taught at reasonable rates' in addition to Latin ibid., 3 April 1750). And there are numerous advertisements for general commercial and navigation schools in New Aberdeen itself (e.g. ibid., 29 November 1748).
54. *Evidence, Oral and Documentary, taken and received by the Commissioners... for Visiting the Universities of Scotland* (1830), iv, 286.
55. Ibid., 286.
56. Op.cit ., 35.
57. *Evidence...taken...by the Commissioners*, iv, 175–7.
58. Ibid., 177–8.
59. *Memorials relating to the Union of the King's and Marischal Colleges of*

Aberdeen (n.p., 1755), 28. Further attempts were made to unite the two universities in 1770 and 1786 and were also unsuccessful despite plans to use *both* sets of buildings. On each occasion the unionists wished to increase the range and number of subjects taught – 'with a view to render the System of Education more complete', as was said in 1786 – in the hope that this would revive the fortunes of both colleges. See R. S. Rait, *Universities of Aberdeen*, 344–6, and W. R. Humphries, *William Ogilvie and the Projected Union of the Colleges 1786–7* (Aberdeen 1940), *passim*.

60. Meston was a philosophy regent in Marischal College in 1714–15, though he may never have taught there : he was deposed in 1716. 'Some years afterwards he commenced an Academy at Elgin, in conjunction with his brother, Mr Samuel Meston, who was remarkably qualified for teaching the Greek language. Here he continued for several years, instructing young gentlemen in all the branches of learning taught at the Universities, whither the flower of the youth of the northern counties resorted to him from all quarters.' (*The Poetical Works of the Ingenious and Learned William Meston* A.M., *Sometime Professor of Philosophy in the Marischal College of Aberdeen, to which is prefixed The Author's Life*, 7th edition (Aberdeen 1802), iv–v.) Meston taught at various times in the next thirty years in Turriff, Montrose, and Perth.

61. Aberdeen University MSS : K.C. 44, ff. 55–9 (31 October 1759).

62. Ibid., ff. 89 et seq. (26 January 1760).

63. For the general background to this point, *see* R. G. Cant, 'The Scottish universities and Scottish society in the eighteenth century' in *Studies on Voltaire*, ed. T. Besterman (Geneva 1967) 1953–66.

9. From Protest to Reaction: The Moderate Regime in the Church of Scotland, 1752–1805

IAN D.L.CLARK

Seldom has an ecclesiastical party been condemned by posterity quite so mercilessly as the 'Moderates' who (at least spasmodically) controlled the General Assembly of the Church of Scotland in the latter half of the eighteenth century. They have, it is true, been admired for their personal accomplishments as historians, philosophers, poets, and even as agricultural 'improvers'; and it has never seriously been denied that for better or for worse they contributed to the erosion of the more austere features of the Scottish Calvinist ethos. Yet if William Robertson, Hugh Blair, John Home, 'Jupiter' Carlyle and their entourage (both clerical and lay) who brought the party to birth in 1752 are remembered today, it is for their cultural rather than their ecclesiastical contribution to Scottish history. Their less many-sided successors, men such as Principal Hill, James Finlayson and Henry Grieve, have left little personal impression upon history, and it is as a faceless party rather than as individuals that the Moderates have been so roundly condemned. Moreover, they have been ambushed both from the front and the rear. Contemporaries (notably John Witherspoon) in the 1750s thought of the party as a radical and dangerous eruption within the life of the Kirk, while subsequent historians have generalized about the alliance of the party with the forces of political and social 'reaction' in the 1790s and first decade of the nineteenth century.

The prevailing picture of the party tends to be far too static. The Moderates in fact emerged in a mood of vigorous criticism of the existing ecclesiastical situation in the 1750s, and only slowly established themselves as a 'regime' within the Church. Because the Moderate Party continued to hold together, in an increasingly ramshackle way, up to the Disruption of 1843, it has too easily been assumed that it predominated comfortably throughout the century of its existence; and because for a time the party found itself revolving in the political orbit of Henry Dundas it has been unhesitatingly censured as 'Erastian' from the start. In actual fact, as we shall see, the Moderate Party's control of the church courts was never as complete as many historians have assumed; and a statement such as that of Dr Ferguson that 'from 1752 onwards the Moderate Party...had a clear ascendancy'[1] needs very considerable qualification. As I have suggested elsewhere, in many ways Leslie's Case in 1805 rather than the Disruption in 1843 provides the logical *terminus ad quem* for a study of the Moderates.[2] In that year the party which in the 1750s had outraged pious opinion by befriending the allegedly 'sceptical' Lord Kames and David Hume, and shown their contempt for current taboos by attending and applauding a stage-play written by a clergyman, found themselves opposing the candidature of a young layman for a university chair at Edinburgh on a trumped-up charge of atheism. The dispute revealed the Evangelical or 'Popular' opponents of the Moderates as plausible defenders of academic freedom, while the Moderates exhibited an unedifying spectacle of internal schism, political chicanery and ecclesiastical obscurantism. Two years later, the Moderates who in 1779 had had their windows smashed because of their unpopular support for Roman Catholic relief now found themselves opposing Catholic emancipation. A *volte face* on this scale demands an explanation. It is the purpose of this essay to examine the background of the Moderate 'protest' of the 1750s, and then to explore some of the reasons for its eventual collapse. 'Moderatism' contained a number of inner contradictions, and it was these which led to ultimate disaster.

Leaning heavily upon the egregious *Autobiography* of Alexander Carlyle, the rather vapid sermons of Hugh Blair, and the strictures of the hostile Popular Party and its post-Disruption Evangelical descendants, it has been tempting for historians to caricature the Moderates. At its most uncritical, history has portrayed them as 'Erastian' supporters of a repressive political regime, allied by class interest to the landed gentry and wealthy borough merchants, implacably hostile to the aspirations of 'the people', and as heretical in the pulpit as they were wordly in private life. Carlyle's own ordination was opposed in 1748 by the honest folk of Inveresk on the grounds that he 'danced frequently in a manner prohibited by the law of the Church', 'wore his hat agee', and had been seen 'galloping through the Links one day between one and two o'clock'; and fifty years later there were still disgruntled parishioners who complained of 'the lean harangues of Moral Philosophy' with which, now in his dotage, he regaled them from the pulpit.[3] Charges of pastoral neglect, 'moral preaching' and a preference for the society of the better educated among their parishioners were, and still are, frequently made against the Moderate clergy, but they are not always just. Carlyle's own deep pastoral concern and his strenuous efforts to help the deserving (and sometimes undeserving) are revealed in his unpublished correspondence and notebooks rather than in his memoirs of genteel society. Similarly, a sympathetic study of surviving Moderate sermons, in their contemporary context, shows a much sharper theological thrust than is commonly supposed. Moreover, any attempt to differentiate between the clergy of the two parties on a 'class' basis fails. Investigation reveals that the majority of the clergy of both parties was drawn from exactly the same strata of society, and (despite the Popular Party's hostility to lay patronage) they owed their livings to the same relatively small circle of landed proprietors, businessmen and government officers.

At its best history has sought to make allowance for the Moderates as typical representatives of a certain mood in eighteenth-century Europe, permissive, undogmatic, optimistic and 'reasonable', who were eventually swept aside by revolutionary currents. Faced from the 1790s onwards by democratic agitation and Evangelical fervour, they rallied to the defence of the *status quo*. This is the more detached interpretation offered by H. W. Meikle and W. L. Mathieson fifty years ago; but on the whole the extreme view has held the field. No nineteenth-century Free Church divine received such universal applause in Scotland as Principal Rainy, when he indignantly rebutted the Anglican Dean Stanley's tentative suggestion that the Moderates might after all be the true heirs of the original (Knoxian) Reformation.[4] More recently, and from a very different ideological angle, the Moderates have once again been exhibited as bourgeois upholders of property and the established order, whose pretensions to 'liberalism' were hollow, and who fostered the rise of artificial 'gentility' in place of the vigorous old communal culture of Scotland.[5] And in the most recent study of the period, Moderatism is acidly dismissed as 'little more than the Dundas interest at prayer, with nepotism and pluralism the main order of service',[6] yet curiously enough the Moderate leaders were the first to complain that Dundas consistently ignored their nephews, and pluralism (except in the very restricted sphere of the universities) was never even heard of in Scotland.

The time seems ripe for a new assessment of the Moderate regime, and a hint of the direction in which this might fruitfully proceed is given by Dr G. E. Davie in his provocative contribution to the modern study of Scottish history. He appeals for 'a more comprehensive point of view which gives the secular institutions of Scotland equal prominence with the sacred, and which sees the distinctive life of the country after [1707] not in its religion alone but in the mutual interaction of religion, law and education.'[7]

This remark takes on significance when we reflect upon the composition of the General Assembly during the heyday of the eighteenth-century Moderate Party. It has often been remarked that, lacking a parliament of her own, Scotland has found in the General Assembly a forum for national debate and self-expression far more resonant than one might expect of a Church Court. The Moderates welcomed and encouraged this, and towards the end of the century actually deplored the fact that the Assembly was being deserted by the judges, statesmen and nobility who had, a little earlier, adorned it as Elders.

A question which is less frequently asked is, what Interests were represented in the Assembly, and to what extent was it subject to non-ecclesiastical pressures? 'Government' was always strongly represented, not only by the Royal Commissioner but often by the Lord Advocate, Solicitor-General and other officers of the Crown, besides a galaxy of judges, all sitting as duly-elected Ruling Elders. The legal profession was usually present in force, and the advocates who sat in the Assembly were commonly related closely to the landed class which held the real strings of political power in Scotland. Most of them were deeply enmeshed in the various Interests which made up the complicated texture of eighteenth-century politics; and, as we shall see, it was through lawyers such as Dundas' political opponent Henry Erskine that the political 'opposition' exercised a strong influence upon Church affairs. The Universities were on the whole in the hands of the clergy, but university patronage was wielded by government, the landed interest and in some cases by Town Councils. In 1801 Dundas claimed that for twenty years past every professor at Edinburgh and St Andrews was appointed 'either actually by myself or upon my recommendation'.[8] To this must be added the fact that the clergy of both parties were either related to or deeply beholden to the landed interest. Finally, it should be remembered that both the Moderate and Popular leaders were adept at 'managing' the election of Elders, and possessed lists of reliable laymen who could be hawked round the presbyteries each spring. Thus in 1789 Carlyle offered his friend Dr Douglas of Galashiels a choice of nine Elders, including Professor Adam Ferguson, Provost Grieve, Sherriff Cockburn and his own lawyer, and asked him to 'Let me know which of them you like best'; and he also mentioned two Edinburgh brewers whom he was 'trying' at Selkirk and Langholm.[9] In 1784 a Moderate minister publicly exposed the Popular Party's manipulation of elections in the Synod of Glasgow and Ayr, and in 1792 the Popular Party was said to have a fund for subsidising Elders of their own way of thinking.[10] In these circumstances it is no wonder if the Assembly was exposed to chilly winds which were not always strictly ecclesiastical.

There can be no doubt that it was the Moderates rather than their opponents who visualized the General Assembly as something more than a purely ecclesiastical body; and it is even arguable that it was the decline of the party which led to the withdrawal of so many prominent laymen at the beginning of the nineteenth century, rather than *vice versa.* Yet in this as in other fields the Moderates found themselves in a dilemma. On the one hand they enthusiastically swam in all the cultural cross-currents of their day, while on the other they genuinely desired to see the Church freed from 'management' from outside. Their ideal was a Kirk fully representative of all aspects of the national life, yet treating with government on equal terms. Within the framework of eighteenth-century society and politics this was a self-defeating programme. But without some understanding of what the Moderates were trying to do it is impossible to appreciate either the scope of the protest which they raised against the existing ecclesiastical situation in the 1750s, or the reasons for its collapse fifty years later.

The driving force in Moderatism was a mood of cultural liberation and optimism which made the Moderate clergy aspire to play not merely a national but a European role. 'Jupiter' Carlyle's famous boast that his Moderate colleagues had made a massive contribution to European culture is today received with derision,[11] but the fact remains that Robertson's histories, Blair's lectures and sermons, and the philosophical writings of Reid, Beattie and Campbell were enthusiastically received as far afield as St Petersburg and Madrid. It is true that their cosmopolitanism led them to make ludicrous and unsuccessful attempts to divest themselves of Scotticisms, and they enjoyed any excuse for a jaunt to London; yet there is an unmistakable national pride in even the most anglicised of the Moderates, which at least partly accounts for their attitude to Henry Dundas. Here was a Scot who, like Lord Mansfield before him, had pushed his way successfully into Whitehall. The Moderates were 'world-affirming' by nature, and had no desire to see the Church of Scotland drawn aside by a narrow and sectarian spirit from the mainstream of Scottish life. Their outlook contrasts sharply with that of their Popular or 'Wild' opponents, who looked back wistfully over their shoulders to a rapidly receding theocratic past, and lifted up a lugubrious testimony against contemporary backslidings. The Moderates did, however inarticulately, grasp the fact that a secular society was emerging. In an age which traced the theoretical origin of society and the state to a contract based upon the rights and self-interest of 'natural man', and in which government increasingly tended to regard the Church as only one among several competing 'Interests' in the national life, they realised that there was little future for a Kirk which was inflexibly dogmatic in its creed and made high claims over the private lives of all Scotsmen, yet drew its skirts away with a shudder from contemporary life and thought. Two alternatives were open to the Church in the middle of the eighteenth century. Either it could retreat into its shell, or it could frankly recognize its new relationship to society by seeking to establish its own independence and freedom of action while at the same time interpenetrating and when necessary criticizing society from within.

In choosing the latter alternative, the Moderates found themselves in conflict with inherited attitudes and vested interests. On the one hand they challenged the highly-articulated doctrinal system of the past. On the other, while fully acknowledging 'the Headship of Christ' they insisted that the Church, at least in its outward and visible aspect, should reflect the patterns of a normal terrestrial society. The Church Courts must be disciplined and efficient, the law of the land obeyed, and government treated as an equal if not always fully reliable partner.

The genesis and development of the Moderates' theological outlook lies beyond the scope of this essay. It should probably be seen partly as a reaction against the rigidity of the old Calvinist categories of the seventeenth century, and partly as a more positive response to new currents of thought from outside Scotland. The alleged 'Socinianism' and 'Pelagianism' of the Moderates has been vastly exaggerated, but it is certainly true that like many of their eighteenth-century contemporaries they set light to precise formulations of doctrine. When the controversy over compulsory subscription of the Confession of Faith came to a head in the 1770s and 80s, Moderate clergy boldly argued that all creeds and confessions, even that of Westminster, must necessarily be partial and incomplete. The Reformation was the product of a particular historical situation, and Luther and Calvin were no more likely to be infallible than their Roman Catholic contemporaries. If a minister of the Church of Scotland repudiates the precise wording of its official standards, it does not follow that he should be deposed forthwith. 'The Reformers had their prejudices', one of them declared, 'These prejudices could not be removed speedily, and we have no reason to think they were removed miraculously':

'Something is still left to reform;...we have the same *right*, nay we have the same calls from duty and conscience, to review received opinions, even though they should be found in our standards, as our fathers had, and to reject them if they are discovered to be erroneous....This age is superior to the age of the Reformation; our sentiments may be presumed juster, and more correct than theirs.'[12]

If we discount the author's naive belief in the inevitability of 'progress' we may still discern a genuine openness to new currents of thought and a willingness to enter into dialogue with the contemporary world. Moderate latitude was shown not only in their own preaching, but in their energetic defence of those who were from time to time formally accused of heresy by the Popular Party.

The immediate context of the emergence of the Moderate Party was not, however, a doctrinal quibble, but the very mundane question of lay patronage. The rights of patrons had been restored in 1712, but it was only comparatively recently that a series of disputed settlements of unpopular presentees had led to alarm and even bloodshed. Moreover, the ambiguity of the Church's own rules for calling a minister in cases where patronage did not apply had led to the Secession of the Erskines in 1733. Then in 1751 the presbytery of Linlithgow disobeyed an injunction of the Assembly to ordain a presentee at Torphichen, and Carlyle describes in his *Autobiography* how he and a group of young ministers and laymen met in an Edinburgh tavern to consider how best they could 'restore the authority of the Church'.[13] When a similar situation arose the following year in the parish of Inverkeithing they were able to carry a reluctant Assembly with them in the deposition of one member of the presbytery of Dunfermline, *pour encourager les autres*. This episode was recognized by the Moderates themselves and their contemporaries as marking the decisive emergence of a new party within the Church, with a consistent policy and increasingly elaborate organization.

The patronage question continued to be the most explicit bone of contention between the parties up to 1843, and formed the subject of endless appeals and debates in the Assembly. To begin with, the Moderates were not committed to the view that patronage was inherently desirable or justified. At least until Robertson's retirement from the leadership of the party in 1780 they argued only that it must be accepted *de facto* as the law of the land, to prevent a head-on collision with government or (what was worse in their eyes) the emergence of a system of unofficial local Independency with congregations calling their own nominee while leaving the stipend in the hands of the lawful presentee. The Moderates frequently pointed out that since no presbytery could be compelled to ordain an unlicensed man, the Church had only herself to thank if she licensed unsuitable candidates in the first place. The Popular Party continued to agitate spasmodically against 'the grievance of patronage' while accepting its fruits in practice; while the Moderates sought the silver lining by pointing out that patronage at least enabled a better-educated type of person to enter the ministry. In fact this turned out to be a dangerous inconsistency in the Moderate position, since while they earned the odium of supporting patronage their opponents, as we shall see, reaped many of the practical advantages.

Patronage was certainly one of the most 'live' issues in contemporary debate, but it is misleading to regard it as more than an outward symbol of a much more fundamental difference of attitude between the parties. It served to bring into sharp focus two conflicting interpretations of the nature of the Church and its role in society. To the Moderates, acquiescence in patronage was the price which must be paid for their ideal of a Church occupying a central place in the national life, Established yet politically independent, disciplined yet comprehensive and tolerant, committed to 'progress' yet conforming to the existing structure of Scottish life. They repudiated the tacitly-held view of their opponents that the Church is a society called out of the world and set over against it. As in their doctrine of salvation they preached the 'wholeness' of man, appealing to his reason as much as to his emotions, so in their doctrine of the Church the Moderates insisted that Christianity caters not for 'man' in the abstract, but for 'man-in-society'. Man is by nature social, and therefore not only must the Church interpenetrate society, but the Church herself bears an analogy to society. Alexander Gerard (1728–95), Professor of Divinity at King's College, Aberdeen, doubted whether 'a society could at all subsist for any considerable time, if its members were generally destitute of all religious impressions', and declared that 'The great end of religion, doubtless, is to fit men for eternity; but it likewise fits them for all the duties of the present life.'[14] William Craig (1709–84), another popular Moderate preacher, similarly insists rather more crudely that 'It is incumbent on every man, not only for his own interest, but as a useful member of society and a lover of his country, to be the friend and encourager of true religion'.[15]

We shall be disappointed if we expect to find in Moderatism a radical criticism of society and a denunciation of social evils. The majority of Moderate preachers were content to take their stand upon the 'Glorious Revolution' which had removed the threat of arbitrary government and ushered in an era of personal liberty, without questioning the justice of the existing social structure. They tended to support the war against the American colonists while the Popular Party opposed it. Carlyle vehemently attacked 'the ungrateful colonies' for their 'foul revolt', relegating to a footnote the fact that the colonists were not represented in parliament, and dismissing this objection on the grounds of 'consuetude'.[16] On the other hand, many Moderates shared the early Wordsworthian enthusiasm for the French Revolution. In 1788 Robertson looked forward to the imminent deliverance of 'so many millions of so great a nation [France] from the fetters of arbitrary government' in a sermon which his son regarded as too 'Jacobinical' to publish after his father's death in 1793. More surprising is a sermon by George Hill in 1792 in which he implies that the revolution was justified by the condition of France under the *ancien régime*.[17] Moderate preachers did insist strongly on the duties and moral obligations of the rich and powerful, and Blair stressed this theme in a vigorous series of sermons from the pulpit of St Giles' which must have made at least some of his aristocratic congregation uncomfortable. When the moderates felt that Scottish interests were at stake they were quite prepared to cross swords with government. For instance the agitation for a Scots Militia in the 1760s and '70s was led (in the famous 'Poker Club') by Moderate clergy, and caused serious annoyance in London. As late as 1793 Carlyle advocated the Burgh Reform movement in a memorandum to Dundas, at least a decade after Pitt and Dundas had ceased to sympathize with the reformers.[18] On at least one subject on which strong feelings were still regarded as a dangerous sign of 'Enthusiasm' the Moderates seem to have been rather ahead of public opinion. In 1755 Robertson warmly attacked slavery in America, and he has more to say to the same effect in his *Charles V* (1769) and *History of America* (1777); and it has even been claimed that through his great-nephew Henry Brougham he contributed to the humanitarian drive of the 'Clapham Sect'.[19] It was certainly a concern shared by other Moderates. Samuel Charteris (1742–1825) and Thomas Hardy (1747–98) have both left sermons on the subject, and Hardy went out of his way to attack the African slave-trade in his Church History lectures at Edinburgh.[20] Likewise Blair, in the 1770s, mentions the abolition of slavery (together with the introduction of 'more equality between the sexes', 'the abatement of the ferociousness of war' and the reform of the penal system) as prime christian objectives.[21]

If man-in-society needs the leaven of religion, the Moderates believed equally that man-in-Church needs the disciplines of society. In *The Reasons of Dissent*, which the young Moderates published during the Inverkeithing Case in 1752, they ask why a minister whose conscience will not allow him to obey the injunctions of a Church of which he is a voluntary member should continue to draw a stipend:

'if he refuses to obey its laws, he manifestly acts both a disorderly and dishonest part : he lays claim to the privileges of the society, whilst he condemns the authority of it...no man ought to become a member of that Church, who is not resolved to conform himself to its administration.'[22]

Later, during the controversy about subscription to the Confession of Faith, the Moderates found themselves hoist on their own petard when the Popular Party argued that if a man cannot bring himself to stomach the official standards of the Church he has no right to occupy a manse. In the case of the allegedly heterodox Dr M'Gill of Ayr his accusers urged that he should either give up his theological crotchets or leave the ministry, for when men enter a society 'they renounce part of their natural rights for its benefit and protection'.[23] This is yet another fatal inconsistency in the Moderate position. How far, and over what matters, is individual conscience to be allowed to weigh against the claims of a disciplined and orderly Church? While the Moderate conscience boggled at the substitutionary theory of the atonement, the Popular conscience stumbled at the forced settlement of unpopular presentees.

In reasserting the authority of the General Assembly the Moderates insisted that they were not innovating but recurring to a central feature of the reformed tradition, in which the parity of ministers must be offset by the subordination of judicatures. Thus Carlyle expressly rebuts the suggestion (which appears in Dugald Stewart's *Life of Robertson*) that the Moderates introduced a new principle in 1752, but claimed that, unlike a secular parliament, a Church 'founded by the laws of Christ' cannot manifestly contradict herself from year to year:

'Church courts that should be variable in their decisions, and inconsistent in their measures, could never acquire or deserve the confidence of the public.... Our supreme court has justly obtained [since 1752] a due authority over the minds of the people, on account of the uniformity of its decrees, and the wisdom of its proceedings.'[24]

In particular, the Moderates objected to the tendency of the Popular Party to ignore the normal rules of procedure and evidence in cases touching the morals or doctrine of the clergy. Thus in 1765 by insisting on what the Popular Party contemptuously dismissed as 'the necessity of what is called Legal Evidence' Robertson saved Carson of Anwoth from deposition by what would have been a virtual Act of Attainder by the Assembly.[25]

Much more incisive, however, was the Moderate demand for the freedom of the Kirk from its bondage to government 'managers' and sectional interests. As this runs counter to the traditional picture of Moderate 'Erastianism', it is worth examining in some detail.

Until the emergence of the Moderates as an organized party in the 1750s the Church had been 'managed' by a succession of influential clergy closely allied to the 'Interests' which at one time or another controlled the Scottish administration. During the brief 'Squadrone' regime of the Marquis of Tweeddale, from 1742 to 1746, Dr Robert Wallace was employed as 'Correspondent' of government, and after Tweeddale's fall the third Duke of Argyll and his agent Lord Milton controlled the affairs of the Church through Dr Patrick Cuming, Professor of Church History at Edinburgh. The Royal Commissioner was reminded annually in his official instructions to ensure that 'nothing be treated of, that is not a fit subject for an ecclesiastical meeting', and in cases of difficulty was to 'advise with such of our Ministers of State,

P

or Members of the Assembly, as you shall think fit'. How literally these orders were taken is seen in the brisk manoeuvres by which the Earl of Leven countered the clergy's demand for a long-overdue augmentation of their stipends in 1749. He knew that if government appeared to countenance the clergy's demand it would fatally alienate the landed interest, out of whose pockets the augmentation would have to come. Accordingly, he promised the Duke of Newcastle to do 'all that is possible' to prevent it, and began to whip up 'all the Interest that can be made to oppose it'; and nine days later he reported that he had contrived to throw 'a little cold water' on the scheme. The following year Leven, who was once again Commissioner, revealed to Newcastle an elaborate plan for scotching the renewed agitation. He recommended the Secretary of State to impress upon the Lord Advocate and Lord Justice-Clerk that the proposed augmentation could expect 'no countenance' in London. Principal Campbell of Glasgow and Professor Pollock of Marischal College, Aberdeen, who were both promoters of the scheme, were to be reminded that the Royal Chaplaincy and Almonership which they held respectively were tenable only during the royal pleasure. Some pretext was to be found for removing two more Chaplains so that more compliant men might be appointed in their place : if the latter proved recalcitrant, 'they might afterwards be dismissed at any time'.[26] Leven himself made a powerful speech warning the clergy to desist, and the Justice Clerk, Advocate and Lord President entered a dissent against the proceedings of the clergy in the Assembly. Thereafter, the demands were quietly dropped.

It was against this kind of interference that the Moderates protested. Their ideal was cooperation with the existing political regime on equal terms, as befitted an Established Church, and they frequently consulted with government; but they were not prepared to tolerate open meddling by Ministers of State. This is underlined by James Finlayson, one of the leaders of the party in the 1790s who says of Hugh Blair that he adhered loyally to 'the great leading principle' of his Moderate colleagues, which was to preserve the Kirk from 'a slavish corrupting dependence on the civil power'.[27] Dr George Cook, who led the party after his uncle Principal Hill's death, likewise praises Robertson for the 'manliness' with which he asserted the independence of the Church, and 'the firmness with which he spurned the dictation of men in office, to which those who went before him in the guidance of ecclesiastical measures too often tamely submitted'.[28] This testimony is corroborated by Sir Henry Moncrieff, a leading member of the Popular Party, and by Robertson's own criticism of the Popular Party in 1766 for 'at one time promoting one set of measures, and at another espousing the opposite, perhaps as one ministry or another prevails at court'.[29] Probably it was Robertson's refusal to abandon his political independence and commit himself to the political orbit of Henry Dundas that led him to withdraw from the leadership of the party in 1780 – a move which puzzled and wounded even his closest friends.

It is fatally easy for a party which sets out in a mood of protest to end up as an immovable regime dedicated to the maintenance of the *status quo*, and to align itself sooner or later with those forces in society which seem to guarantee support. Frequently, from about 1790 onwards, the Moderates countered the radical demands of their opponents with the bland argument of 'inexpediency'. Thus, in 1790, agitation for the repeal of the Test Act was met from the Moderate side by a claim that the time was inopportune for weakening the principle of ecclesiastical establishment. The famous Evangelical Overture on Foreign Missions in 1796 foundered on the Moderates' suspicion of Missionary Societies which (like the politically radical 'Friends of the People') were 'affiliated' and 'corresponded', and were thus likely to be hotbeds of sedition and republicanism. In 1807 'expediency' was again invoked to explain the Moderate opposition to Roman Catholic relief.

This instinctive conservatism naturally found an ally in the political conservatism of Pitt and Dundas, who were preoccupied with preventing a revolutionary outburst in Britain while mobilizing the national resources for war with France. Fear of 'sedition and fanaticism' were certainly responsible for the Moderates' attempt to bring the licensing of Chapels of Ease under the control of the Assembly in 1795 (although in fact the Popular Party seem to have been equally convinced that some form of control was necessary). Carlyle thankfully reported to Dundas in 1793 that the clergy had done their part in preventing a revolutionary movement in Scotland, and reckoned that 'the tide has turned in favour of Government' – in fact he had recently had the gratification of baptising an infant 'George Loyalty'.[30] In 1799 the Royal Commissioner, Lord Haddington, informed Carlyle that 'The General Assembly ended well, and by proper attention Church and State going hand in hand, a proper check will be given to innovators and we shall have comfort and quiet'.[31] The only danger lies in attributing too much to the complaisance of the Moderates alone. During the years of crisis the Popular Party were equally quiescent. Thus in 1792 Hill reported that all the clergy had been 'kept very quiet' after instructions to that effect had been sent down by the Duke of Portland to the chief Popular firebrands in the Assembly; and in the same year Dr Finlayson informed the Lord Advocate that in the Synod of Lothian and Tweeddale he had found only one minister who had shown any sympathy with 'the licentious spirit of the times'.[32] In the same month the Sherriff-Depute of Ayr reported that in his district there was only one minister 'a little tinged with French Revolution principles' – and was obviously puzzled by the fact that the man was a Moderate![33] It was actually Dr Erskine, the Popular leader in the famous Missions Debate, who urged that a sermon on *The Distinction of Ranks* by the Moderate Dr Drysdale should be printed and circulated. It had already caught the attention of Robertson as 'a very useful antidote' against 'some of the wild tenets of the present day'.[34]

All this can to some extent be attributed to the natural reaction of the 'Establishment' in Church as well as State to the revolutionary currents of the 1790s. Such, at any rate, is the usual explanation. It is arguable that the 'democratic' threat brought out Moderatism in its true colours. On the other hand it is doubtful whether this is not really an over-simplification, which fails to do full justice to the evidence. There is still something disturbing about the sweeping verdict of a nineteenth-century historian who condemns the Moderates as 'that party which, dreading change more than it loved improvement, has since been called "Tory"',[35] when we recall that they have been accused of innovating in everything from farming to the use of organs in church, and themselves convicted their opponents of being old-fashioned and illiberal. One suspects that in the last resort a simple theory of 'reaction' does not provide a completely satisfactory explanation.

Rather, the changeover of the Moderates to a defensive attitude should be seen against a much wider background of British politics. During the ministry of Lord North events tended to polarize political opinion, and the Moderates found themselves confronted by a clear-cut choice between 'government' and 'opposition'. Issues such as the American War (which many of them supported) and the burgh reform movement (which some but not all opposed) were reflected in the debates of the General Assembly, and prudence and an instinct for self-preservation almost inevitably led the Moderate leaders to side with government while their ecclesiatical opponents sided with the political opposition. It is probably no accident that at this same period the two Moderate philosophers Beattie and Oswald were abandoning academic restraint and good-manners in their attacks upon David Hume, and raising the spectre of 'dogmatic atheism'; while as early as 1774 from the opposite camp the 'Whig' Professor John Playfair was laughing up his sleeve at the trouncing which Joseph Priestley's recently-published *Institutes of Natural and Revealed Religion* had given to the Moderate exponents of 'common sense'.[36] Long before 1789 some at least of the more second-rate minds in the Moderate Party had become convinced that political opposition to government went hand in hand with sceptism and infidelity in theology.

Up to the time of his retirement in 1780 Robertson was dedicated to securing harmony within the Church, and even his opponents paid tribute to his 'reasonableness'; but under his successors there was an increasingly sharp series of clashes between the parties on major issues, and a very marked political alignment which certainly ante-dates the French Revolution. This is the period during which Henry Dundas was beginning to cement the elaborate network of 'influence' by which eventually he was to control not only the electoral system in Scotland, but also the handling of much of the patronage in the Church. Robertson's family connections had lain outside the Dundas circle, and in some cases his relatives were in direct political oppo-sition. The new generation of Moderate leaders, consisting of two separate and not always harmonious groups in Edinburgh and St Andrews, were united by their almost total dependence upon Dundas for patronage for themselves, their friends, and those they sought to influence. The Moderates, who in theory stood for the independence of the Church and cooperation with government on equal terms, found themselves increasingly committed to a political alignment which in turn threw their opponents into the arms of the political opposition groups. Yet, as we shall see, Dundas' attitude towards the Moderate Party was ambiguous, and did not always bring them the advantages which they expected. Moreover, the rather scattered elements in what I have called the 'Moderate Protest' of the 1750s looked much less convincing when erected into a permanent system of ecclesiastical policy. The inconsistencies in the Moderate programme became increasingly apparent, and in order to maintain their always rather precarious control of the Assembly they were compelled to compromise with their original principles. Thus in seeking an explana-tion of the transition from 'Protest' to 'Reaction' in the eighteenth-century Moderate Party, two things must be kept in mind. One is the vulnerability of the Moderates when new and unforeseen circum-stances made their original ideals irrelevant. The other is the effect upon the Church of the rise to political prominence of Henry Dundas.

Detailed study of the composition of the presbyteries between 1752 and 1805 suggests that at no time did the Moderate Party have a de-pendable majority except in a few lowland and east coast areas. Even in those districts which were considered notoriously 'Moderate', such as Ayrshire and Fife, the parties were in fact surprisingly evenly bal-anced. The presbytery of Ayr has always been regarded as a hotbed of

Moderatism, yet in 1780 only twelve out of the twenty-nine clergy can be identified as active and consistent supporters of Moderate measures. In 1784 the Popular Party in the presbytery suceeded in passing an overture attacking patronage; and in 1786, at the start of the proceedings against the allegedly 'Socinian' Dr M'Gill, the presbytery was evenly divided. In 1791 Blair warned the Lord Advocate that the presbytery of Linlithgow (another so-called Moderate stronghold) was evenly divided, and the presentation of a Popular minister to a Crown living would tip the scales against the Moderates.[37] In Edinburgh, where historians have often assumed a Moderate majority, the Popular Party defeated the Moderates by four votes in a motion on patronage in 1784. In 1791 a violent altercation took place in Edinburgh over the election of Elders to the Assembly, and it was reported that 'In this contest, what is called the Moderate interest in the Presbytery prevailed. *For seven years past they have been in a minority*'.[38] In 1808 and 1810 there is evidence that the presbytery was once again evenly divided; and it is probably this that accounts for the warmth generated there during Leslie's Case in 1805. The traditional picture of a deeply-entrenched Moderate majority in the 1780s is further undermined by the fact that between 1781 and 1786 seven synods sent up overtures strongly attacking patronage, while only two expressed approval of Moderate policies.

In these circumstances we may wonder how the Moderates ever had a majority in the Assembly at all. The answer would seem to lie in their superior tactics, and their ability to 'manage' the elections in lethargic or indifferent presbyteries. A full-scale 'canvass' was an energetic affair, and entailed anxious calculations and correspondence, discreet hints by party leaders to men of substance and influence, and the priming of local agents with information. For example in 1805 Dr Finlayson (known from his adept handling of such matters as the 'Jesuit' of the party) urged Carlyle's *quondam* assistant Dr Lee to persuade his former pupil Sir John Johnstone to put pressure on the minister of Westerkirk. The latter was said to lie under 'deep obligations' to the baronet, and 'could scarcely refuse a request from him'.[39] In 1784 Lord Dalhousie promised Carlyle to influence the clergy in his vicinity to elect a more satisfactory [i.e. Moderate] commissioner than they had done the previous year.[42] Many of these letters survive and show the complexity of Moderate 'management' and the attention to detail which made it so successful.

Yet all this anxious canvassing represents a serious compromise with the avowed Moderate aim of making the Kirk free from outside pressure-groups. While Robertson preserved his political independence his successors certainly did not. Thus in the letter to Dr Lee

quoted above, Finlayson unblushingly urges him to remind Johnstone that 'the rights of Patrons and the future good order of the
Church establishment are in some degree dependent on the success
of the Moderate Party', and that 'the interests of Moderation in the
Church, and the interests of the great Landholders are inseparably
connected'. Such a statement may be symptomatic of political panic
during the revolutionary years, but it is far more a reflection of a basic
inconsistency in the Moderate position which has nothing to do with
the French Revolution. In their determination to procure an annual
majority in the Assembly the Moderates were compelled to seek help
from those who held the real strings of power, and in maintaining
this annual majority they were inevitably caught up in the machinery
of patronage and the conflicts of competing political 'Interests'. This
was a vicious circle, but unavoidable for a party which refused to
contract out of the eighteenth-century structure of politics and society.

If the Moderates failed to find a way of escape from dependence on
the landed interest, there is no sign that their opponents were any
more successful. The more the Moderates became tied to the apron-
strings of Dundas, the more the Popular Party found themselves in
the arms of the political opposition groups. This meant that in fact for
many years the lay leader of the Popular Party was Dundas' political
foe Henry Erskine. These groups (loosely referred to by contemporaries as 'Foxites') were no less 'landed', and no less dependent upon
the all-pervading system of patronage. Moreover, Popular canvassing
and 'management' was just as thorough as that of the Moderates, and
as the latter ruefully admitted, often equally successful.

The War of American Independence was the first issue which
clearly revealed the extent to which the Popular Party was prepared to
bring secular politics into the debates of the Assembly. In 1776 they
tried to persuade the Assembly to send an Address to the King asking
him to recall troops from America and 'put an end to so unnatural a
war'. This was countered by Robertson and the Royal Commissioner,
with the help of the Lord Advocate and the Moderator, and an innoc-
uous Address acceptable to both parties was eventually despatched.
In 1782 William Porteous, one of the Popular clergy, proposed to include in the reply to the annual Royal Letter a clause criticizing the
recently dismissed ministry of Lord North and welcoming the appointment of a Whig administration under Rockingham, Fox and
Shelburne. When the motion was rejected as improper by the Assembly, a Dissent was entered by twenty-seven members, of whom
twelve can be identified as clergy who regularly voted with the Popular Party, and six were well-known 'Whig' laymen.

In 1789 Carlyle was put forward, unsuccessfully, as Moderate candidate for the vacant Clerkship of the Church. Before the previous Clerk had even been buried, and at a time when the Moderates did not feel it seemly to mention the matter, the Popular Party began an energetic canvass for their own candidate. According to the *Caledonian Mercury* for 21 May, Carlyle was 'strenuously supported' by Dundas and 'all the ministerial interest'; and two days later the newspaper reported that 'the contest is, in a great measure, a political trial of strength betwixt Mr Dundas and the Scottish Opposition. Both that gentleman and Mr Pitt, it is said, have personally interfered in the canvas in favour of Dr Carlyle.' Reporting ruefully to Dundas after Carlyle's defeat, Hill confessed that 'The Foxites are triumphant', and admitted that Henry Erskine had shown superior tactical skill.[41]

In 1790 the question of the Test Act was raised by the Popular Party. In theory this Act discriminated against members of the Church of Scotland by making it impossible for them to hold an official post or military commission in England without first receiving the sacrament according to the rites of the Church of England, although in fact it seems rarely to have been enforced. Despite Moderate protests, the Assembly appointed a committee to seek redress from the grievance, and a petition was sent to parliament. Hill and Carlyle felt that the committee should have begun by 'corresponding with Ministers of State in order to learn the sentiments of Government' – a good illustration of the way in which the Moderates thought relations between Church and State should be conducted. They certainly supplied the Lord Advocate and other Scottish officials with arguments against the petition; and Dr Somerville of Jedburgh, the proposer of the motion, noted regretfully that the business soon became a party issue, and was used by 'those who were at that time hostile to the existing administration [of Pitt]' as a stick with which to beat the government.[42] Again, Hill's report to Dundas is illuminating. He criticizes the Lord Advocate for failing to perceive that 'his political opponents had laid hold of some good well-meaning ministers as their tools for bringing forward a discussion of which they mean to make all the mischief they can'. He continues in words which rather call in question the traditional picture of Moderate hegemony in the Kirk at this period:

'I must be allowed to add that the situation of the moderate Interest in the Church has become very distressing. We have to combat our old Enemies [i.e. the Popular Party] who are accustomed to oppose us at all points; and in every question that trenches upon politics these old Enemies are reinforced and led by a desertion of all the Foxites. The Summit to which Harry Erskine's ambition is allowed at present to reach, is to appear the Governor of our Church.'[43]

During the dangerous 1790s party politics were seldom heard in the Assembly, after the Duke of Portland had ordered Erskine and the Popular leaders to desist. Nevertheless, it is possible to detect more than a hint of political partisanship in the Popular Party's rejection of the Moderate proposals for a uniform system of licensing of Chapels of Ease in 1795, and still more in some of the arguments used on both sides in the 1796 debate on Missions. Both episodes have been grotesquely exaggerated by historians who have seen in the Moderate attitude positive disapproval of missionary activity and active discouragement of church-extension at the behest of a reactionary government. The Moderate leaders and the Lord Advocate consulted one another as a matter of convenience to both, but even in the most intimate correspondence of Hill and Dundas there is no evidence of improper interference by government in the affairs of the Church. At worst, the Moderates can be convicted of an instinctive tendency to rally to the *status quo* at a time of social unrest.

The fall of Dundas certainly contributed to the discomfiture of the Moderates in Leslie's Case in 1805, and the Opposition was jubilant. In 1806, however, despite the active support of the Whigs, the Popular candidate for the post of Procurator of the Church was defeated in the Assembly.

In 1807 the battle between 'Whigs' and 'Tories' in the Assembly reached a sensational climax. As in 1776 and 1782 trouble started with the debate on the Address. The version proposed by the Moderates was alleged to contain an insolent clause congratulating George III on the dismissal of the Whig government, approving the royal veto on Catholic emancipation, and condemning in advance renewed Popular agitation against the Test Act. But more serious was the question of the vacant Clerkship of the Assembly. In November 1806 the Moderates put forward Dr Dickson of Leith as their official candidate, while the Popular Party adopted Mr Duncan of Ratho. Hill described Dickson as 'a steady friend of the Moderate Interest, much liked in the Church, and not recommended by any political Interest', and added 'I was willing to hope that these circumstances...would have prevented a political opposition to this ecclesiastical choice, but Sir Henry Moncreiffe has started his friend Mr Duncan of Ratho, and I suspect [Grenville's] Government mean to give him their decided support'.[44] This was an understatement. The Solicitor-General virtually ordered the Moderates to drop Dickson – which, says Hill, 'was not be born'. Hill seriously expected to lose his Royal Chaplaincy, but was resolved not to desert his principles or his friends, even though he feared the necessity 'to retrench my present way of life, that I may not encroach on my Stock'.[45] In January Dr Grieve (one of the Moderate 'managers' in Edinburgh) was visited by an agent of Lord Spencer, the Home Secretary, who demanded the withdrawal of Dickson's candidature forthwith and hinted that the government expected the Chaplains to vote for Duncan. Grieve sent a dignified reproof to Spencer, intimating that although the Moderates had always cherished a 'Spirit of Subordination and of Submission to lawful Authority', and had always 'been desirous to maintain a good Correspondence with His Majesty's Ministers', yet they had never asked or received specific directions from government, and were not disposed to listen to the inclinations of the Home Secretary on this or any other occasion. Grieve also mentioned the Solicitor-General's intervention, and branded it as 'an unprecedented step, which would have a tendency to subvert the independence of the Church'.[46] Finlayson claimed that the Moderate canvass was made 'as little thro' political interest as possible'.[47] Nevertheless, although the Whigs lost office in March, Duncan was elected by 180 votes to 132 – a defeat which shook the Moderates and hastened the rise of their opponents.

These circumstances should, I think, make us chary of accepting at face value the charges of 'Erastianism' which have been levelled at the Moderates. It is true that the Moderate alignment with Dundas drove their opponents into alignment with the 'Foxites' – but the reverse is also true. It does seem to be apparent that, whether the chicken or the egg came first, the Popular Party was used deliberately and not unwillingly as a 'front' by the opposition political groups, and notably by Henry Erskine and his backers.

It remains to be considered how far the Moderate alignment with Dundas really furthered the interests of the party. The rather unexpected conclusion emerges from the evidence that Dundas was far less committed to supporting the Moderates than has sometimes been supposed. This is another example of the vicious circle in which the Moderates found themselves entangled, and shows clearly the limits which were set to their control of the Kirk. They sincerely believed that their loyalty entitled them to consideration by Government in the exercise of Crown patronage and the distribution of royal Chaplaincies and and Deaneries and other offices. At the same time they urged government to ignore the protests of the Landed Interest and institute legislation for the long-awaited augmentation of clerical stipends. Yet, with the exception of the clergy's exemption from the Window Tax, extorted by Carlyle on a trip to London, government remained blandly indifferent to the demands of the clergy for financial relief, up to 1790. When augmentation finally came, it was thanks to the Lord President of the Court of Session, not Dundas.

Complaints of neglect by government were frequently voiced by the Moderates. As early as 1766 Robertson theatened that he would 'entirely withdraw from all sort of church business and management' unless 'the ministry choose to bestow those marks of their countenance upon such clergymen as are friends to government and law'.[48] Carlyle's dissatisfaction with the attitude of Ministers of State (including, as time went, Dundas) was perennial. In 1781 he complained of 'the total negligence of administration, almost ever since the accession of this King', which had allowed 'a very great number of illiterate Fanaticks to slip in amongst us'[49] and he was probably the author of a memorandum to government in 1783 which begged that the Kirk should be 'carefully look't after' by a timely augmentation of stipends and a more careful exercise of Crown patronage.[50] In 1793 he again complained that 'the Moderate clergy if not upheld by government however individually they may maintain their character will soon be annihilated as a Party and give way to the intrigues of their opponents'; and he held out the awful prospect of the Assembly being filled with 'Burgh Elders raging with democratic zeal'.[51]

How far were these complaints justified? In 1808 Dundas' nephew tried to persuade government to present a Moderate to the Canongate Church, and pointed out that on the whole the Popular Party had been much more successful in obtaining presentations for their supporters:

'The Popular Party in the Church, like the opposition in the State are infinitely more assiduous in their Measures...and by applying through every possible Channel they have in the case of every Vacancy of a Church in Scotland, succeeded as often in putting in Clergy of their way of Thinking, that many Presbyteries... are now gradually converted into Wild Presbyteries, and uniformly send to the Assembly Members of that Description'.[52]

Analysis of effective royal presentations between 1752 and 1810, in cases where it is possible to gauge the party proclivities of the presentees, suggests that government favour was shown fairly equally to clergy of both parties; and in the case of Chaplaincies, Deaneries and the Royal Almonership the Popular Party received at least some share (about one third) of the loaves and fishes.

From the *Scottish Correspondence* in the Public Record Office it appears that from 1783 onwards Dundas kept a very close eye on the distribution of Crown livings, either personally or through his nephew Robert Dundas. In sifting the multitude of applications and recommendations which flowed in, Dundas was normally guided by the preferences of the resident heritors of the parish, and the MP (unless he was in 'Opposition'). While willing to gratify the Moderates when this could be done without inconvenience to himself, he was very far from being disposed to follow their dictation. The strongest motive that weighed with him was undoubtedly political advantage. Thus in 1784 Lord Leven recommended a notorious adherent of the Popular Party to the parish of Markinch, and Dundas allowed him to be presented despite an agonized protest from Dr Drysdale, who warned the Lord Advocate that 'it will discourage the Moderate Party whose exertions will be much needed for next Assembly'.[53] In 1791 he rejected two Moderate candidates for a vacancy at Linlithgow, despite Blair's warning that the presbytery was evenly divided, and that the presentation of a Popular minister would 'raise discontent...among all the Moderate clergy'.[54] In 1789 a similar *contretemps* arose over the appointment of a 'Wild' chaplain at Stirling castle;[55] and in 1799 Finlayson protested in vain against the presentation of a Popular minister to the Crown living of Denny after he had been recommended by the 'Wild' parishioners through the agency of the principal heritor.[56] In 1794 Dundas secured a presentation for the vehement opponent of the Moderates, Dr Burnside, after being informed by the Lord Provost of Edinburgh that Burnside had shown 'the most steady attachment to Government' and was 'much connected with many of your warm friends in Edinburgh and Leith'.[57]

Carlyle noted with chagrin that the recommendations made by himself and his friends were often ignored altogether. In 1786 he wrote to Dundas on behalf of four ministers 'who were very active in my service, who should if possible be rewarded', but nothing was done for any of them for twelve years. Between 1803 and 1805 he again made desperate applications for a Crown living for his own assistant Dr Lee but without success.[59] Like the other Moderate leaders, Carlyle was gravely upset by the decision of Dundas to give an equal share of royal Chaplaincies to members of the Popular Party in 1793. He bluntly warned Dundas that the Popular Party were a bunch of 'Fanaticks and Demagogues' unworthy of government favour, and Hill thanked him for his courageous letter : 'If the scheme of equalising Court favour goes on, the Moderate Interest will soon vanish from the face of the earth : and Government may have more trouble than they are aware of'.[60] Years later Robert Dundas referred to this incident, and made it quite plain that he and his uncle had 'concurred in opinion that both sides of the Church should have a fair share of the King's Patronage'.[61] In private Dundas repudiated any sense of dependence upon the Moderates, and gave instructions that a rumour that he was consistently taking Moderate advice should be scotched forthwith.[62] His attitude is well summed up by his son, in a letter written during his last illness:

'It is rather too much to expect that in all cases whatever, where the Crown is patron...the Patronage of the Crown is to be bestowed from no other Motive and with no other view than to uphold what

is called the Moderate Party in the Church of Scotland'.[63]
Much the same pattern is to be seen in Dundas's handling of university patronage. Potentially, the universities provided the Moderates with their chief strongholds, since the professors sat *ex officio* in every Assembly. Yet even at Edinburgh and St Andrews, which he controlled absolutely, Dundas did not always listen to Moderate pleas; and at Aberdeen and Glasgow he usually allowed himself to be guided by the wishes of their respective Chancellors. One of the most vigorous opponents of the Moderate regime was Principal W. L. Brown, whose appointment Dundas sanctioned in 1796.

Occasionally the Moderate Party even found itself ranged in public opposition to Dundas. Thus in 1798 Finlayson protested on behalf of the Moderate leaders against the royal presentation of a Mr Geary to a vacant Charge at Brechin, on the grounds that he was not only a 'Jacobin' but a fervent supporter of the Popular Party. Geary was, moreover, technically disqualified from accepting a presentation, having been licensed outwith Scotland by a congregation of English dissenters. Dundas was approached by the Popular leaders, who argued that the Moderate accusations were untrue and malicious, and he decided to allow Geary's presentation to stand.[64] This compelled the Moderates to try different tactics. They referred the matter to the Assembly, where their usual majority enabled them to declare Geary unlicensed and therefore not qualified to receive a presentation in Scotland. In this case the Moderates were able to use their control of the Assembly not only to discomfit their ecclesiastical opponents, but also to defeat the declared wishes of their 'patron' Dundas.

In 1782 Dr Thomas Hardy, professor of Church History at Edinburgh and a staunch supporter of the Moderate Interest, put his finger unwittingly on the real weakness of his party. In a pamphlet aimed at the Popular Party he denounced 'the ruinous system of making the settlement of ministers subservient to election-politics in the counties and boroughs of the kingdom'.[65] Coming from a Moderate, this looks like the pot calling the kettle black; but the significant thing about it is the fact that it antedates the political rise of Dundas. Had Hardy been writing ten years later, he might well have done so more in sorrow than in anger, since by then Dundas had gathered into his own hands the administration of Crown patronage in the Church, and thereby controlled the right of presentation to at least a third (and probably far more) of the parishes in Scotland. This could have been a source of enormous strength to the Moderate Party; in fact, as we have seen, it proved just the opposite. This, it seems to me, is the clue to the failure of the Moderates to maintain and extend their regime within the Kirk, and for the collapse of confidence which became apparent in the party at the turn of the century. It cannot be stressed too strongly that the Moderates were a minority regime. In order to maintain their control of the Assembly they came to rely increasingly upon the support of the predominant political 'Interest', and this turned out to be a broken reed. The French Revolution and the consequent social unrest in Britain made government less, not more, ready to commit itself to any one party in the Church; and the result was that the Moderates were left on the defensive, touchy, disappointed and ultimately 'reactionary'. Their alignment with Dundas served only to cement the political alliance of their opponents with the political opposition, and in the fullness of time this brought a political nemesis upon the party.

Moreover, as we have seen, there were a number of inconsistencies in the Moderate programme which became apparent when the party found itself in control of the affairs of the Church. Their original 'protest' of the 1750s represents an attempt to free the Kirk from what they regarded as its backward-looking and negative attitude to new currents in Scottish life and thought, and its subjection to 'management' by government and sectarian interests. Their ideal was a Kirk broadly-based and undogmatic, with its Assembly serving as a focus for all aspects of the national life – the peculiarly Scottish version of the 'Enlightenment'. In practice, what they believed to be their eminently 'rational' and harmonious regime was undermined almost from the start by 'irrational' forces beyond their control. Their vision of an independent Established Church cooperating with government foundered on the indifference of government and the intrusion of secular politics into the ecclesiastical arena. Their appeal for 'discipline' in the Church was turned against them by the upholders of theological orthodoxy. Their 'world-affirming' acceptance of the existing patterns of society became irrelevant when that society began to disintegrate. Even in theology the Moderates found themselves outflanked. In Leslie's Case in 1805 the Evangelicals vigorously criticized the traditional eighteenth-century armoury of 'proofs', 'evidences', 'Natural Religion' and the appeal to 'Reason' which the Moderates had taken for granted. These had already been undermined by the corrosive effect of David Hume, and while the Moderates sat appalled in the wreckage the Evangelicals were actually beginning to hail Hume as the guide to a new exploration in theology.

The Moderates can perhaps be compared to typical eighteenth-century 'Improvers', who canalized the stagnant stream of the Kirk to form an attractive ornamental water, spanned by elegant balustraded bridges and flanked by well-planted policies and the classical country seats of gentlemen who (of course with a Moderate as tutor) had made the Grand Tour in their youth. Before the century was out, Nature began to reassert herself, and landscaping in the Moderate manner passed out of fashion.

NOTES

1. W.Ferguson, *Scotland, 1689 to the Present* (1968), 127.
2. I.D.L. Clark, 'The Leslie Controversy, 1805', *Records of the Scottish Church History Society*, Vol. XIV (1963), 179–97.
3. Anon. to A. Carlyle, n.d. [Watermark 179?] (NLS, 3431, f. 238).
4. A.P. Stanley, *Lectures on the History of the Church of Scotland* (London 1872); R. Rainy, *Three Lectures on the Church of Scotland* (1872).
5. D. Craig, *Scottish Literature and the Scottish People, 1680–1830* (London 1961).
6. W.Ferguson, *Scotland*, 227.
7. G.E. Davie, *The Democratic Intellect ; Scotland and her Universities in the Nineteenth Century* (1961), xiv.
8. H. Dundas to T. Pelham, 14 Dec. 1801 (BM Add. MSS 33,108, f. 452).
9. A. Carlyle to Dr Douglas, 18 Apr. 1798 (NLS, 3116, f. 182). Six years earlier Carlyle wrote to Douglas, 'I must trust you for your Presbytery...Can you tell us how to Gain the Burgh of Jedburgh ?', 7 July 1783, ibid. f. 148.
10. P. Wodrow, *Copy of a Printed Letter signed John Gillies...with Observations Moral and Theological* (n.p. 1784), 12 ; *The Procedure of our Church Courts in the Case of Dr William M'Gill of Ayr* (n.p. 1792). 157.
11. *Autobiography of the Rev. Dr Alexander Carlyle of Inveresk, 1722–1805*, ed. J.H. Burton (1860), 561.
12. J. Mackenzie, *The Religious Establishment of Scotland Examined* (London 1771), 73.
13. Op. cit. 246.
14. A. Gerard, 'The Influence of Piety on the Public Good', in *The Scotch Preacher* (1775–89), 311.
15. W. Craig, *Sermons on various Subjects* (1808), i, 37 f.
16. A. Carlyle, *The Justice and Necessity of the War with our American Colonist Examined* (London) 1777.
17. G. Hill, *Sermons* (London 1796), 406 ff.
18. A. Carlyle to H. Dundas, n.d. [1793] (NLS, 3464, f. 96).
19. C.W. New, *The Life of Henry Brougham to 1830* (Oxford 1961), 126.
20. R. Lundie to C. Lundie, 17 Jan. 1792 (NLS, 1675, f. 89).
21. H. Blair, *Sermons* (1777–1801), i, 155.
22. N. Morren, *Annals of the General Assembly of the Church of Scotland, 1739–66* (1838–1840), i, 231.
23. *Narrative of the Whole Process respecting some late Publications of the Rev. Dr William M'Gill* (n.p. 1790), 1.
24. A. Carlyle, *The Usefulness and Necessity of a Liberal Education for Clergymen* (1793), 32.
25. W.L. Mathieson, *The Awakening of Scotland* (Glasgow 1910), 222.

26. PRO, S.P. 54/40, ff, 81, 92, 93, 181, 196, 204–6; 54/41 ff. 10–12.
27. J. Finlayson, 'A Short Account of the Life and Character of Dr Hugh Blair', (1801), in vol. 5 of Blair *Sermons*, 504.
28. G. Cook, *Life of the Late George Hill, D.D.* (1820), 115.
29. *Scots Magazine*, vol. 28 (1766), 338.
30. A. Carlyle to H. Dundas, n.d. [1793] (NLS, 3464, f. 95).
31. Ld Haddington to A. Carlyle, 12 June 1799 (EUL MSS Dc. 4. 41).
32. G. Hill to H. Dundas, 25 May 1793 (PRO HO. 102/5 f. 60); Dr Finlayson to R. Dundas, 14 Nov. 1792 (PRO HO 102/6 f. 13).
33. W. Craig to H. Dundas, 24 Nov. 1792 (ibid. f. 82).
34. C. N. Innes, *Memoir of Andrew Dalzel* (1861) 97; Robertson to Douglas [bishop of Carlisle] 15 Feb. 1793 (BM Egerton MSS 2182 f. 78).
35. C. Innes, op. cit. 62.
36. J. Playfair to W. Robertson, jnr, 6 Nov. 1774 (NLS, 3941, f. 168).
37. H. Blair to R. Dundas, 10 Dec. 1791 (NLS, 6, f. 37).
38. *Scots Magazine*, vol. 53 (1791), 151 f. [my italics].
39. J. Finlayson to Dr Lee, 10 Oct. 1805 (NLS, 3432, f. 61).
40. Ld Dalhousie to A. Carlyle, 30 Aug. 1784 (EUL MSS, Dc. 4. 41, f. 111).
41. G. Hill to H. Dundas, 2 June 1789 (St Andrew's UL MSS 4756).
42. *Minutes of the Proceedings of the Committee of the General Assembly on the Subject of the Test Act, 1790* (MS vol. in SRO); T. Somerville, *My Own Life and Times, 1741–1814*, ed. W. Lee (1861), 229.
43. G. Hill to H. Dundas, 2 June 1790 (St Andrew's UL, 4758).
44. G. Hill to H. Dundas, 13 Dec. 1806 (St Andrew's UL, 4817).
45. G. Hill to the Rev. F. Nicoll, 14 Dec. 1806 (NLS, 3432, f. 99).
46. Dr Grieve to Ld Spencer, 29 Jan. 1807 (NLS, 1057, ff. 29 et seq.).
47. J. Finlayson to F. Nicoll, 8 Dec. 1806 (NLS, 3432, f. 97).
48. *Memorials of the Public Life and Character of the Rt Hon. James Oswald of Dunnikier* (1825), 120.
49. A. Carlyle to Dr Douglas, 14 Mar. 1781, (BM, Egerton MSS 2185, f. 103).
50. PRO HO. 102/1, f. 137.
51. Copy of letter to Dundas, enclosed in a letter to Hill, Nov. 1793 (NLS, 3464, f. 44).
52. R. Dundas to R. S. Dundas, 4 July 1808 (NLS, 352, f. 6).
53. Dr Drysdale to I. Campbell, ? June 1784 (PRO HO 102/2 f. 90).
54. H. Blair to R. Dundas, 10 Dec. 1791 (NLS, 6, f. 37).
55. PRO HO 102/60, f. 53.
56. J. Finlayson to R. Dundas, 25 May 1799 (EUL, Laing MSS II, 501).
57. Ld Prov. Elder to H. Dundas, 31 Dec. 1793 (PRO HO 102/9, f. 347).
58. BM Add. MSS. 41,084 ff, 56, 58.
59. NLS, 3432, ff. 31–49.
60. G. Hill to A. Carlyle, 20 Aug. 1793 (EUL, Dc. 4. 41, 76); cf. NLS, 3464, f. 44.
61. R. Dundas to R. S. Dundas, 12 Feb. 1810 (NLS, 352, f. 54).
62. H. Dundas to [?], 25 June 1787 (PRO HO 102/3 ff. 137/8).
63. R. S. Dundas to [?], 6 Mar. 1811 (NLS, 352, f. 129).
64. PRO HO 102/16 ff. 1–7.
65. T. Hardy, *The Principles of Moderation, Addressed to the Clergy of the Popular Interest in the Church of Scotland* (1782), 65.

10. *The Social Background of the Scottish Renaissance* *

JOHN CLIVE

The question of the origin of the 'Scottish Renaissance' – that remarkable efflorescence of the mid-eighteenth century, with its roll call of great names: Hume, Smith, Robertson, Kames and Ferguson – is one of those historical problems which have hitherto stubbornly resisted a definite solution. This is not to imply that attempted explanations have failed to be forthcoming. On the contrary, ever since a learned Italian named Carlo Deanina applied himself to the problem in *An Essay on the Progress of Learning among the Scots* (1763), historians have suggested different reasons for that striking and apparently sudden outburst of creative energy. Macaulay saw the principal cause for what he considered to have been 'this wonderful change' from the barren wastes of seventeenth-century theology in the act passed by the Estates of Scotland in 1696 which was designed to enforce previous legislation setting up a school in every parish. Buckle, sounding a suitably Darwinian note, observed the energies displayed in the Scottish political and religious struggles of the seventeenth century surviving those struggles and finding another field in which they could exert themselves.

There is something to be said for both these points of view. The national system of education, though in practice never quite as ideal as in conception, enabled many a poor father's boy to go on to one of the universities as well prepared as his socially superior classmates. Nor can it be denied that in spite of the Fifteen and the Forty-five the general atmosphere of eighteenth-century Scotland was more conducive to peaceful pursuits than that of the strife-torn decades of the seventeenth century. But it requires no more than a little reflection on cultural history to perceive that neither peace nor public education,

* This essay was first written some years ago, as a part – eventually not published – of the author's *Scotch Reviewers : The Edinburgh Review, 1802–1815* (London 1957). In bringing it up to date for this volume the author would like to acknowledge the help of Dr Nicholas Phillipson and Professor H. J. Hanham. He also acknowledges occasional quotations from John Clive and Bernard Bailyn, 'England's Cultural Provinces: Scotland and America', *William and Mary Quarterly*, 3rd Series, xi (1954), 200–13.

nor their conjunction, guarantees the intellectual achievements suggested by the word 'renaissance'.

Similar objections can be advanced concerning some of the other so-called 'causes' of Scotland's golden age. Thus it is certainly true that the eighteenth century, in contrast to the seventeenth, was for Scotland a period of increasing economic prosperity. However, the disastrous Darien scheme of the 1690s ate up that capital fuel without which even the most rigorous Protestant ethic could not become economically efficacious. The immediate effect of the Union of 1707 was not the expected sudden prosperity, but, rather, increased taxation and loss of French trade. Nor, until much later, was there a compensatory expansion of commerce with England and the colonies. Real economic advancement did not come until later in the century, too late to serve as a satisfactory reason for the first stages of Scotland's great creative period.[1]

The Union, of course, had effects more immediate than those in the economic field. It was not only the sixteen Peers and forty-five Members of Parliament making the annual pilgrimage to London who acquired English tastes and aped English fashions. Scottish society did not want to lag behind its southern counterpart, and the tremendous popularity of London literary periodicals among its members exemplifies only one of the countless means by which English cultural influence reached the North. What a mere listing of English influences leaves unexplained, however, is the high degree of receptiveness to those influences which might, after all, have fallen on barren ground. That school of thought which sees Scotland 'forced back upon herself' by the Union avoids this problem by laying prime stress on the vernacular revival and the strength of native Scottish literary tradition. There is no gainsaying the importance of a tradition that helped to inspire Ramsay, Macpherson, Burns and Scott. But it must be remembered that their achievements were part of a literary production bifurcated throughout in terms of 'pure' English and Scottish vernacular.[2]

As for the influence of 'New Light' Hutcheson, his Glasgow lectures – effusions on the marvellous powers of the 'moral sense' by an enthusiastic disciple of Shaftesbury – no doubt 'contributed very powerfully to diffuse, in Scotland, that taste for analytical discussion and that spirit of liberal enquiry, to which the world is indebted for some of the most valuable productions of the eighteenth century'.[3] But holding them solely responsible for the Scottish enlightenment is surely expecting a little too much, even from the most lucid philosopher. Furthermore, it is worth noting that after Hutcheson's first year at Glasgow, at least one contemporary observer singled him out for praise because he was maintaining the cause of orthodox Christianity in a university shot through with free thought. The fact is that by the time Hutcheson began his lectures, considerable breaches had already been made in the dam of orthodox austerity so laboriously constructed during the embattled decades of the previous century.

Adequate explanations of the origins of the Scottish Renaissance, therefore, must take account not only of a variety of social factors at the moment of fullest flowering, but also of the conditions of growth in the previous period. It is always dangerous to confuse origins and causes, but a knowledge of the former often helps to elucidate the latter. To what extent had enlightened ideas broken through Presbyterian orthodoxy by 1729, the year of Hutcheson's appointment? Did this process date from the Union, or had it begun before? What kind of people were interested in secular intellectual activities? What was the role of the Scottish Kirk and the Universities in these developments? The city of Edinburgh is bound to be the principal focus for seeking answers to such questions. For one thing, it is well to keep in mind Lecky's caution that intellectual currents such as Moderatism in the Church were almost wholly confined to the big cities; so that, for instance, over the greater part of Scotland, the empire of the old Kirk was little shaken in the course of the eighteenth century.[4] For another, Edinburgh remained, even after 1707, the administrative, legal, ecclesiastical, and intellectual centre of Scotland, a position which could be disputed only by the growing commercial wealth and the influential university teaching of Glasgow. Studying the genesis of eighteenth-century Edinburgh culture is thus really tantamount to studying the origins of the Scottish enlightenment.

Any such study – and here no more is intended than to suggest possible lines of investigation – would have to begin with the consideration that apart from David Hume there were no professional men of letters in eighteenth-century Scotland. We find Dugald Stewart, in his *Life of Robertson*, commenting on the fact that in the 1730s the trade of authorship was unknown in Scotland, and that her high rank among the learned nations of Europe had, for many years, been sustained entirely 'by a small number of eminent men, who distinguished themselves by an honourable and disinterested zeal in the ungainful walks of abstract science'.[5] Boswell, writing in 1763, noted after a supper with Johnson and Goldsmith that 'I had curious ideas when I considered that I was sitting with London authors by profession'.[6] The main reason for the difference between Scotland and England in this regard is not far to seek. The Scottish reading public was not sufficiently large for the support of professional authors; and, whereas in London patrons and booksellers had in turn assumed a tutelary function – with authors bound to them in varying degrees and often in unsavory fashion, but free to devote their entire time to writing–inEdinburghliteratureremained,forthemostpart,theby-product of men engaged in other professions. Lawyers, professors and clergymen produced most of the outstanding literary works of the Scottish Enlightenment.

Of the three, the lawyers undoubtedly played the most important role. Not only do individual names, such as those of Mackenzie, Kames, Monboddo, Scott, Jeffrey and Brougham indicate the significance of the legal profession for Scottish literary history. But lawyers and judges of lesser renown contributed as much through their active interest in literature and philosophy which formed part of their continuous concern for intellectual and cultural pursuits, a concern that befitted their aristocratic class standing in Edinburgh society. Peter Williamson's first *Edinburgh Directory* (1773–4) which listed citizens in an order of rank originally sanctioned in 1532 was headed by Lords of Session, Advocates, Writers to the Signet, and Lords' and Advocates' Clerks, in that sequence. The category of 'noblemen and gentlemen' followed after.[7] It must, of course, be remembered that both the Faculty of Advocates and the Writers to the Signet were closed corporations of gentlemen, with high entrance fees and exclusive regulations. Dr Phillipson has shown that between 1707 and 1751, 96 per cent of entrants to the Faculty of Advocates came either from landed families or from families with close landed connections. The corresponding percentage for the period 1752–1811 was almost as high, i.e. 88 per cent.[8] In any event, because Scotland kept her own legal system after the Union, and the principal Law Courts were located in Edinburgh, judges and lawyers there possessed an importance that transcended their rank by birth.

Such a desirable profession naturally attracted a great many unsuccessful aspirants. An English visitor to Edinburgh, writing shortly after the publication of Williamson's *Directory*, commented on the 'almost innumerable' number of gentlemen styled advocates, few of whom had much business. He added, more acerbly than accurately, that 'every man who has nothing to do, and no better name to give himself, is called advocate'.[9] One wonders whether this same observer who declared himself vastly impressed with the literary attainments of Edinburgh society, was aware of the intimate, though hardly illicit, connection between the Law and the Muses which had long characterized the city.

A good example of this connection is provided by an analysis of the membership of the Select Society, founded in 1754 for the dual purpose of philosophical inquiry and improvement in public speaking.

By 1759 this society had come to include all the Edinburgh literati, in addition to many of the nobility and gentry. A membership list of that year totalled 135; of whom 119 can readily be identified by profession. Of these at least 40 were associated with the law in one way or the other.[10] A generation earlier, the membership list of the Rankenian Club, a philosophical society of 'learned and respectable men', founded in 1716, had included five lawyers, as against only four university professors.[11] Is there any explanation for this affinity between Scottish law and Scottish culture? Why did the lawyers indeed constitute 'a body of men who in Scotland had all along taken a decided lead in matters of taste and literature'?[12]

In dedicating his *Institutions of the Laws of Scotland* to Charles II (in 1681) Viscount Stair, perhaps the greatest legal mind produced in Scotland during the seventeenth century, made the proud boast that Scottish law could be compared to any in the world, noting that 'those that applied themselves to that profession amongst us, have given great evidence of sharp and piercing Spirits, with much Readiness of Conception and Dexterity of Expression'.[13] He might have added that it was not just the professional lawyers who concerned themselves with the study of Scottish law. An edict by James I (of Scotland) and an Act of Parliament under James IV had decreed that all barons and freeholders must have their oldest sons instructed in the law.[14] The tradition, thus dating back to the fifteenth and sixteenth centuries, which linked the Scottish gentry with the attainment of legal knowledge and which, in this way, helped to give the law such an influential place in society, was steadily carried on; so that Blackstone, in 1758, could single out Scotland as a place where 'it is difficult to meet with a person of liberal education, who is destitute of competent knowledge in that science which is to be the guardian of the natural rights and the rule of his civil conduct.[15] He made a contrast between Scotland and England in this respect and connected the more pervasive role played by the law in the national life of 'the northern parts of our own island' with the fact that municipal laws were there frequently related to the civil [i.e. Roman] laws. And there is no doubt about the crucial significance of this relationship for the theme of this essay.

Roman Law came to Scotland mainly at second hand from French practitioners and the French courts, through Scottish students who studied in France in the course of the sixteenth century.[16] On the one hand, it is well to guard against over-estimating its influence: though Scottish municipal law was in many respects founded upon it, the instances in which customs and statutes differed from it were in fact so numerous that it could be said that to understand Justinian was far less difficult than to perceive his application to Scottish practice.[17] On the other hand, the undoubted emphasis placed upon Roman Law in the training and qualification of Scottish lawyers meant that many law students pursued their studies on the continent, first mainly in France, later in Holland, and were thus exposed to the intellectual influences current there. A reliable estimate reveals that between 1600 and 1800 approximately sixteen hundred Scottish students (many of them future lawyers) studied at the University of Leyden alone, the greater number during the latter part of the seventeenth century.[18]

The continental course in 'natural jurisprudence' made for a close association of legal studies with moral philosophy and political science, and brought a philosophical and scientific tinge into the realm of Scottish Law.[19] The influence of Grotius and Thomasius is particularly important in this context, since it tended towards a humanistic rationalism alien to the prevailing intellectual temper of seventeenth-century Scotland, and since it helped to cement a fruitful union between law and philosophy at the Scottish universities. It is of some significance that Hutcheson's predecessor at Glasgow, Gershon Carmichael, edited Grotius (1724), and that Hutcheson's own lectures on moral philosophy can be said 'to form perhaps the most complete view of legal philosophy of the time'.[20]

Grotius had carried his secularism so far as to assert that the laws of reason would remain valid, even if no God existed.[21] Stair, whose *Institutions* long remained the most influential commentary on Scottish Law, was a militant Presbyterian, in spirit far removed from the Dutch jurist; though significantly enough, he had begun his career as a regent in philosophy at the University of Glasgow. Stair denied the validity of the Decalogue for all nations and all times not because Roman Law had taken its place, but because man's 'pravity' had so much increased vice and deceit since then that what had been sufficient in the simplicity of the time of the Old Testament now fell short of what was needed. Stair specifically cited Grotius in support of the doctrine of law as a rational discipline, having principles from which its conclusions could be deduced; and, exalting law as the dictate of reason, he adduced the argument that even God chose to determine Himself by His goodness, righteousness, and truth.[22] But Peter Stein has acutely observed that Stair differs from continental natural lawyers such as Grotius and Pufendorf in maintaining that a rational theory of law cannot be independent of theological assumptions. Law is founded primarily in the will of God. Reason remains a subsidiary instrument. Logic has its limits. No legal system can dispense with authority. Law is neither entirely logic nor entirely experience, but a mysterious mixture of the two. Professor Stein points out that Stair was only the first of a succession of Scottish legists who challenged natural law theory and thus paved the way for a socio-historical conception of the law.[23]

The study of Roman Law, and the study of history, were in any event in close alliance. In 1689, when Sir George Mackenzie delivered his inaugural address as the opening of the Advocates' Library in Edinburgh – while the town was swarming with his Whig enemies – he declared that this library was to be purely legal, differing in this way from all other libraries. Nevertheless, historical works had to be included, as essential adjuncts of legal studies.[24] It was thus entirely appropriate that in 1719 the Faculty of Advocates sponsored the appointment of Charles Macky, a lawyer, as the first Professor of Civil History in the University of Edinburgh. The names of Hume, Robertson and Ferguson bear witness to the important place of history in eighteenth-century Scottish letters. The Scottish Bar can rightly claim a share in planting the seed from which these fruits were to spring.

The share Edinburgh lawyers had in the appointment of a history professor in 1719 did not mark the first such contact between the University and the legal profession. In 1590, only a few years after the founding of the College of Edinburgh, Lords of Session, Advocates, and Writers to the Signet joined the Town Council in making provision for a professor of law.[25] But the appointees under this grant never taught law, perhaps because the ministers of Edinburgh followed the example of the Venerable Pastors of Geneva who had remonstrated strongly against the law faculty there, and had singled out the dissolute habits of the young men of quality who wanted to study under that faculty.[26] Whatever the reason, the failure of this project is indicative of the failures that were to mar Scottish university education during the seventeenth century. In the *First Book of Discipline* the early Scottish reformers had made radical proposals for the improvement of higher education, but these were never carried into effect. The Scottish nobility and gentry generally went abroad to study; the majority of the student body at the College of Edinburgh consisted of theological students 'from the middling ranks of society'; and the quality of learning in the School for Theological Studies is reliably described as 'very slight'.[27]

To what extent can the Kirk of Scotland be held responsible for the low state of higher education during the seventeenth century? Can that revisionist history which has exonerated the New England Puritans from obscurantism be made to yield the same results for the Scottish Presbyterians? It must certainly be granted that there is no ineluctable antithesis between Calvinism and secular culture; though Max Weber's reference to its fundamental antagonism to sensuous culture of all kinds does have particular validity for Scotland. What must be kept in mind, however, is the fact that the spiritual distance between Geneva and the Scottish Kirk remained far smaller than that, say, between Geneva and English Puritanism. The fundamental and irreconcilable conflict between the English Independents and the Scottish Presbyterians illustrates one aspect of a difference which, as Tawney suggested, may have 'depended, above all, on the question whether Calvinists were, as at Geneva and in Scotland, a majority, who could stamp their ideals on the social order, or, as in England, a minority, living on the defensive beneath the suspicious eyes of a hostile government'.[28]

It may be argued that even an authoritarian theocracy can buttress itself with learning; and that the classics can be persuaded to declare the glory of the Lord even as the Heavens. But, perhaps on account of its embattled state, perhaps because its original alliance with the nobility was only briefly resumed during the seventeenth century, the Scottish Kirk, for most of that century, constituted an inhibiting force in matters of culture and learning. The universities naturally tried to free themselves from this inhibition. Thus a joint Universities Commission, in 1647, advocated freedom from church control in all except ecclesiastical matters, and drew up a uniform course of studies. But the last sentence of one of the reform proposals submitted reveals the fate of all of them: 'This is to be understood ordinarily, and in peaceable tymes.'[29]

If the Church of Scotland is to be held solely responsible for the low state of university education, it is only proper to ask whether the period of the Restoration produced any remarkable changes for the better. To raise this question is to open up a complicated field of inquiry which will yield no simple answers. If one is to believe Dr Alexander Monro, Episcopalian Principal of the University of Edinburgh from 1685 to 1690, those years in particular were a golden time, 'when the government of the city of Edinburgh was lodged in the hands of the first and best order of citizens and gentlemen', – note this social emphasis! – and the Masters of the College 'had all the encouragement they themselves could wish', guarded by the magistrates against 'the little efforts of censorious and talkative Fanaticks'.[30] Monro is no unprejudiced witness; since, in 1690, he along with four other professors, was dismissed from the University as a non-juror. It is, none the less, undeniable that a certain upswing took place during the 'seventies and 'eighties, especially in the sciences. By 1690 David Gregory had begun to lecture on Newton, thus making the University of Edinburgh the first in all Europe where the *Principia* were publicly taught; and Sir Robert Sibbald had established the Medical

School, soon to become justly famed far beyond Scotland. Before their day the Scottish universities had hardly concerned themselves with science.[31] The fact that neither Gregory nor Sibbald was a Presbyterian may serve as a warning to those who would apply too readily to Scotland Robert Merton's thesis in regard to the elective affinities between Puritanism and science in seventeenth-century England.[32]

Yet to conclude from this that the new winds of doctrine which were blowing so hard all over Europe during the last four decades of the seventeenth century left the Scottish Presbyterians unaffected would be inaccurate. The Kirk itself was changing in character, especially in the course of the second half of the century; approximating less and less to the ideal type postulated by Buckle. Hume Brown writes about the 'mighty force of Presbyterianism', broken by repression and concession, the latter in the form of three Indulgences (1669; 1672; 1679) issued by Charles II which were accepted by the majority of the Presbyterian clergy. In so doing these ministers compromised the essential principles of their creed – by accepting the King's supremacy – but supplied a potent stimulant for the idea of toleration.[33] Meanwhile, the more liberal currents of Dutch theology had begun to exert increased influence, specifically the *De Veritate Religionis Christianae* of Grotius, whose steadily growing popularity foreshadowed the intellectual orientation of the eighteenth-century Moderates in the Church of Scotland.[34]

The main argument against crediting Episcopalians alone with the new spirit of the Universities, which found one means of expression in the falling off in attendance at 'dictation' sessions by students dissatisfied with the antiquated teaching methods, is the continuance of this spirit after the re-establishment of Presbyterianism. This is not to say that the difference between the two confessions had by then disappeared. On the contrary: while during the period of the Restoration their liturgical disagreements had been remarkably small, these were greatly intensified after the Revolution Settlement, when the Episcopalians 'drifted in a definitely English direction'.[35] And there was no lack of occasion for conflict in the political and social realms. But Covenanting days and ways were over. A man such as William Carstares, elected Principal of Edinburgh University in 1703, exemplifies this change. Though twice tortured with 'thumbikins' for his knowledge of the Rye House Plot, he continued to count several Jacobites among his close friends. His great dream was of a revival of learning through the importation of professors from abroad; and although he was unable to accomplish this, under his administration the university curriculum was increasingly modelled on that of Utrecht and Leyden, the old 'regenting' system being replaced by formal lectures.[36]

Glasgow University, meanwhile, had begun to send its theology students to Holland on an increasingly large scale, usually for post-graduate studies.[37] One of the results was a greater spirit of tolerance, which made itself felt in frank theological discussion. To observe the extent to which this tendency developed in a relatively brief time it is instructive to examine the comments of the Rev. Robert Wodrow, a Presbyterian of the old school, on the activities and attitudes of Edinburgh and Glasgow University students in the mid-1720s; remembering that this was some years before Hutcheson 'officially' inaugurated the Scottish enlightenment.

In December 1724, Wodrow (not one to take these matters lightly) noted that the divinity students at Glasgow were openly opposing the Confession of Faith; that there was much reading of Deists and anti-Confessionists; and that thirty to forty students, finding these conditions unbearable, were reputed to have left for Edinburgh. He added that the Professor (of theology) allowed the students 'lightness and liberty of speaking'.[38] A few months later (February 1725) Wodrow once again voiced concern over Glasgow where student clubs were debating such questions as 'The role of moral goodness' and 'Whether God could make the sun better than it is' ; where other clubs ventured to 'declare against reading, and cry up thinking'; and where, *horribile dictu,* a farce about the ministers of the town had been composed. Little more than a year after this, accounts reached Wodrow of atheistical clubs in Edinburgh, meeting very secretly, and taking their origin from a Hell-fire club in London. Wodrow's comment about all this was succinct and to the point : 'Wickedness is come to a new height!'[39]

It was not the first time that club life in Edinburgh had supplied material for Wodrow's Jeremiads. In December 1724, in the course of the very month in which the band of pious Glasgow students was reported to have sought the reputedly more orthodox atmosphere of the capital, word had reached him that for some years Edinburgh had been harbouring a club whose members, including several ministers, were convinced that 'we're in a way of too narrov [sic] thinking in this country; and that some of the younger students inclined to have some great freedom of thoughts'.[40] This club, as is clear from the names of the members supplied by Wodrow, was none other than the Rankenian Club, the Philosophical Society whose membership list of nineteen we found to have included five lawyers.[41]. The number of clergymen amounted to no less than seven. The old Kirk still had its adherents. But a Presbyterianism mollified to the point where it produced (in Ramsay of Ochtertyre's phrase) 'cluster[s] of clerical *literati*' was in the ascendant. An Edinburgh philosophical club consisting mainly of lawyers, ministers and professors, its membership in sympathy with the desire for greater freedom of thought on the part of university students – there could be no better illustration of the thesis of this essay up to this point. What must be primarily emphasized is the fact that while by the 1720s the cultural results of the Union had certainly begun to take effect, autonomous developments in the realms of the law, the church, and university education, dating back at least as far as the end of the seventeenth century, had done much to prepare the ground for the reception of English influences.[42]

The diffusion of those influences owed a great deal to the Scottish nobility and gentry, especially to those among them not prosperous enough to look on London rather than Edinburgh as their proper metropolis. In the course of the seventeenth century, the old alliance between the Scottish Presbyterians and the nobility had only been briefly revived. That revival was impelled by Charles I whose Act of Revocation (1625) threatened to annex to the Crown all church and crown lands alienated since the accession of Mary Stuart. The nobles saw, at this point, that their interests were tied to the anti-Royalist cause, and a majority of them signed the Covenant of 1678. The General Assembly of the Kirk, in its sittings that year, might have established a moderate Episcopacy, embracing all ranks of the people. But its intransigence on all issues involving theology and church organization prevented this compromise whose political and cultural results would have been considerable.[43] By mid-century the nobility found itself still in the possession of its estates; while the Bishops, of whose new powers it had been jealous, had ceased to exist. From this time on it drifted away from Presbyterianism; working very hard for the restoration of Charles II, and, after this had been accomplished, loyally supporting Episcopacy and the Stuarts. Hume Brown goes so far as to state that after the Revolution and William's accession, only one solitary Scottish noble, Crawford, displayed pronounced Presbyterian sympathies.[44] Most of the nobility and a large part of the gentry certainly remained Episcopalian and – what almost invariably followed – Jacobite.[45]

In matters of taste, manners and culture they were thus unencumbered by those ascetic proclivities against which even the growing body of moderate Presbyterians still had to struggle; and this made it easier for them to supply the essential froth for the potent mixtures starting to brew around the turn of the century.[46] Their study and travel abroad had given them at least a modicum of cosmopolitan propensities, from which Edinburgh derived much benefit. For the Darien failure left many of them too poor to travel abroad, and brought them to the capital each winter.[47] They had already played the principal role in the amusements and – as some said – the excesses which shocked and delighted the citizens of Edinburgh after the Restoration.[48] And their strong hold on Edinburgh society continued in spite of the return of Presbyterianism. For their religion was not proscribed; and they were not persecuted for their politics. They kept alive the spirit of sports, concerts, dancing, gaiety, and general *bonhomie*; and thus set a tantalizing example for the more liberal-minded of the Presbyterians.[49]

There is little doubt about the fact that in the years immediately following the Union, Episcopalianism became increasingly fashionable – perhaps because it was considered an emollient for the painful wound left by a growing awareness of provincialism. 'Such was episcopal influence among the professional classes and gentry in the early years of the century', Douglas Duncan writes about the Jacobite Thomas Ruddiman, 'that his beliefs seem to have helped rather than hindered his career'.[50] As usual, Wodrow found the *mot juste*. There was, he noted, 'a disrelishing of Presbyterian Government'.[51] Some Presbyterian ministers, seeing which way the wind was blowing, changed their tack : 'The peculiar doctrines of Christianity would, they hoped, be more acceptable to the nobility and gentry for being set forth in a language worthy of a Tillotson and an Atterbury whose works were universally admired in those days' (i.e. after 1714).[52] And while a large proportion thus appealed to remained equally loyal to Episcopalianism and Jacobitism, there is a good deal of significance in the strangely sweet modulations with which they were now being enticed. Episcopalianism had already acquired something of the aura which, many years later, impelled Boswell to end a catalogue of the things he wanted most to do during his lifetime with the desire to attend the 'Church of England Chapel' in Edinburgh.[53]

The cultural stirrings of the early eighteenth century owed much to the Jacobites, and not just to those of noble birth. Nearly all the Edinburgh printers and booksellers at this time, among them the anthologist James Watson, were Jacobites and Episcopalians.[54] So were two of the most influential figures in the city's intellectual life: Dr Archibald Pitcairne – physician, wit, and, by repute, close to a freethinker; and Thomas Ruddiman, Librarian of the Advocates' Library, publisher and scholar. One must not forget, furthermore, the debt of the vernacular revival to 'disaffection'. Opposition to the Union meant an intensified patriotism which found cultural outlets. The works of Ramsay, Burns and Scott serve as the best illustration of Jacobite influence on Scottish literature.[55]

One reason for the important part played by Jacobites in the cultural life of Edinburgh derives from the fact that this cultural life was largely fostered by gentlemen's clubs and societies, many of whose members were politically 'disaffected'. The significance of the legal profession for Scottish culture has already been emphasized. In 1707 the great majority of the Faculty of Advocates was strongly attached to the Stuarts, as were most of the Writers to the Signet.[56] Ramsay of Ochertyre reported that 'near a majority' of the Lords and Earls of Session were similarly inclined, and raises the question of how they could reconcile this inclination with their oaths of allegiance. His answer is the cynical one that oaths of allegiance will not make men refuse lucrative and honourable offices.[57] However that may be, the fact that these judges and lawyers, whose political sympathies were, of course, well known, could keep their positions shows that the seventeenth-century atmosphere of struggle and persecution had been largely dissipated. When the Jacobite scholar Thomas Ruddiman founded Edinburgh's first purely literary society, for the purpose of mutual improvement in the classics, the original members declared in their charter that there was to be no meddling with the affairs of Church and State. That this injunction was indeed followed is proved by the membership of the society, which came to include Presbyterian ministers as well as Jacobite lawyers.[58] It may well be taken as symbolic of a new era.

The attempt has been made to show that the cultural revival in Scotland can best be understood in the light of the social and intellectual background of the late seventeenth and early eighteenth centuries; and that this approach yields a clearer view of the causes of that revival than those hitherto set forth, which have generally concentrated on the educational system, the Union of 1707, and assorted mysterious forces. English influence resulting from the Union fell on fertile soil: The Scottish Bar constituted a force congenial to new philosophical currents, historical studies, and other intellectual activities. The Kirk had changed greatly since Covenanting days and had begun to develop within itself the roots of that Moderatism which was to come to flower in the course of the eighteenth century. This process went hand in hand with a more liberal spirit among faculty and students at the universities, where curricula and teaching methods had also begun to undergo some improvement. In all these fields Dutch influence, transmitted through the large number of Scottish students at Dutch universities, had a significant and fruitful part to play. A portion of the Scottish nobility and gentry stood ready to foster cultural activities, with Edinburgh as their focus. And these activities owed something to the Episcopalianism and Jacobitism which many of these leading families professed.

One further question should be asked. When the flowering came, did Edinburgh's provincial cultural situation *vis-à-vis* London serve to inhibit or to enhance it? Throughout the century, certainly, life in Edinburgh was affected by the mere fact of physical removal from the cosmopolitan centre. For though the Scottish border lay less than three hundred miles from London, as late as 1763 only one regular stagecoach travelled between Edinburgh and the British capital. The trip took about two weeks, and those few who could afford to make it considered it so serious an expedition that they frequently made their wills before setting out. As far as the English were concerned, Smollett's Mrs Tabitha, who thought one could get to Scotland only by sea, represented no great advance over those of her countrymen earlier in the century to whom 'many parts of Africa and the Indies... are better known than a Region which is contiguous to our own, and which we have always had so great a concern for'.[58A] Even towards the middle of the century, there were occasions when the London mailbag for Edinburgh was found to contain only a single letter.

But isolation, as the late Perry Miller pointed out, 'is not a matter of distance or the slowness of communication: it is a question of what a dispatch from distant quarters means to the recipient.'[59] News, literature and personal messages from London did not merely convey information. They carried with them standards by which men and events were judged. In them was involved a definition of sophistication. *Tatlers* and *Spectators* were eagerly devoured in Edinburgh. Scottish ladies ordered all sorts of finery, from dresses to wallpaper, from England. And Wodrow complained that 'all the villainous, profane, and obscene books and plays, as printed in London, are got down by Allan Ramsay, and lent out, for an easy price, to young boys, servant weemen of the better sort, and gentlemen'.[60]

Communications from England exerted such authority because they fell upon minds conscious of limited awareness. A sense of inferiority pervaded eighteenth-century Scottish culture, affecting the great no less than the common. It lay behind David Hume's lament, in 1756, that 'we people in the country (for such you Londoners esteem our city) are apt to be troublesome to you people in town; we are vastly glad to receive letters which convey intelligence to us of things we should otherwise have been ignorant of, and can pay them back with nothing but provincial stories which are in no way interesting'. And it led Adam Smith to admit that 'this country is so barren of all sorts of transactions that can interest anybody that lives at a distance from it that little intertainment is to be expected from any correspondent on this side of the Tweed'. A young Scot returning to Edinburgh after a journey to the continent and London felt he had to 'labour to tone myself down like an overstrained instrument to the low pitch of the rest about me'.[61]

The manners and idioms that labelled the provincial in England were stigmas that Scotsmen tried strenuously to avoid. There was no subject about which they were more sensitive than their speech. Lieutenant Lismahago may have proved to his own satisfaction that 'what we generally called the Scottish dialect was, in fact, true, genuine English'. But Dr Johnson laughed at Hamilton of Bangour's rhyming 'wishes' and 'bushes'. And when in 1761 Thomas Sheridan, the playwright's father, lectured in Edinburgh (and in Irish brogue) on the art of rhetoric, he had an attentive audience of three hundred nobles, judges, divines, advocates, and men of fashion. Hume kept constantly by his side a list of Scots idioms to be avoided, and was said by Monboddo to have confessed on his deathbed not his sins but his Scotticisms.

The sense of inferiority that expressed itself in imitation of English ways, and a sense of guilt regarding local mannerisms was, however, only one aspect of the complex meaning of provincialism. Ramsay of Ochtertyre, for example, inveighed against the slavish imitation of English models as such a confession of inferiority 'as one would hardly have expected from a proud manly people, long famous for common-sense and veneration for the ancient classics'.[62] Awareness of regional limitations frequently led to a compensatory local pride. It was the conviction that in spite of its 'familiarity', life in Edinburgh possessed a congeniality and vigor all its own that made Robertson refuse all invitations to settle in London. Hume, too, in the midst of his Parisian triumphs, longed for the 'plain roughness' of the Poker Club and the sharpness of Dr Jardine, to correct and qualify the 'lusciousness' of French society.[63] Hume's complex attitude toward his homeland is significant. It is typical of a psychology which rarely failed to combat prejudice with pride.

For Scotsmen this pride was reinforced by the treatment they received in England, where their very considerable successes remained in inverse proportion to their popularity. One day Ossian, Burns and Highland tours would help to wipe out even memories of Bute. Meanwhile, in spite of their own 'Breetish' Coffee House, life in London was not always easy for visitors from north of the Tweed. 'Get home to your crowdie, and be d—d to you! Ha'ye got your parritch yet? When will you get a sheepshead or a haggis, you ill-far'd lown? Did you ever see meat in Scotland, saving oatmeal hasty pudding? Keep out of his way, Thomas, or you'll get the itch!'[64] The young Scotsman thus recounting his London reception added that little real malice lay behind such common jibes. But Boswell's blood boiled with indignation when he heard shouts of 'No Scots, No Scots! Out with them!' at Covent Garden. Yet only a few months later, he can be found addressing a memorandum to himself to 'be *retenu* to avoid Scotch sarcasting jocularity', and describing a fellow country-man as 'a hearty, honest fellow, knowing and active, but Scotch to the very backbone'.[65]

The deepest result of this complicated involvement in British society was that the provincial's view of the world was discontinuous. Two forces, two magnets, affected his efforts to find adequate standards and styles : the values associated with the simplicity and purity (real or imagined) of nativism, and those to be found in cosmopolitan sophistication. Those who could take entire satisfaction in either could maintain a consistent position. But for provincials, exposed to both, an exclusive conception of either kind was too narrow. It meant a rootlessness, an alienation either from the higher sources of culture or from the familiar local environment that had formed the personality. Few whose perceptions surpassed local boundaries rested content with a simple, consistent image of themselves or of the world. Provincial culture in eighteenth-century Scotland was formed in a mingling of these visions.

Undoubtedly, provincialism often served to inhibit creative effort. But there existed important factors which more than balanced its deleterious effects. The complexity of the provincial Scotsman's image of the world and of himself made demands upon him unlike those felt by the equivalent Englishman. It tended to shake the mind from the roots of habit and tradition. It led men to the interstices of common thought where they found new views and new approaches to the old. It cannot account for the existence of men of genius, but to take it into consideration may help us to understand the conditions which fostered in such men the originality and the creative imagination that we associated with the highest achievement of the Scottish Renaissance in the eighteenth century.

NOTES

1. Cf. T. C. Smout, *Scottish Trade on the Eve of Union 1660–1707* (1963). Smout dates significant economic advancement from about 1730.
2. This bifurcation is strikingly illustrated by the Easy Club, in whose founding (1712) Allan Ramsay had a part. Its members 'met in a Society By themselves in order that by a Mutual improvement in Conversation they may become more adapted for fellowship with the politer part of mankind and Learn also from one anothers happy observations.' Originally the six founding members picked English literary pseudonyms such as 'Bickerstaff', 'Rochester', and 'Newton'. By 1713 all except 'Newton' had assumed names connected with native literary history, Ramsay undergoing

a metamorphosis from 'Bickerstaff' to 'Gavin Douglas'. A. Gibson, *New Light on Allan Ramsay* (1927), 42 and 48.

3. D. Stewart, 'Account of the Life and Writings of Adam Smith, LL.D.,' in W. Hamilton, ed., *The Collected Works of Dugald Stewart* (1854–60), x, 82.

4. W. E. H. Lecky, *A History of England in the Eighteenth Century* (New York, 1878), ii, 97.

5. [D. Stewart], *Account of the Life and Writing of William Robertson* (London 1802), 4.

6. F. A. Pottle, ed., *Boswell's London Journal 1762–1763* (New York, 1950), 287.

7. H. W. Thompson, *A Scottish Man of Feeling* (New York 1831), ix.

8. Cf. N. T. Phillipson, 'The Scottish Whigs and the Reform of the Court of Session 1785–1830' (Cambridge University Doctoral Thesis, 1967).

9. [E. Topham], *Letters from Edinburgh, 1774–1775* (Dublin 1776), ii, 121.

10. The list, dated 17 Oct. 1759, is printed in Dugald Stewart's *Life* of Robertson, 214–20. The Rev. Alexander Carlyle, who supplied Stewart with the list, notes in his *Autobiography* (1910), 311–12, that it is incomplete. But he lists only two additional members, one of whom is a lawyer. Ibid. 312.

11. For a list of members (undated, but probably compiled in the 1720s) cf. A. F. Tytler, Lord Woodhouselee, *Memoirs of the Life and Writings of the Honourable Henry Home of Kames* (2nd edn., 1814), iii, 75–6. It totalled nineteen.

12. J. Ramsay of Ochtertyre, *Scotland and Scotsmen in the Eighteenth Century* (1888), i, 39.

13. James, Viscount Stair, *Institutions of the Laws of Scotland* (3rd edn., 1749), [ii].

14. Woodhouselee, *Kames*, i, 12.

15. W. Blackstone, *Commentaries on the Laws of England* (Chicago 1876), 4.

16. D. B. Smith, 'Roman Law', in *An Introductory Survey of the Sources and Literature of Scots Law* (Stair Society edn., 1936), 176.

17. Baron [David] Hume, *Lectures 1786–1822* (Stair Society edn., 1939), i, 2.

18. J. C. Gardner, 'French and Dutch Influences', in *Survey of Scots Law*, 233. Utrecht and Bourges also attracted many Scottish law students throughout the century. Dr Phillipson has found that the influence of Dutch law schools on Scotland began to decline by the beginning of the eighteenth century, at a time when sons of gentlemen were starting to desert the Bar for other forms of employment, and when Scottish law schools were beginning to grow in importance.

19. S. G. Kermack, 'Natural Jurisprudence and Philosophy of Law', in *Survey of Scots Law*, 440.

20. Ibid. 441.

21. On the works of Grotius as the antithesis of rigorous Protestantism, cf. E. Troeltsch, *The Social Teaching of the Christian Churches* (New York 1931), ii, 636; and the same author's *Die Bedeutung des Protestantismus fuer die Entstehung der modernen Welt* (Munich and Berlin 1911), 79.

22. Stair, *Institutions*, 2, 5–6, 13.

R

23. P.G. Stein, 'Legal Thought in Eighteenth-Century Scotland', *Juridical Review* (N.S., 11, 1957), 1–20.

24. A. Lang, *Sir George Mackenzie His Life and Times* (London 1909), 299.

25. A. Grant, *The Story of the University of Edinburgh During Its First Three Hundred Years* (London 1884), I, 202.

26. Ibid. I, 188.

27. A. Grant, *University of Edinburgh*, I, 188 ; and A. Bower, *The History of the University of Edinburgh* (1817), I, 214–15.

28. R.H. Tawney, *Religion and the Rise of Capitalism* (Pelican ed., New York 1947), 99–100.

29. Curriculum proposed by King's College, Aberdeen, cited in A. Morgan, *Scottish University Studies* (London 1933), 69.

30. A. Monro, *Presbyterian Inquisition*, quoted in 'Letters of Alexander Munro, 1690–1698', W.K. Dickson, ed., *Miscellany of the Scottish History Society*, 3rd Series, v (1933), 199.

31. A. Bower, *University of Edinburgh*, I, 269–70.

32. R.K. Merton, 'Puritanism, Pietism, and Science', in *Social Theory and Social Structure* (Glencoe Ill. 1940), 329–46. It is, however, worthy of note that some Presbyterians perceived no dangers in Cartesianism because they took it to show God's rational plan. Cf. G.D. Henderson, *Religious Life in Seventeenth-Century Scotland* (Cambridge 1937), 133. And by the 1720s the 'Literary Reformers' among the clergy began to approve of science because it ennobled the soul, 'leading it to contemplate and adore the Author of nature, in all his works and ways'. Ramsay, *Scotland*, I, 222.

33. P. Hume Brown, *History of Scotland* (Cambridge 1909), II, 414–15.

34. G.D. Henderson, *Religious Life*, 71–5. Hutcheson was thus not undertaking anything radically new when he conducted special classes on the *De Veritate* at Glasgow. Ibid. 260.

35. Ibid. 157.

36. A. Grant, *Story of University of Edinburgh*, I, 228–30 ; 262–3. See also D.B. Horn, *A Short History of the University of Edinburgh 1556–1889* (1967), 36–47.

37. L.W. Sharp, ed., 'Early Letters of Robert Wo[o]drow, 1698–1709', *Publications of the Scottish History Society*, 3rd Series, XXIV (1937), xl and xliii.

38. R. Wodrow, *Analecta* (1842–3), III, 170–2. These contemporary comments, by a Presbyterian minister who looked back nostalgically to Covenanting days, are invaluable for any study of Scottish culture in the early eighteenth century.

39. Ibid. III, 309.

40. Ibid. III, 175.

41. See above, p. 7. For a brief but very important essay about the significance of the Rankenian Club for Scottish intellectual history, see G.E. Davie, 'Hume in his Contemporary Setting', *David Hume : University of Edinburgh 250th Anniversary of the Birth of David Hume 1711 : 1761 A record of the Commemoration Published as a Supplement to the University Gazette* (1961), 11–15. Davie shows that members of the Rankenian Club introduced Berkeley into the Scottish curriculum, and that some of the problems raised by Berkeley's philosophy supplied important raw materials for Hume.

42. Cf. H.W. Meikle, *Some Aspects of Later Seventeenth-Century Scotland*

(Glasgow 1947), 6 : 'So in the later seventeenth century, beneath the surface of Scottish life, dominated by bitter religious strife and persecution, and by tyrannical government, there were currents of thought and even cultural achievement which made their own permanent contribution to Scottish national well-being.'

43. P. Hume Brown, *History*, 11, 286–308.

44. Ibid. 111, 4.

45. For evidence on this point, cf. Woodhouselee, *Kames*, 1, 161–2 ; Ramsay, *Scotland*, 11, 5–52 ; Wodrow, *Analecta*, 1v, 84 and 415. Trevelyan is more cautious and sees the gentry of the lowlands divided not unevenly into Presbyterians and Episcopalians. G. M. Trevelyan, *England under Queen Anne : Ramillies and the Union with Scotland* (London 1932), 183. On the contribution of Scottish landowners to the development of a dynamic economy in the eighteenth century, see T. C. Smout, 'Scottish Landowners and Economic Growth, 1650–1850', *Scottish Journal of Political Economy*, x1, 1964, 218–34.

46. This statement, citing Episcopalianism in contrast to the ascetic aspects of Presbyterianism, may err on the side of simplification. The diffe rences, certainly through 1688, did not turn on forms of worship. What *did* distinguish the two Confessions was a definite spirit of anti-dogmatism on the part of the Episcopalians who generally looked askance at what seemed to them narrow and fanatical in Presbyterianism ; deriving, as they did, from a theological tradition still close enough to Catholicism to be naturally amenable to both rationalism and latitudinarianism. It should be noted that the cleavage between the two came to rest not only on political but to some extent on class lines. (Cf. Ramsay's statement that while in a few shires Presbyterians formed a great proportion of the gentlemen, they constituted the vast majority of burgesses and commonalty in Scotland as a whole, with the Episcopalians dominating the upper classes. Ramsay, *Scotland*, 11, 55.) Many of the Episcopalian clergy were men of good family who had travelled and had acquired some formal culture. G. D. Henderson, *Religious Life*, 257–8.

47. See the description of an Edinburgh musicale in the early eighteenth century, with the Laird of Newhall playing the viola da gamba, Sir Gilbert Elliot of Minto the flute, and Lord Colville the harpsichord, in H. G. Graham, *Scottish Men of Letters in the Eighteenth Century* (London 1901), 22. On the poverty of the gentry and minor nobility in the early eighteenth century, see Sir Walter Scott, 'General Account of Edinburgh', *Provincial Antiquities and Picturesque Scenery of Scotland with Descriptive Illustrations* (London 1826), 11, 71–82.

48. H. Arnot, *The History of Edinburgh to 1780* (1816), 127.

49. Cf. J. Colville, 'Social Life in Edinburgh after the Union', *The Union of 1707 : A Survey of Events* (Glasgow 1907), 123–33.

50. D. Duncan, *Thomas Ruddiman : A Study in Scottish Scholarship of the Early Eighteenth Century* (1965), 21.

51. Wodrow, *Analecta*, 1, 218. (5 Dec. 1709).

52. Ramsay, *Scotland*, 1, 221.

53. *Boswell's London Journal*, 201.

54. Wodrow, *Early Letters*, xxxvii ; Graham, *Men of Letters*, 10. On

the importance of Watson, originally Roman Catholic, see W. Ferguson, *Scotland 1689 to the Present* (1968), 98–100.

55. See D. Daiches, *The Paradox of Scottish Culture : The Eighteenth-Century Experience* (London 1964) on the literary importance of the Jacobite movement. On Jacobite circles in Rome, significant in the diffusion to Scotland of Italianate tastes in art and architecture, see B. Skinner, *The Scots in Italy in the Eighteenth Century* (1966) and A. Smart, *The Life and Art of Allan Ramsay* (London 1952).

56. A. Bower, *University of Edinburgh*, 11, 66–7.

57. Ramsay, *Scotland*, 1, 85.

58. G. Chalmers, *The Life of Thomas Ruddiman* (London 1794), 83–4.

58A. J. Chamberlayne, *Magnae Britanniae Notitia : or, the Present State of Great Britain* (London 1708), iii.

59. Perry Miller, *The New England Mind : From Colony to Province* (Cambridge, Mass. 1953), 6.

60. Wodrow, *Analecta*, 111, 515.

61. David Hume to John Clephane, 20 April 1756, J. Y. T. Greig, ed., *The Letters of David Hume* (Oxford 1932), 1, 229 ; Adam Smith to Lord Fitzmaurice, 21 Feb. 1759, quoted in W. R. Scott, *Adam Smith as Student and Professor* (Glasgow 1937), 241 ; George Dempster to Adam Fergusson, 5 Dec. 1756, J. Fergusson, ed., *Letters of George Dempster to Sir Adam Fergusson, 1756–1813* (London 1934), 15.

62. Ramsay, *Scotland*, 1, 5.

63. William Robertson to Baron Mure, Nov. 1761, Dugald Stewart, 'Account of the Life and Writings of William Robertson, D.D., 'W. Hamilton, ed., *The Collected Works of Dugald Stewart* (1854–60), x, 136 ; David Hume to Adam Ferguson, 9 Nov. 1763, Greig, *Letters of Hume*, 1, 410–11.

64. William Tod to William Smellie, 29 Nov. 1759, R. Kerr, *Memoirs of the Life, Writings, and Correspondence of William Smellie* (1811), 1, 46.

65. *Boswell's London Journal*, 71 ; F. A. Pottle, ed. *Boswell in Holland, 1763–1764* (New York, 1952), 137 and 260.

Index